RE-IMAGINING THE DIVINE

Re-Imagining the Divine

Confronting the Backlash

against

Feminist Theology

LAUREL C. SCHNEIDER

THE PILGRIM PRESS
Cleveland, Ohio

For my mother, Pat Schneider

The Pilgrim Press, Cleveland, Ohio 44115

Pat Schneider, "Confession" and excerpt, from *Wake Up Laughing* (Montgomery: Negative Capability Press, 1997). Reprinted by permission of the author. • Donna S. Gates, "Untitled," 1996. Reprinted by permission of the author. • Marjorie Power, "Why I Gave Tishku Shampoo," in *Tishku: After She Created Men* (Omaha: Lone Willow Press, 1996). Reprinted by permission of the author. • Janie Marshall, "Untitled," 1997. Reprinted by permission of the author. • Cindy Davenport, "Untitled." Reprinted by permission of the author. • Cynthia Trenshaw, "Sickness and Death: The Anointing of Acceptance," 1997. Reprinted by permission of the author. • "Bar Mitzvah" reprinted by permission of the author. • Joann Heinritz, CSJ, "The Winter of My Life." Reprinted by permission of the author. • Inna Jane Ray, "To the Road Crew," in *Ruah: Power of Poetry—A Celebration*, vol. 2 (Berkeley, Calif.: Graduate Theological Union, 1992–93). Reprinted by permission of the author. • Dianne Bilyak, "Canyon" and "Mindfulness." Reprinted by permission of the author. • Pat Schneider, "Temple," in *One More River* (Amherst, Mass.: Amherst Writers and Artists Press, forthcoming). Reprinted by permission of the author.

Biblical quotations are from the New Revised Standard Version of the Bible, © 1989 by the Division of Christian Education of the National Council of the Churches of Christ in the U.S.A., and are used by permission

Printed in the United States of America on acid-free paper

03 02 01 00 99 98   5 4 3 2 1

Library of Congress Cataloging-in-Publication Data

Schneider, Laurel C., 1961–
     Re-imagining the divine : confronting the backlash against feminist theology /
Laurel C. Schneider.
        p.   cm.
     Includes bibliographical references and index.
     ISBN 0-8298-1289-x (alk. paper)
     1. Feminist theology.   I. Title.
BT83.55.S446   1998
230'.082—dc21   98-36260
                                                                          CIP

Contents

Preface

THIS BOOK IS about the roots of feminist theology and the challenges that theology now faces as a result of those roots. I came to this inquiry by way of studying the rich fruits of feminist theology and by my personal commitments to deeper critical reflection on the racist, sexist, ethnocentric, heterosexist, and otherwise socially malicious tendencies that can persist in all theologies. I am personally motivated by the healing possibilities for renewal and spiritual growth that I also believe persist in theological reflection and re-imagining.

Over the years, I have observed with interest the robustness of new spiritual practices and communities among feminist-minded people in North America. As individuals or in small, diffuse, or even large gatherings, women and men have put the ideas and theological reasoning of various feminist theologies to use, generating and incorporating new and dramatically revised images and ideas of divinity. The vitality of these practices and the experiences that people report from their participation in them speak of a spiritual energy that is not likely to diminish very soon.

Although I am deeply motivated by personal commitments to the work of justice-oriented theologies, this project is also the result of my concern that these theologies more effectively address accusations of idolatry, heresy, and self-aggrandizement that tend to emerge in more traditional settings where women and men have attempted to put new feminist ideas and images to work in their home communities. I have been struck by feminist theology's general incapacity to face these charges with consistency and philosophical depth. The brilliant and powerful ease with which womanist, white feminist, *mujerista*, Asian feminist, and other feminist theologies critique traditional theological ideas and images of divinity is usually not matched by an equally strong defense of new ideas put into ritual practice or into radically concrete forms. I have heard some feminist theologians suggest, for example, that women and men who actually believe that they experience the divine as "she" or as "black" or as particular and present in any concrete way are deluding themselves and do not understand the negative dimension of theological language. Theologians do this to protect the theology itself from such charges of idolatry and self-aggrandizement (they are less concerned, perhaps, about heresy). But in the act of protecting theological space for constructing new concepts of divinity, theologians tend to sacrifice the concrete, multiple, untheorizable, and often incommensurate space in which experiences of real people in real communities occur because such experiences are not negative, not metaphoric, not universalizable.

Theologians are right to invoke negative traditions to protect divinity from the caprices of human acquisitiveness, but there is also something poignantly ironic about the dismissal of direct comprehension of divine presence in concrete and fully embodied forms. Indeed, I have come to see that there is internal inconsistency in feminist theologies when some experiences serve as foundational warrants for theological work (experiences of oppression and liberation, for example) while others are deemed delusional (experiences of divine presence in embodied ways). This is the challenge, both in its epistemological form and in its constructive form, that I attempt to address in this book. The epistemological question pursues the most basic intellectual and authoritative foundations upon which feminist theologies rest, and the constructive question asks what such theologies can say with clarity about divine existence given those foundations. From their twin roots in skepticism and experiential confession, I conclude that feminist theologies best support more concrete (and hence even more radical) multiplicity in their concepts of embodiment, and more unlimited dimensions of immediate possibilities for presence in its concepts of transcendence. I have therefore set myself the task in this book of clarifying the foundations upon which feminist theologies stand so that they can more adequately address the difficult position and space in which women and men committed to justice and to re-imagined possibilities for religious life find themselves.

Although I address feminist theologies specifically in this book (I self-consciously use this term as a generalization for a more complex chorus of perspectives that address dynamics of racism, sexism, and other forms of social malice in religion), I hope that my real motive of saying something meaningful about contemporary constructive theology in general comes through between the lines. I believe that my basic critique applies to any contemporary theology that strives to make sense of the social constructedness of history and tradition and that argues for reconstructed and re-imagined images and ideas of the divine. Womanist, white feminist, Asian feminist, and other feminist theologians have something to contribute to this more general task, and we share the same ground as others who seek to better understand the human dilemma of speaking of divine things. Feminist theologies face challenges—of coherence, relevance, prophetic insight, and accountability to community and tradition—that all of contemporary constructive theology faces. How they address these challenges will determine their wider relevance in the coming years.

Acknowledgments

I AM VERY THANKFUL for the many women and men who shared their thoughts and insights with me through the course of working on this book. My heartfelt gratitude belongs to those who trustingly provided written material and ideas for my use. I have quoted quite a few in the text, but there are others who provided materials that I did not end up quoting, though they still helped to shape my thinking about experiential confession. My thanks, therefore, to Laura Frazier (Woman!), Dion Devon, David Harper, Jane Falla, Stephanie Palladino, Max Rivers, Celeste Downing, Treece James, John Wright, Laura Impanevo, Diane Moore, and Ellen Goldberg.

This project grew out of my dissertation work at Vanderbilt University, and I am profoundly grateful to a number of individuals as I write the last few lines of this book in preparation for its publication. I thank Howard Harrod and Victor Anderson for their unflagging support and advice through a sometimes difficult and challenging process of integration, and I thank Edward Farley and Sallie McFague both for their contributions to this project and for their confidence in it. Sandy Grande, Julie DeSherbinin, and Tom Longstaff of Colby College, and Jack Shindler, Susan Traverso, Fran Navakas, Ann Keating, Howard Mueller, Dan Lloyd, Richard Paine, Don and Mary McVicker, David Fisher, Sarah Fowler, and members of the faculty seminar group of North Central College are invaluable colleagues who understand the importance of collegial guidance and criticism, and of sharing bread and cup as necessary nourishment to the life of the mind. I am also deeply indebted to the confidence and patient guidance of Timothy Staveteig and Ed Huddleston at Pilgrim Press.

I owe my deepest gratitude for getting this first book anything close to publication to an astoundingly powerful and articulate community of intimate support and accountability. It includes my parents, Pat and Peter Schneider, and my family, Cindy, Rebecca, Paul and Nina, Bethany and Katie Louise, Sarah, and Nathaniel. It also includes Anne McWilliams,

Nancy Tatum, Ginger Morgan, Holly Toensing, Helene Russell, Chandra Taylor Smith, David Livingston, Mark Justad, Darby Ray, Georgie Finn, Billy Wilcox, Lisa Stenmark, and *especially* Rev. Nancy Stillman. Without their love, patience, enthusiasm, laughter, cooking, and critical thinking, I could not have come this far, no way. Thanks, Mary Dell, wherever you are, for the scribbled instructions I still carry in my bag. I *am* remembering the women.

And C.J., you particularly saw me—and this—all the way through. Thank you.

Prelude

The dream was utterly, vividly clear, and she never forgot it. She was nine-teen years old in the fall of 1980, and she was stunned by it. She could never explain how she knew that this was an encounter with a divine reality, but it was.

IT WAS NOT WHERE SHE WAS GOING. The train had unceremoniously stopped and left her there. It was not home or anywhere she had ever been before. And the train, what she thought was an unerring steel conduit between city and home, had silently disappeared altogether. Not even the tracks remained. Where was she? How would she get home to the family expecting her? She shivered a little and looked around her. She seemed to be in a wild place, on the sloping edge of a mountain. Below her were rough fields studded with boulders hunched against the persistent wind and anxious clouds, their edges diminishing into the chilly gloom of a late fall evening. What was she doing there?

Still a bit dulled by shock, before the sour clench of panic could goad her to move, she heard something off to her left—or did she hear it? Was it an electriclike humming, or did she sense it in her skin, the way dogs can sense things below sound? She could not see anything in that direction because a tall outcropping of rock jutted out in the way, making the slope to her left a steep edge. Whatever it was, it was just around that edge of rock.

Careful of her footing, she eased around the outcropping. There the rock face flattened into a comfortable ledge. Out of the nearly night clouds a powerful, self-contained shaft of light angled onto the rock. That was the cause of the vibrant electric sound-sense. She almost laughed at the cinematic absurdity of it. It had to do with God, she somehow simply knew that. "What is this?" she wanted to ask. But it was not a light shaft you could talk to. Something was going on inside. A figure was slowly forming within the bright pillar of light.

The sudden realization struck her hard and with it an exultant thrill. This was God becoming human again! *Surely*, she thought, *this one will be a woman.* The humanlike figure was still not clear, not fully formed, but gradually it took on shape and substance. Soon she would be able to tell if it was female or yet another god-made-man. Then another certainty slammed into her consciousness as she squinted hard into the incandescent fabric. Once this god-human finished forming, it would be here for good, no going back. It would be here, and even more particularly, it would be in her face, irrevocable, undeniable, certain. A new, truly divine incarnation, not from a book, recorded in hymns, or recited in creeds, but here, in front of her, in real flesh, beyond the control of doctrine, theology, or the rationalizations of her well-educated friends. Her exultation withered into fear.

She was not afraid of the still-forming figure—why could not she tell if it was male or female? That mattered! But she was afraid of God. Particularly of God-as-man-again. That would shatter her. She had just finished *Gyn/Ecology,* after all. And here God was about to show her the truth, irrevocably. This would tell her, once and for all, if God's relationship, at least to the human race, was fundamentally male. She did not know why it should, but she did know that it would. Dreams are like that.

The folds of light shimmered in creative action. The whole thing reminded her ridiculously of *Star Trek* or the movie *The Ten Commandments.* But now she was somehow in it, and everything rested on her. The consequences of the moment, she knew, were inalterable. With a slow, dead, cold certainty she realized that the decision was hers. In her lay the power to stop it until the instant that the human figure was complete and walked out of the light and into her life, her real life, not just this dream life (how did she know that?). She could stop it just by turning and walking back around the rock. Even in the dream she wondered at her knowledge of this simple fact.

The urgency of decision lay heavy on her, clutching at her breath. She was angry that God would do this to her. Was this a cruel joke? Few seconds remained before the truth would take its first step out of the light and say hello. She stared into the shimmering pillar, at the features of a face she could almost see. And with a despairing moan she fled back around the rock.

Slowly, the humming energy left her skin. She knew that the light had gone, and all that remained was the empty, dark ledge on a forsaken mountain. The world, ignorant, was the same. She was alone, and the wind blew. She felt empty and sad. Oddly, she was not afraid—it had not been a trick question or a test. But it had been real. She felt lost and wondered if she had made a terrible mistake.

PART I

Questions the Backlash Has Raised

CHAPTER ONE

How Disclosive of Reality
Are Symbols of the Divine?

SYMBOLS ARE THE STRANGEST and best of human inventions. Whether they come to us from the loam of dreams or from simple and pragmatic assignments of metaphor, they are the creative product of a distinctly human need to tell all, a product of our genius for approximation. Language itself is an immoderate testimony to our necessary flair for making present the ineffable, the maybe, the no-longer-here, the not-yet, the big-one-that-got-away. Whether made of words or images, fabricated in stories, pictures, or spaces, symbols are the elemental bedrock of our communication with one another and with the world. They are the marvelously rich and varied stuff of human being.

The complexity and intricacy of symbols affect every dimension of human thought and communication, and nowhere more poignantly than in theology. Theology is faced with the particularly thorny task of speaking intelligently of what is beyond all symbols and beyond all ideas, yet having only symbols and ideas for tools. The words "God," "El," "Christ," "Allah," "Yahweh," "She Who Is," "Goddess," "the divine," and the rest, being names for divinity, are just symbols, but they are symbols with enormous power in part because of the enormous power they attempt to name. Every theologian is faced with the awareness that these names do not, in the end, suffice. But every theologian is also faced with the awareness that all names, in the end, produce.

What does this somewhat cryptic statement mean? It refers to the foundational challenge of coherence that is now before contemporary theology in general, and feminist theologies in particular. The double edge of modern consciousness recognizes human construction in every symbol for the divine, yet recognizes the agency of symbols in the constructedness of humans, and still wagers on divinity that is "really there" and that really responds through veils of cultural fabrication.

There are histories and consequences, in other words, to the words we use and to the ideas we associate with words. We shape and are shaped by these symbolic structures. There is no innocence. This is the greatest and most damning insight of postmodernism, and it is, in all of its complexity, the most important challenge before all feminist theologies. Every name and symbol for divinity takes its meaning and power from that to which it refers, but this does not cancel the fact that the name, the image, the idea itself has considerable efficacy in the social marketplace and shapes social understanding of the divine. Names and ideas may refer to someone or something, but they also instruct, they "participate" as Paul Tillich says, and sometimes they bring into being.

The intricacies and complexities of symbols and their functioning in the human realm are vital subjects to theology. The purpose of this book, however, is to address only part of that complexity as it relates to the dynamic world of feminist theology in the Western, predominantly monotheistic cultures as they tip toward the millennium. Specifically, I will suggest that pressures internal to feminist theologies from their twin roots in modernist skepticism and spiritual experience shape their commitments and their possibilities and raise troubling challenges for monotheism.

Before attempting another word, however, I must attempt a working description of feminist theologies. To begin with, feminist theology is a collage of voices that is best named in the plural. Taken together, they constitute a thoroughly modernist (which I believe includes postmodernist) enterprise facing the ironies and stubborn courage of their work and commitments for justice and liberation. They are intimately concerned with the marketplace of symbols in human life precisely because of the meaning and power that symbols of divinity play in the structuring of social systems and because of the importance that symbols can have for re-imagining new possibilities. Feminist theologies have powerfully critiqued the roles that traditional symbols of the divine play in the maintenance of sexism, racism, heterosexism, and other structures of social malice. They have also worked to legitimate new understandings of religion, spirituality, and divinity through the construction of names, ideas, symbols, and images for the divine that focus human attention on justice, liberation, empowerment of the oppressed, and structural transformation of society.

Even in their most radical critiques of essence, feminist theologies engage the assumption that human beings structure their actions and values in response to ideas of divinity, and that divine reality *in some way* corresponds or responds to human constructions of it. Feminist theologies, in other words, do not generally undertake lightly the construction of new and sometimes dramatically nontraditional ideas and images of the divine. They do not assume that divinity itself (whatever that word means) is a completely passive, empty, or innocent vessel for the aspirations of human imagining.

As a multiple and multivalent set of discourses, practices, and communal orientations, feminist theologies no longer reside on the intellectual margins of contemporary religion and spirituality. In North America at least, their basic concerns are familiar to most people, even if acceptance does not always accompany familiarity. The chorus of voices that in whole or in part contribute to the feminist theological circle is growing, edging out into new territory, and curving back ever deeper and with more critical strength into the historical discourses and particular traditions out of which it arises. Indeed, the time is past (and it never really was) when the term "feminist theology" can refer to a single approach or to a handful of scholars. The identity of the particular feminist theologian herself or himself—including ethnicity, economic and social class, culture, national location, and other shaping influences—has become a significant aspect of this work for theologians and their readers.

To look closely at the general feminist theological movement, we must recognize the limits of a general name to capture the important differences in strategies, cultures, and starting points that inform specific theologians and the communities for whom they labor. Generalizations are immensely helpful in some tasks like the one that guides this book, which sets about looking for common ground in a contemporary conversation among multiple contributors. But generalizations can also diminish the integrity and individuality of distinct approaches and significant disagreements that guide the work of liberation and cross-cultural understanding, particularly in theology. Feminist theologies are, in some circles, associated narrowly with the work, experiences, and concerns of white, academic, middle- and upper-class women.[1] Although historically white feminists have made serious errors in assuming their cultural patterns to be both generic and normative, I think that the term "feminist" is still helpful as a general signifier for what is now a multicultural discourse that addresses multiple layers and dynamics of oppression.

To use a term that has become most associated with white middle-class concerns and patterns may perpetuate the erasures that privileged people have always unthinkingly visited upon others. But I remain convinced that despite the dangers, there are commonalities between the concerns of straight white middle-class women and other women and men concerned with dynamics of prejudice, oppression, and liberation in contemporary theology. The term "feminist" continues to seem to be the one more appropriately generalized than other, more culturally specific identifiers such as womanist, *mujerista*, queer, or white feminist. It continues to represent basic concerns with sexism and culture that are shared and argued over among women and men who are also black, white, Hispanic, Asian, African, Native American, straight, lesbian, Jewish, Christian, pagan, and so on. I am also mindful of the inadequacies of a term already popularly associated with one mostly privileged group. Because the purpose of culturally specific signifiers is their specificity rather than their generality, I have not yet come upon a better term than "feminism" for the general task that I am attempting here. I look forward, however, to the time when it may be eclipsed by another, less burdened term.

So, what are these feminist theologies that I claim refer generally to persons who have worked so hard to distinguish themselves clearly with dignity and respect? To have general, rather than specific, relevance, feminist theologies refer to the work of women and men from a variety of cultural contexts who yet share concerns about institutionalized and foundational values and beliefs that feed oppression and prejudice. White feminists have slowly learned what nonwhite feminists have always known, that concerns with sexism in theology or in any other discipline are inseparably linked to other forms of social malice, such as racism, classism, and heterosexism. This book is therefore concerned with the intellectual bases that legitimize and undergird the shared ground of contemporary feminist theologies in general. Furthermore, I suggest that these liberationist-oriented theologies evolved in response to the modernist insight that religious ideas function in the construction and maintenance of social systems.

Since feminist theologies are engaged in the work of attempting to speak both of divinity and of the social consequences of names for the divine, they cannot be understood apart from the creative trouble they have caused in the work of symbolizing divinity. It may indeed be most accurate to say that feminist theologies are founded on the notion that symbols of God "function." What does this mean? Contemporary theologians such as Elizabeth Johnson claim that it means our language about divinity and our symbols for divinity, whatever they may be, act upon our consciousness in complex ways, influencing and sometimes directing how we understand divine relationships to the world.[2] What is more, symbols and ideas of the sacred, of divine power, glory, love, and so forth, are weighted by culture, history, and the interpretive labor of centuries-old traditions. What we communicate through the symbols of language, pictures, and ritual about divine things is neither inert nor innocent. It matters what we say about sacred things not just because it behooves us to avoid delusion about such potentially powerful things as divine realities, but because it behooves us to avoid delusion about ourselves. As the history of ideas, of ideologies, and even of fashion suggests, we seem to be infinitely suggestible beings, capable of the grandest fabrications, no doubt a fault that also founds our genius.

Sharon Welch sums up both sides of this equation with the claim that "ideas have the effects of truth."[3] For feminist theologies, this insight has been dynamite. In particular, the deleterious effects of traditional ideas (such as an exclusively male deity) on Western society form the cornerstone of feminist theological criticism while the therapeutic effects of new ideas (images that include the female) are the cornerstone of feminist theological construction. The resulting smoke of explosion is still so thick that we cannot yet tell how much the landscape of religion has changed.

The argument that symbols of God play a role in the smooth functioning of society is not new to feminist theologies or even to the twentieth century. Nevertheless, feminist theologians have been making use of this insight for years, dating back at least to Mary Daly's claim in 1973 that "if God is male, then the male is God"[4] and even farther back to Elizabeth Cady Stanton's claim in 1895 that the "canon law, the Scriptures, the creeds and codes and church discipline of the leading religions bear the impress of fallible man, and not of our ideal great first cause, 'The Spirit of all Good.'" She concluded from this that it is "no wonder [that] the majority of women stood still, and with bowed heads, accepted the situation."[5] Stanton and the other early feminist critics of religion were products of their time, thinking thoughts about "the fallible impress" in a milieu of increasing confidence in human creativity to re-create the world, on the one hand, and despair over the apparent inability of human society to build heaven itself, on the other.

Perhaps, given the tendency of troubling insights to take a long time to settle in, the no longer new notion that symbols of divinity work in the public and political sphere is finally drifting onto the sedimented floor of general consciousness, the murky underground where things are taken for granted and where they slowly, under the pressure of habit, become bedrock. Or it is equally possible that the opposite has occurred, and this insight (that God, in whole or in part, may be a humanly constructed symbol, vulnerable to and even necessitating reconstruction and adaptation) has erupted out of the undiscussed depths into the bright contrasts of public conversation. In either case, it is clear that at the close of the twentieth century, communities of worshipers both within and outside traditional church structures are beginning to experience the malleability of divine symbols with greater regularity and perhaps even greater distress.

On an academic level, all things theological are open for investigation. It is, however, generally disorienting and perhaps even inappropriate to take the historicity of language about God into the church or other realms of spiritual focus. In the traditional monotheistic religions, spiritual attention does presume, after all, a stable and independent object of that attention.

The idea that divinity is even partly a product of complex social processes is hard on the worshiper. Feminist activists and scholars in religious communities already know well the levels of discomfort that simmer in contemporary churches over decentering theological issues as narrow as inclusive language. The 1993 ecumenical Re-Imagining Conference and the hyperbolic reactions to it in the conservative Christian press, the Drew Divinity School eucharist that made news for its supposed heresies, and any number of other examples of public feminist religious expressions and backlash against them in recent history confirm this.[6]

Nevertheless, the central question here is not one of popular discomfort or comfort over the notion that symbols of God function in oppressive social systems. The primary focus of my inquiry has to do with the ultimate strength and coherence of feminist theologies themselves in light of the necessary notion that symbols of God function in the social sphere. Their dual roots in modern theological epistemology and in pragmatic commitments to specific communities establish a tension between the rational demands of social constructionism, on the one hand, and the supposed authority of lived experience, on the other. This tension does not have to result in a dead end of incommensurate claims, but it does present difficulties for feminist approaches to constructive theology. Although I will argue that this tension presents feminists in theology with fertile possibilities for more coherent and bolder new work, I also contend that, left unexamined, this tension threatens to undermine the long-term viability of their many important and compelling constructive propositions.

The problem, in one sense, is relatively simple. Feminist theologians in general have stated that symbols of God function in the creation and maintenance of social structures of authority. Most feminist critiques of Bible, tradition, doctrine, and ecclesiastical authority depend upon this claim. But what about "true" divinity? The old ontological question of divine being joins up with the old epistemological question of whether that divine being is at all accessible to human knowing. Feminist theologians have explored in depth the functioning of religious symbols in patriarchal culture, but have not yet adequately addressed the implications of their own new constructions for the integrity and coherence of their ontological and epistemological claims as a whole. The theologians who come closest are those who are most willing to dispense with ontological foundations altogether. But the question remains, at least for theologians still wedded to some notion of independent divine existence, that if new images and language for the divine are justified primarily in terms of their benefits to society, are these benefits merely by-products of a larger task concerned with divinity itself, or is social betterment the sum of the feminist theological enterprise? Is a claim of divine reality even necessary to feminist work, or is it ultimately satisfied by what Edward Farley calls "culturally originated symbols of ultimacy called God . . . projective image[s that] could 'found' the human being"?[7]

Feminist theologies in general reflect historicist assumptions that the social function of theological images is of utmost importance. At the same time, however, the divine is traditionally understood even by feminists to entail—to "be"—something more than social function alone. Thus, the true work of theology—logos about theos—is presumably also more than just politics attempting to manipulate public affections through carefully crafted reasoning for presumably noble civic ends. But politics is always present. Largely out of necessity, feminist theologians choose highly political avenues to unmask the highly political nature of traditional theology. Traditional theology turns out to be, after all, susceptible to the machinations of public manipulation. But having taken this route, can feminist theologians claim that they are talking about something greater, more real even, than socially constructed political reality? Is there enough of a basis upon which to build the argument that there is something substantive in divine being apart from human imagining? Moreover, is there something substantive apart from human imagination that weeps for the lost and thunders against injustice, even in so-called sacred sources?

I will attempt to argue in the following chapters that a feminist concern with divine reality is important, not only for the sake of philosophical and theological coherence in a historicist age, but also for the sake of persons directly experiencing the heat of backlash who must somehow answer to themselves and to their accusers that they are not simply re-creating divinity in their own image for their own parochial purposes. Although it is true, and may be therapeutic, to say that men have been making God in their own image for millennia, and it is time to take turns, this argument is not sufficient to answer some of the deeper questions raised by the general and institutional retaliations against religious feminists popularly referred to as backlash. The argument that there are "turns" is sufficient only if feminist theologies are purely functional in the social sphere, only if we concede that there is nothing more to divinity than a political fiction, for then the efficacy of a symbol or image is its substance and is the full measure of its value. The basic courtesy of sharing becomes then entirely a social tool of reparation.

THE EVOLUTION OF FUNCTIONAL SOCIAL CONSTRUCTIONISM IN FEMINIST THEOLOGIES

The fully developed contemporary idea that the symbol of God functions in the social sphere is the product of several hundred years of a mounting historical consciousness in the West, commonly described in terms of the

Enlightenment and of modernism. Feminist claims about the social functioning of religious symbols are therefore best understood within the larger context of Enlightenment propositions about the historical nature of human thought. This movement has steadily undercut premodern assumptions about divine reality and omnipotence, so that by the nineteenth century, figures such as Karl Marx could denounce religion and its contents entirely as a numbing drug serving the interests of ruling classes, and Ludwig Feuerbach could extol religion and its contents on the basis of its ability to project the best in human values onto a heavenly scale, providing a never-ending goal of humanist progress.

Part I briefly traces this development in terms of its impact on feminist theological work and introduces the idea of functional social constructionism as the product of this intellectual evolution. The notion of functional social constructionism tells us that symbols and ideas of divinity are not socially or politically inert, but they sustain, support, challenge, or undermine the dynamic structures of social and personal meaning within the fabric of the cultures they inhabit. As so-called knowledge of God is constructed and not given, experience of the world is also implicated and no longer direct. We must account for the act of interpretation, its qualitative sources, and its shaping influences.

To make their claims for new, more inclusive symbols, feminist theologies depend on the historicist insight that experience itself is a constructed filter for the production of meaning. Because, for example, we know that language and images of God as male, as monarchical, as disembodied, and as independent have far-reaching effects on the structure of human relationships and human valuations and thus human experience, feminist scholars undertake to change these images and to offer new language about God and about divinity that supports feminist, liberationist, ecological, and antiracist goals and claims for human life. Both symbols and experiences of symbols are implicated and open to inquiry on functionalist grounds. This is the philosophical problem of epistemology, and it is important to feminist theologies because increasingly persons who argue for changes in ritual practice and who offer new theological images must address questions about how we discern truth or accuracy in the new constructions.

Cultural theorists since the late nineteenth century have developed and honed functional social constructionist ideas of religion to expose its fundamental role in what Peter Berger calls the twin activities of world construction and world maintenance.[8] If human beings are primarily social beings, necessitating shared understandings of the world, then we are also dependent upon symbols to help construct and sustain these understandings. Reality, according to this view, is symbolically constructed and transmitted, and ideas of God and divinity serve the production and mainte-nance of reality rather well—that is, so long as the substance of religious ideas is taken to be real. But through sociology of knowledge critiques, the gods tend to topple into history and pile up like so many puppets, the strings leading back to the transcendence of human collectivity rather than to some extrahuman force, to a God, for example, beyond history.

Functional social constructionism, the epistemological claim that hu-man beings collectively create perceived reality, provides even more than a toppling of the traditional deities, however. Human life, thoroughly depen-dent upon socially shared meanings, requires deity or symbols of transcen-dence in order to exist. This theory, then, turns into an acid bath for ontol-ogy, supporting the view of all reality as a complex of shared symbolic constructions born wholly out of human need for meaning and order. This includes the constructions of sacred ultimacy called God, even perhaps ge-netic codes, the Big Bang, Gaia, and so forth. The compelling tenacity of functional social constructionism is not founded on its ability to explain the so-called secularization of modern life by revealing the "true" socially for-mative and ultimately atheistic root of sacred symbols. Rather, its strength in feminist theologies comes from its ability to explain the way that symbols of any kind function in this most basic symbolic ordering of human life.

Functional social constructionism did not jump directly from the late Enlightenment social theorists of the nineteenth and early twentieth cen-turies into feminism. Although feminist theologies are deeply influenced by it, functional social constructionist ideas traveled through neoorthodox theology on their way to the late twentieth century. The questions they raised for theology were taken up by the humanist theologians of the nine-teenth century and by the likes of such neoorthodox luminaries as Karl Barth, Paul Tillich, Rudolph Bultmann, and H. Richard Niebuhr in the early twentieth. Indeed, many of these theologians can be characterized by their attempts to deal creatively with the challenges of functional social constructionism in their constructive work. This theological legacy pro-vides a critical foundation for the powerful emergence of feminist theolo-gies and their strategic appropriation of what I call the metaphoric exemp-tion, which is the critical reminder that all ideas of the divine are metaphors, unremittingly constructed in the social sphere.

Even though they are characterized primarily by the particular tradi-tions and communities out of which they come and in which they attempt to stand, it is no surprise that feminist theologies share a basic confidence in the idea of reordering society through symbolic means. Marjorie Hewitt Suchocki begins an essay on God with the claim that the "doctrine of God is developed so as to ensure that there is an answer to the problem of evil as defined by the society," and she goes on to suggest that this social function implicates sexism in Western culture.[9] Sallie McFague argues in many places that "Christian hierarchical dualism of spirit over flesh, male over female, and human beings over the natural world has been a factor in the Western utilitarian and imperialistic attitude toward the earth."[10] The idea of God for these theologians is ineradicably linked to ethics and the structure of social relations, thoroughly implicating theology in the social-political work of constructing metaphors for divinity.

Womanist theologians tend to work more with the functional vitality of socially constructed images of Jesus, and Kelly Brown Douglas argues that "the Black Church leaders who want to take down images of White Christs in their churches are right: a blond haired, blue-eyed Christ does not empower or nurture self-esteem for Black people."[11] Delores Williams takes on the soteriological symbol of Jesus' death, arguing that his "surrogacy, attached to this divine personage, takes on an aura of the sacred. . . . If black women accept this idea of redemption, can they not also passively accept the exploitation that surrogacy brings?"[12] Biblical scholar Elisabeth Schüssler Fiorenza has made the point that the "revelation of God in Scripture is expressed in human language and shares culturally conditioned concepts and problems. . . . This hermeneutical insight is far-reaching when we consider that Scripture as well as theology are rooted in a patriarchal-sexist culture and share its biases and prejudices."[13] Rosemary Radford Ruether sums up the functional argument, stating bluntly that "male monotheism reinforces the social hierarchy of patriarchal rule through its religious system."[14]

The beginnings of difficulty for feminist theologies lie in these vibrant strains of criticism. In addition to the theory that undermines the independent "truth" of all socially constructed images of the divine, feminist theologians at times see their work as faithful response to a divine call or sacred presence that becomes known in dramatically embodied ways. Nelle Morton writes of her intellectual conviction but emotional reluctance to engage female imagery for divinity until she was directly addressed by what she knew to be a sacred, female presence.[15] Mary Hunt and Diane Neu founded WATER (Women's Alliance for Theology, Ethics and Ritual) precisely because of the importance they attach to the experience of divine presence in theology, in ritual, and in the production of nonpatriarchal images.

FEMINIST SPIRITUALITY AND THE CHALLENGES OF EMBODIED EXPERIENCE

Despite the difficulties that they pose to theory, emerging patterns in feminist spiritual practice and experience are important to feminist theological work, and part 2 turns to these patterns. Feminist theologians must begin to navigate the difficult terrain of theological substance without losing critical ground gained by the metaphoric exemption. The knowledge that male-dominated discourse about God has produced male images of divinity supporting male-dominated society has justified the critical work of feminist theologies in vibrantly creative reconstructions of female and other divine images.

But now, even avowed feminist antifoundationalists such as Sharon Welch and Kathleen Sands can see that not only are they right—ideas do have the effects of truth, especially when they are enacted in ritual ways—but their opponents understand them all too well and understand what is at stake in theological reconstruction. The issue is not just the ontological question of God's existence (though, god knows, that is a big enough problem) or even the question of idolatry, which worship and spiritual attention always risk. At issue is the enduring possibility that ideas of divinity are creative in the profoundest sense, that the divine reserves for itself the possibility of responding to, becoming even, the symbols and names that human beings construct in multiple, embodied, and temporal ways. In other words, ritual enactment and spiritual focus may turn function, or metaphor, into substance. More precisely, divine realities may choose to enact themselves in metaphor, to "come forth" in substantive and worldly ways in constructions.

Are feminist theologians sufficiently in awe of what can happen when their work is taken with utter and religious seriousness? Enthusiastic appropriations of and popular resistances to new constructions are both resilient and passionate. While much of either kind of response can be shrugged off as evidence of misunderstanding and ignorance, some elements of the backlash against feminist spirituality in particular beg, of feminist theologians at least, a new seriousness concerning the place of revelatory experiences of goddess, divinity, Gaia, She Who Is, and other constructions in devotional contexts. Another way to look at this is to see that feminist theologies are at something of a crossroads, evidenced not so much by boundary transgressions—feminists have known that they were crossing boundaries from the start—but indicated by the success and the vitality of feminist theological scholarship and public rituals. As many have observed, the virulence of the backlash against religious feminism is an excellent indicator of success. But what of value, if anything, is there to learn from the attacks and campaigns against feminist enactments of faith?

It is too easy, and even unwise, to assume that the powerful smear campaigns of the likes of Jerry Falwell, Pat Buchanan, the Christian Coalition, and the conservative United Methodist Good News and Presbyterian Layman movements against feminist theologies represent the defensive but dying gasps of patriarchy. Catherine Keller argued, after the Re-Imagining controversy reached fever pitch, that "many feel their power diminished by women's growing leadership in church and theology, and . . . they recognize that female imagery of the divine—even used along with male imagery—empowers women. So they are desperate to put a stop to it."[16] Representatives of the Good News movement called this "an unfortunate use of amateur psychology that fails to take evangelical concerns seriously or even attempt to address them."[17]

Who is right? Most likely both, to some extent. It is possible that the boundary transgressions of feminists in liturgies with explicit female content, resisted by Christian traditionalists, in fact touch on the ultimate concern of both—the foundational claims that both make about a God who then functions in the maintenance of social order and meaning. In a study on clergywomen in the Berkshire hills of western Massachusetts—a unique area where fully 50 percent of the United Church of Christ clergy are women—Allison Stokes has discovered that congregants, for the most part, continue to resist gender changes in language about God and in ritual, although their attitudes toward women as clergy have become quite open. This finding supports the idea that traditional theological language and symbols remain tenacious and embedded, even among the most open of liberal Christian communities (with the authority to select their own pastoral leaders) who call women as senior ministers.

Stokes has found that the willingness to receive, support, and accept the authority of women in the human role of *minister* is not followed by a great deal of openness to revise internalized ideas of *divinity* and of God. She reports that 90 percent of her respondents held that women pastors should not be outspoken on women's issues, and a full 83 percent do not appreciate hearing female metaphors for God. Part of the resistance could be generational; younger congregants were somewhat more open on these issues, particularly if they perceived them to be important to the minister. Part of the resistance could also be explained in evolutionary terms; as long as the practice of incorporating female language and images of God into worship is unfamiliar, it remains suspect, but over time and with increased exposure, the worshiping community may acclimate and come to accept these images as valid and worthy of incorporation into sacred vocabularies. Sixty-three percent of Stokes's respondents did say that they are "better able to think of the Divine in female terms as long *as they are thinking abstractly*."[18]

This relatively small study of a liberal church environment may be most helpful as an illustration rather than a scientific analysis of the strange tenacity of divine masculinity. This tenacity persists even within a locale long renowned for its tolerance, feminism, and openness to liberal and even radical social ideas. Something is at stake when feminist theologies move into the enacted sphere of ritual and worship that goes deeper than the feminist cries for justice, arguments from logic, or appeals to biblical references to Sophia.

Functional social constructionism suggests that what is at stake is everything—the whole constructed social order; the sacred canopy of meaning dependent on gendered notions of the autonomous deity. Certainly, the arguments against feminist changes in worship are partly about the simple resistance humans tend to exhibit to small but deep changes in their lives. But resistance to feminist theology may also be about idolatry and the enduring possibility that divinity may relinquish its abstract transcendence from time to time and enter into the particularistic constructions of a community.

Feminist theology as a whole is at something of a crossroads but not perhaps the foundational or antifoundational split it appears at first. Function is the scandal of substance in feminist theological work, and substance is the scandal of function. These feminist theologies are well articulated at the point of function and social construction, and perhaps wisely, until now they have been weakest at the point of substance. As McFague has argued clearly, we understand the devastating effects of idolatry all too well and do not wish to repeat them by claiming that our ideas and language about God are anything other than metaphorical.[19]

This argument, careful and important as it is to the work of numerous feminist projects of theological construction, is weakened in the context of ritual enactment and invocation. No feminist theologian wants to suggest that feminist worship or ritual is playacting. But what answer can theologians give to those who incorporate new metaphors into their personal meditations, their collective worship in local, communal settings, or their large gatherings such as the Re-Imagining Conference, and who are then bullied by the likes of United Methodist Bishop Cannon, claiming that "Sophia worship is idolatry—these extreme feminists have made for themselves an idol and they call that idol God. Without knowing it they are worshipping themselves"?[20] The fact is, feminist spirituality and worship that incorporates female imagery or other forms of symbolism drawn from life as we know it do constitute a form of self-representation. We *are* worshiping an idea of ourselves in the new constructions coming from the best feminist theologies, an idea of the way we desire ourselves, desire the world, and desire ourselves and the world to be, with good functional reasons for doing so. It is not enough to say that protests of idolatry such as the bishop's can be applied to the traditional male canon as well. Because they can—

male dominance has set itself up as God and pronounced itself good and is thereby idolatrous. But where does that leave us? What, then, is *not* idolatry?

Traditionally, the answer to the charge of idolatry has been a variety of forms of negative theology (God is never conceivable, even in symbols or metaphors). However, the problems attending the *via negativa* are particularly thorny for feminist theologies that tend to extol divine embodiment and the virtues of embodied religious experience. If all constructions are never descriptive of true divinity (which is what the metaphoric exemption insists), then the methodological difficulties for feminist theologies mount. Despite the vitality of internal debate concerning the status of experience, feminist theologies of all kinds ground their work in descriptive claims about the experiences of women and men in the communities for which they are written. It would be profoundly ironic if experiences of divine encounter were excluded from the experiential fund that shapes and informs feminist theologies. But from the perspective of the metaphoric exemption, lived experiences of divine encounters can have no place without jeopardizing the strictly nonreferential status of images and metaphors.

On the other hand, despite the vitality of experiences of divine presence, the metaphoric exemption cannot be dismissed. It preserves for feminist theologies their critique of the tradition and at the same time preserves the option of imaginative model building by recognizing the functional social constructedness of all such attempts. Negation of this sort is very Barthian— reserving for God an identity wholly removed from the partial and awkward attempts of human naming in theology and in worship. Barth, however, retained the Bible as a source of unmediated divine revelation and so did not have the added difficulty facing feminist theologians of the status of their constructed images in the liturgical context. It is this that makes negation a strong tool for the intellectual process of theology, but a nearly useless one for the process of enacting that theology in ritual.

The nature of feminist spirituality and experiential confession confounds the metaphoric exemption insofar as it embraces ritual enactment, resists abstraction, employs imagistic narrative, and emphasizes the vitality of informed "direct" experience.[21] We cannot adjudicate accuracy or truthfulness in individual experiences of divine presence, but we can trace the outlines of an authoritative move, properly rooted in feminism's attempts to validate women's professed experiences over against systematic cultural erasures or trivializations of them.

What emerges finally is a foundational shape to feminist theologies that rests on two principal supports. More precisely, feminist theologies are like a river churning at the vibrant confluence of two divergent but powerful sources. One source is the important and skeptical insights of the metaphoric exemption, producing and legitimating the transcendent core of metaphoric creativity. The other source flows from the embodied reality claims of women and men who put theological metaphors into action, so to speak, and find that spiritual attention invokes a more profound substance than the metaphoric exemption allows. They experience, with robust regularity and particularity, the presence and discernible shape of divinity in the world, in worship, in things, in dreams, in life.

Part 3 takes up the challenges and implications for feminist theologies of this dual, tensive foundation in the opposing impulses of skepticism and experiential confession. I suggest, on the basis of the historical analysis in part 1 and the analysis of spiritual and ritual experience in part 2, that constructive feminist theologies are ineradicably founded on both the skepticism of the metaphoric exemption and the affirmation of experiential confession. Each root informs and corrects the other, and within each root resides specific constitutive strengths and vulnerabilities. This is an organic relation between opposing impulses that depends on deep, constitutive relationality between transcendent (metaphoric) abstraction and concrete (experiential) particularity. This tensive and dynamic confluence cannot, however, resolve into a theological construction of the divine as One as in traditional ontology. Feminist constructions of divine reality must remain both open and multiple. Divinity conceived within the web of metaphoric exemption and experiential confession must be profoundly free, not limited to transcendence or even to the abstract embodiments of more traditional theologies. It is for this reason that I suggest that, apart from their many differences, feminist theologies most coherently support notions of the divine that are suitably open, suitably mobile, suitably multiple.

A critique of exclusive monotheism and suggestions for constructive resolution through the concept of dynamic plurality form the conclusion of this book. The tensive foundations in functional social construction and experiential assertion mirror a constructive relation between the traditional theological poles of transcendence and concrete embodiment. Divinity is never one or the other, but always and already both. Feminist theologies have never denied this, but they have not fully developed it, wanting usually to preserve a nostalgic notion of the one God in a more organic relation to the embodied world. But I argue that even this distinction is too static. (Many post–Christian, process, and ecofeminist theologians may see points of overlap here.) To be truly inclusive of both embodiment and transcendence and to allow feminist theology as a whole its dual foundations in criticism and enactment, divinity itself must be understood as more open and more variously concrete, more transient, more particular, and ultimately more great.

The possibility that feminist theologies in the West are moving away from the exclusivist limitations of traditional monotheism without losing their characteristic focus on wholeness may set them in even greater opposition to conservative traditionalists than they are already, but give them greater methodological strength and value in more liberal religious settings. The idea that the theoretical unity of divinity (the adjective) is not compromised by multiple real embodiments of real divine being (the noun) in a multitude of forms is an ancient and therefore not unfamiliar or wholly unorthodox concept even in the West. The Christian Trinity is just one example of this concept of divinity. And for spiritual feminists, that troublesome, rich, chaotic source of inspiration, namely, sacramental experience, remains central to the theological task and neither embarrasses nor threatens the validity of its work. Quite the contrary, on the basis of an organic and dynamic plurality in divinity, feminist theologians can now more clearly and boldly claim both the heritage of negation that preserves divine greatness from idolatrous impulses and the heritage of sacramental attention that remembers—and honors—the presence of the divine.

The One and the Many, an ancient theological and philosophical conundrum expressed in myriad ways through the centuries, crouches now before feminist theologies like the grinning Coyote of so many First Nation traditions. Like Coyote, this conundrum will not be resolved or killed, except briefly and then to ill effect. Rather than be resolved once and forever, the ancient problem awaits our creativity, our attention, and offers itself to further our understanding. The stasis of the traditional one deity no longer can hold the multiplicity of the world over which it is supposed to preside. It is lost in the din of competing voices, competing cultures, competing Ones. The One has become the Many, and we must better understand that turning in order better to recognize divinity before us and in order better to understand ourselves.

> Apprehended on the slant
> of air between two trees
> crow-fractured morning
> after morning, I would
> name you if I knew how.
> I don't. Know. How
> you leap over naming,
> sidle under, squeeze around,
> you lilac, thistle, burr,
> belonging to no species,
> you chipmunk-sudden,

slug-utterly unaccommodating—
you rainfall prism beautiful,
earthquake terrifying,
still of night-deep darkness
comforting,
you rock, you rock,
you unnamable, unknowable known
how you scamper/swim
creep/crawl soar/sink
stride/fly—you mountain, you
desert, delicious, delirious
madness-making
you ocean, you faucet, you ripple,
erupt! Spray! Spout, you silence,
you suggestion, you
impossible, unbelievable
god

—Pat Schneider[22]

CHAPTER TWO

Can Feminist Theologies
Be Historicist and Disclosive?

I MPORTANT IDEAS HAVE HISTORIES. Like great flooding rivers, they start some-
where as innocuous and small streams and grow only as others contribute to them. At the greatest width of the Mississippi, the Amazon, or the
Nile, it is difficult to picture the tiny spring so many miles away, and as you
straddle the spring, it is hard not to shake your head at the thought of the
mighty earth-carving river. Feminism has become something of a great
river. It is an influential phenomenon in religion and theology that did not
jump whole and all grown up, like Athena, out of the head of a single
person. Feminist theologies actually are rooted in a long and bumpy history
of rethinking life, the universe, and everything that began roughly five hundred years ago. They are the product of sometimes conflicting responses to
that long history and possess at heart a deep and important tension between
the critical skepticism borne by the scientific revolution and the theological
affirmation that persists in religious feeling. Understanding these roots is
crucial to understanding feminist theologies and their challenges today.

"Feminist theologies" is a collective term for a profoundly diverse group
of voices and communities addressing sexism in relation to racism and other
social structures of oppression in contemporary religious communities. However, the specific and diverse cultural and communal influences that characterize the many voices that come together as streams in the feminist theological river are all part of a theological realm of discourse that is shaped by
a shared intellectual history. Certainly, all contemporary theological discourse must trace its roots to the prehistoric past presented by tradition and
sacred texts. And feminist theologies are no different, evidenced by the
breadth and depth of work that is being done by feminist scholars on Christian, Jewish, and pagan origins. But in the overall character of their debates,
feminist theologians are part of a particularly modern movement fueled
and bedeviled by the intellectual and social legacies of the Enlightenment,
legacies that can be described in three largely secular phases of modern
epistemology—the scientific revolution, the philosophical turn to subjec-

tivity, and finally the emergence of functional social constructionism. In addition, feminist theologies are deeply influenced by neoorthodox theological responses to modernity in the twentieth century. Taken together, these developments illuminate the intellectual roots of feminist theologies; the depth of their history, and the intensity of the challenges they now face as a result of this history.

Feminist theologies do not represent merely one more in a line of theological responses to the modernist insight that religious ideas function in the construction and maintenance of social systems. On the whole, they go farther in that they thoroughly depend upon modernist skepticism for their most basic critiques of the Christian tradition. Feminist theologies generally ground their warrants for constructive innovation in a skepticism that exempts all language, metaphors, images, and ideas from corresponding directly to independent divine substance. I call this strategy the metaphoric exemption. As a strategy rooted in Enlightenment historicism both modern and postmodern, the metaphoric exemption has profoundly important consequences both for feminist theologies and for feminist religious experiences. That is because experience, messy and untheorizable and generally inaccessible to skeptical criticism, is also a foundational category for feminism across the board.

Feminist theologies in general, therefore, are deeply shaped by skepticism and by affirmations of lived experience in all of its robust particularity. Feminist theologians have tended to skirt the problems that stem from obvious tensions between these two foundations, with the result that deeper inconsistencies tend to creep into their theological proposals. Some theological constructions (like monotheism) are glossed and uncritically adopted, while feminist spiritual practices and experiences, with their implications for embodied divine multiplicity, tend to be ignored.

It is not enough to assert that feminist theologies are generally structured and shaped by two opposing taproots. Most theologians engaged in constructive feminist work know that their proposals are resisted in mainstream religious communities and that they have little to offer by way of defense except the repetitive claim that traditional theological ideas about divinity and related ethical ideas are marred by prejudice. The position that new images and ideas more sympathetic to excluded groups are warranted simply because of traditional abuses may be true, but as an argument, it does not provide a foundation upon which to answer charges of reverse idolatry. Feminist theologies can answer these charges in the long run only if their own skeptical, historicist foundations are firm and yet do not contradict their claims about experiential authority. Understanding the evolution of modernist skepticism in the theological form of the metaphoric exemption clarifies the critical underpinnings of feminist theologies and highlights the challenges for feminist experiential claims about divine existence that result. Thus, examining the two main streams of skepticism and experiential confession that flow into the feminist theological river is crucial for theologians who are concerned about the long-range viability of liberationist discourses and theological constructions.

HISTORICISM IS AN ENLIGHTENMENT TALE

Five hundred years ago navigational skills and inventions such as the printing press, the telescope, and the gun began to alter the landscape of ideas by altering the possible and the known. It is hard for us today to appreciate the magnitude of these otherwise small inventions in terms of their impact on the world, the heavens, and history. Intellectually, they enabled a deep skepticism about earlier truths to develop along with an emphasis on empirical experience. Perhaps the most dramatic early forebear of feminist theology's skeptical heritage is the colorful Galileo, not because he looked through a telescope and saw a different universe, but because he dethroned the past masters by arguing so convincingly against the revealed truths of the ancients in favor of his instrument's evidence.

Perhaps Italians have always been hot-blooded, or perhaps he just had the misfortune to live too close to a threatened Vatican, but Galileo Galilei took the rap for emerging skeptical ideas about traditional and sacred truths. There were quite a few others engaged in similar investigations, such as the Englishman Francis Bacon and the Frenchman René Descartes. Like them, Galileo argued that truth is made not by the authority of elders or of tradition but by its example in the present. Whether present example would bear up the traditional truths remained (and in many ways still remains) to be seen. But they all argued in their own ways that errors can last a very long time and can even be mistaken for the most sacred truths by the worthiest of people. Galileo directly impugned Ptolemy and Aristotle, but he was put under house arrest by the church rulers for indirectly impugning the inerrancy of the Bible and the authority of the church fathers. Bacon and Descartes were doing much the same thing, but one was a baron with English manners living in a land of marginal Vatican influence and the other was a Frenchman with enough savvy to write placating, God-fearing introductions to his essays and enough sense to immigrate to the relatively tolerant Netherlands.

The idea that errors about the world and heavens could occur on such massive scale as Galileo and his fellow philosophers suggested was disturbing, but it was actually less so than the implication that error could lurk in sacred texts and traditions. If tradition and the wisdom of the ancients cannot be trusted except by present display, then how can the tradition and wisdom of religion's ancient founders possibly hold up? Is God supposed to repeat miracles on demand for them to be credible? Most certainly, according to Bacon, who was thoroughly convinced that for God to exist, God must be a reasonable chap. Barring that, Bacon argued, the Divine One would at least make sure that enough credible observers are present to give reliable reports. In any case, the idea that *truths* about the world and the composition of the heavens revealed by God in the Bible could be proven incorrect by human observation was the beginning of a long history of struggle for understanding the world and its increasingly problematic ruling deity. Galileo was officially silenced, but as we all know, the ideas that he and his contemporaries contemplated were seeds let loose on a busy wind.

Feminist theologies can trace their ancestry in this skeptical intellectual tradition. Feminist theologians are able to take for granted the rightness of questioning traditional authorities because of a long intellectual history that made doing so a sound and even recommended practice. Starting from the position that theological traditions should be questioned, especially those that portray God as exclusively male or that privilege dominant groups in any way, feminist theologies assert that sacred and theological traditions are open to critical interrogation, regardless of ancient or sacred standing. The conclusion that traditional theology misrepresents the divine and does damage to women (and all that is not designated "man") is widely dispersed throughout feminist literature.[1] Bacon and Galileo would approve, if not of the conclusions, at least of the critical premise.

But behind feminism's sweeping and damning conclusions about the functional complicity of theology in the subjugation of all women (and designated women, nonwhite men, and the earth) lies a fundamental concern with the power of religious language, symbols, and traditions to affect the *epistéme,* the social ordering of shared meanings, particularly as these meanings denote normative gendered realities. This concern goes far beyond Galileo's or Bacon's complaints against traditional authorities. It reveals an assumption, woven deeply into the fabric of feminist theologies, that much of what we call reality is a social construction and that ideas of divinity function to maintain or to subvert that reality. The scientific revolution of the sixteenth and seventeenth centuries was only the start of the ideas that would eventually form the fabric of feminist theologies. The assumptions of social constructionism—that reality itself is the product of human imagining—and of functionalism—that symbols of divinity play supporting roles in the smooth running of society—represent the mature result of questions about traditional authority that began with the scientific revolution and grew into critical insights about history and social change through the Enlightenment.

Social constructionism is the creative product of one of the core epistemological insights of modernity, namely, that history (and all of its attendant meanings and claims to truth) is a series of complex human fabrications. It is not that historians make things up or that they manufacture evidence. Rather, it is the awareness that any given history, being a process of interpretation, is also partly fictional. All historical accounts are stories that can never tell the whole tale, no matter how carefully the evidence is treated. Every good historian knows this. No account of an event is true from every angle, and the job of historians is to identify what they believe to be the best angle—to see which evidence has meaning and to give the best interpretation of that evidence. History works this way for everyone. Even individual histories, as memories, are worked into personal stories that filter, sort, and edit. Over time, the distinction between filter and truth becomes hard to discern.

The more radical consequence of this insight about history is that reality "itself" is a complex matter of human interpretation, its contents a sleight of language and habit serving social and cultural ends first and last. The most extreme way of stating this is that there is no reality except what we have manufactured together. Reality is what we agree it to be at the deepest, most taken-for-granted levels. Even so-called direct observation does not protect us from the possibility that everything in the end is a fiction founded only on common belief. A colleague has posted on his door, for example, a sign that says, "I believe it, therefore I see it." What is more, common belief is fraught with suggestion and the potential for error. Has anyone been spared the experience of a belief or perception proven false at some time or another? Ultimately, of course, we depend upon the pragmatic assertion that the world is really there, firm and placid in its existence apart from our unruly and traitorous perceptions. No one could get through a day without making this wager. But we can prove nothing in favor of the wager when our instruments (ultimately, none other than our minds) are so prone to breakage, misalignment, and fault.

The persuasive power of critical skepticism in relation to questions of ultimate reality has become so strong over the past two hundred years that theology, in general, has increasingly had to engage the possibility that God is merely a product of human imagination. As I suggest in the next chapter, twentieth-century theologians have had to structure their arguments within the relatively hostile canopy of an intellectual age that suspects, if not believes, that culture is the paper on which human beings rather than deities author truth itself for their own functions and purposes. This phe-

nomenon is functionalism and social construction together, a linked notion that has become foundational to constructive theology in its most
creative, but precarious, work. I call this linked notion the metaphoric
exemption, a critical tool of constructive theology that recognizes the social constructedness and powerful political functioning of *all* language, ideas,
and images of the divine. To make clear the connection between the metaphoric exemption and contemporary theology, and ultimately to make the
argument that feminist theologies are founded upon and funded by the
metaphoric exemption's critical insights, we must first briefly trace its historical development and main themes.

THE CHALLENGES OF HISTORICISM

Most Western theological discourse since the seventeenth century has been
filtered through the lens of so-called Enlightenment thought. The mounting evidence of vastly different worlds of peoples and their religions pour-
ing into the European world over the course of several hundred years of
exploration and expansion began to eat at the assurance most felt about the
self-evident primacy of their religious beliefs. German philosopher
Immanuel Kant took up this unease in the eighteenth century and con-
ceded that no knowledge, even knowledge of God, could come to us
unfiltered through human interpretation. Conducting most of his work
alone in an isolated study, Kant was confident that he could locate a truly
sure foundation for absolute truth claims in the careful application of reason to practical and moral questions.

Because he concluded that most of what we know is not knowledge
but interpretation, Kant could find no objective basis for religion except as
moral sentiment, or for God except as an abstract regulative principle
grounded in the structure of reason. In other words, we can only be rea-
sonably sure of ideas that withstand reasonable tests, and we can only be
absolutely certain of ideas that withstand tests with universal conditions.
God, he concluded, is a reasonable reality only insofar as the absolute measure of universal conditions is met.

Although he was satisfied that this conclusion provided a basis for human appreciation of real divinity, in effect it was a radical and not very
satisfying reduction of divinity to moral necessity. Kant did not, in the end,
apply his skepticism of reason critically enough to satisfy a more gregari-
ous young contemporary named Georg Wilhelm Hegel who questioned
the sources of reason itself and concluded that ideas, including reason, are
subject to the vagaries of intellectual fashion, in other words, to history.
Thus, in the most radical move yet of an epoch committed to the disman-

tling of tradition, Hegel redefined philosophy as the articulation of *Zeit-geist* (loosely translated "the spirit of an age"). Truth claims, he concluded, are firmly embedded in and emerge out of the overall spirit, or culture, of an era, meaning that reason and truth themselves may be relative and can change over time.[2]

The profound epistemological shift from absolute to relative represented in Kant's and Hegel's ideas, coupled with the earlier shift from traditional authority to experience represented in Bacon's and Galileo's ideas, ushered in the self-reflective age of subjectivity we call modernity. These profound innovations in thought were motivated by a search for certainty, but they ended up making certainty a more elusive mirage. If traditional authorities such as Aristotle and the Bible are no longer reliable sources of scientific certainty, and if human reasoning itself is subject to epochal textures and paradigms, certainty about ultimate truths recedes farther and farther from human grasp. Thus, these ideas ultimately undercut the foundations of metaphysical and ontological claims and opened the door to an understanding of ideas uprooted from the stasis of traditional notions of the Absolute and located them anew in the historical, and hence mobile, fabric of culture.

The birth of modern skepticism in the Enlightenment is so crucial to the eventual emergence of feminist theological criticisms of patriarchal sacred history that it is worth tracing the development of these ideas more closely. Claude Welch has made the helpful suggestion that the very heart of the Enlightenment was not so much the "omnipotence of reason" as is commonly claimed, but the "omnicompetence of criticism, understood as the assertion that everything is properly subject to rational criticism . . . in the confidence that such criticism will recognize and mark its own limits, thus finally showing its competence and certainties."[3] That is, everything is open to question, even the standards by which answers can be found. Because Kant turned the omnicompetence of criticism onto religion, he subjected religious truths to rigorously rational criticism and reduced religious truth claims to a universalized morality, based not in the paternal edicts of an external sacred realm, but in the structures of human rationality.[4] In so doing, he created an opening for the self-critique of religion and theology. His preoccupation with laws as the source of certainty established the limits of his critique. A reduction of ethical judgment to human happiness as the standard for moral action allowed him to locate moral certainty in a notion of the greatest good, the categorical imperative.[5]

Perceiving the self-referencing limits of Kant's conclusions and remaining dissatisfied with what he understood to be the static and ahistorical limits of categorical absolutes, Hegel sought to locate the foundations of knowledge elsewhere. He overturned philosophy's preoccupation with absolute ideas and replaced it with a foundational preoccupation with self-critical, dialectical movement, or what he called Absolute Spirit.[6] Hegel was not ready to historicize and hence relativize all thought, and so he developed notions of "absolute knowledge" to deal with this problem. However, in later years the so-called young Hegelians began a process of inquiry that eventually abandoned Hegel's retreat to absolute knowledge, leading them to conclude that everything is a product of human history. They set about the task of revealing the human hands (or minds) behind all aspects of culture, religion, and knowledge.

At one extreme of this new historicized view of culture, a passionate young German Hegelian named Karl Marx articulated his view of human agency in the production of history. He replaced Hegel's notion of absolute knowledge with one of absolute materialism in order to account for the massive dehumanization frothing in the wake of new industrialization. His neo-Hegelian theory of history made the production of culture primarily an affair of competing human interests, exempting no social institution, especially the institutions concerned with truth claims and consciousness. Religion therefore made an important, if overly determined, target for Marxists.[7] Because ultimate reality is material, rather than supernatural or spiritual, religion is false insofar as it points beyond the material realm to a supposed greater reality. Religion functions on behalf of the ruling powers; it drugs the downtrodden, distracting them from the immediate systems that oppress them with promises of a distant heaven.

This omnicompetence of criticism undercut confidence in ontological claims about divine existence and about epistemological hopes that the divine could somehow be known. Perhaps God was a delusion, since the traditional sources for certainty were increasingly criticized. Nineteenth-century theological responses were, we could argue, creatively defensive. The valorization of human agency implied in Hegel's concept of *Zeitgeist*[8] was developed in a more personalistic form by Friedrich Schleiermacher, a young German pastor whose excellent education in German philosophy could not douse the warmth and experiential authority of his childhood religious life. He saw hope for affirming divine existence and power in pietism, the direct and incontrovertible evidence of personal experience. This strategy, the genius of evangelists throughout history, served a particular purpose in combating the crisis of confidence engendered by historicism.

Schleiermacher was convinced that he could persuade his most skeptical friends that belief in God is rational by providing them with a universal experiential basis for faith. He also sought to shore up the foundations of certainty for believers by turning them inward to the incontrovertible evidence of their own experience. His strategy required a turn to the authority of personal feeling. For Schleiermacher, the heart of the matter, so to speak, was epistemological and existential. Knowledge concerning the Absolute, or God, cannot be obtained through reason, scientific observation, or admittedly fallible textual sources. Rather, the only incontrovertible knowledge of divine existence comes through feeling, the common experience of radical (absolute) dependence. We feel and know dependence, we cannot help it, and so intuitively we know God. This entails a kind of reduction of theology to claims about human experience and perception that he argued reveal a universal subjective relationship to divine being.[9]

But the slippage of theology's moorings in the certainty of tradition and sacred text only increased in Schleiermacher's neo-Hegelian turn to the self. Despite the fact that by the nineteenth century Descartes's famous ontological proof ("I think, therefore I am") had long been discredited among philosophers, the concepts of self and subjectivity as final arbiters of reality were taking root because of their fluid adaptability within history. The self, if nothing else, could be a refuge of subjective certainty. Needless to say, pietism and the makeshift pulpits of traveling evangelists flourished in the nineteenth century.

The idea that history implicates and swallows up the perceived truths of an age allowed Hegel his evolutionary optimism concerning freedom, Marx his optimism about the inevitable downfall of capitalism, and Nietzsche his pessimism about both. The idea that human cultures and perceived truths can change over time for the better is the same idea that whole societies can be endlessly deluded. Thus, out of the fabric of *Zeitgeist,* Marx developed his key notion of false consciousness to explain the willing acquiescence of millions of factory laborers in exploitive and degrading work. He spoke not of the spirit of an age, but more cynically of "the illusion of an epoch."[10] He was influenced by yet another young German Hegelian named Ludwig Feuerbach, whose enthusiasm for the humanist potential of historicism led him to posit the notion that divinity is a product of human imagining, serving symbolic purposes of inspiration and self-improvement.[11] Feuerbach's contribution to the growing torrent of modernity that was sweeping away the foundations of certainty was a complete reduction of theism to human projection. His isolation of God as the imaginative symbol of the best in human longing influenced not only Freud and the developing fields of psychology and sociology but, as we shall see in the next chapter, took hold of Christian theology and would not let go.

The idea that some gods are illusory was by no means an innovation of the elite nineteenth-century German community of theologians and philosophers. But the idea that *all* gods and concepts of divinity are illusory and that they exist within a kind of false consciousness that serves human imaginative functions was the fullest expression of historicism yet. With Feuerbach, the way was paved for a thoroughgoing critique of religious practices and beliefs, no longer exclusively in terms of their doctrinal comprehensibility or coherence within theological norms, but in terms of their functioning in individual and social formations of human knowledge and culture.

Walter Lowe suggests a helpful way of viewing the development of the Enlightenment backdrop to theology. He identifies two formative points or phases that are critical to understanding the position in which theology finds itself today. The first phase, he suggests, is characterized by Newtonian physics. Isaac Newton's science (which followed closely on the heels of Galileo, Bacon, and Descartes) established nature for the first time as an autonomous, mechanized *order*, ultimately transparent in its structure and impersonal in its effects. The initial importance of this innovation for theology was in the realm of ethics, counteracting the prevailing belief that all suffering and tragedy was the consequence of moral action. By positing nature as autonomous and rationally structured, tragedy and evil could be divided into natural and moral categories, relieving human beings of culpability for the events, such as floods and other disasters, now understood as "natural" occurrences. The separation of moral and natural evil in the Newtonian cosmos supported a theological turn to the self since moral culpability now resided more discretely in self-willed action—in the realm of subjectivity—rather than in divine retributions acted out on the world.

The second phase, Lowe argues, was political. This phase developed in opposition to a myth supported by the first phase, namely, that prevailing social orders (including their injustices), like volcanoes, childbirth, and the weight of things, were also natural and, being so, were rationally structured and autonomous and thus preordained and ahistorical. The Hegel/Marx phase of the Enlightenment discovered history and, in so doing, historicized the structures of legitimacy in politics and society, including eventually, religion and theology. Again, the implications for theology were, at first, primarily ethical. By historicizing social and political orders and making them human products, injustices stemming from them could be understood in moral terms, and persons in positions of authority could be held responsible not only for their individual actions but also for the working of the whole. This historicization of politics entailed a rethinking of culture and social structures as no longer divinely given.

The actual implications of this shift for theology and religion run deep. Marx's argument that religious institutions fall into the category of social structure, for example, made explicit the functional dimensions of religious orders in the maintenance of society. It was a relatively small step from the condemnation of religious institutions as flawed and interest-laden social constructs to the condemnation of the theological arguments underpinning those institutions. The divinely ordained order of things, from kings and queens to the authority of the church to interpret God's will, was becoming a humanly ordained order and thus could be revised or chucked altogether. Feuerbach's argument that divinity is a human ideal writ large on the heavens followed easily from the argument that cultures are historical products of human action governed by human self-interests. And these steps were made easier (although not determined) by Hegel's earlier work historicizing human thought.[12]

The Enlightenment, however its progress and processes of thought are understood, is not remarkable for its engagement of philosophy with theology. Among others, Plato, Origen, Plotinus, Augustine, and perhaps most notably Thomas Aquinas predate the philosophers of the Enlightenment in their engagement of theological claims with philosophies of their time. Indeed, theology and philosophy are, for the vast majority of recorded human history, indistinguishable. What is notable about the Enlightenment mix of theology and philosophy is the import of the idea of human agency into history itself. Plato's divinized universe of ideas, characterizing the development of theology through its first thousand years, was gradually eclipsed in philosophical theology by Aristotelian naturalism, worked out by Aquinas into a governed universe of natural laws. While the differences between both the Platonic and the Aristotelian systems of thought occupied the lives and work of generations of theologians and philosophers, both were concerned with the explication of truths about the world independent of human understanding or construction, a concern that had radically changed shape by the beginning of the twentieth century.

Whether the historicization of social meaning that developed through the Enlightenment was a pessimistic acquiescence to the inaccessibility of independent truths or an optimistic retrieval of human capability to construct meaning in the absence of such truths remains unanswered. The innovations of the Enlightenment touched religion and theology in new ways with lasting significance, especially for the latter. The historicization of human knowing could not help including theological knowing. First ecclesial and then liturgical structures slipped out of the realm of the Absolute into history and the realm of human construction, opening themselves to reforms of all kinds. This made possible ever deeper questions about theology's foundational warrants, first concerning church authorities, next concerning ritual patterns and structures of worship, and finally concerning the language of God "himself," the central work of theology and the particular concern of feminist theologies.

SOCIAL THEORY AND RELIGIOUS IDEAS

By the end of the nineteenth century, the idea that knowledge is socially constructed and historically malleable gave birth to a new breed of scholarship concerned entirely with the evolution and maintenance of human societies. No longer considered a more or less null backdrop on the divine and the human stages, the realm of the social—society—with all of its fashions, morays, fetishes, tyrannies, and beliefs was suddenly a foreground topic, a remarkably clever and influential human invention worthy of investigation and comparison. The final pieces of the modernist foundations underpinning feminist theologies fall into place with the contributions that sociological theory made to the evolution of the idea that gods are social constructions serving political and sociological ends.

Emile Durkheim was a thoughtful French boy born in the mid-nineteenth century. His less serious-minded schoolmates dubbed him "the metaphysician," and he assumed he would become a rabbi like his father. However, after an adolescent mystical experience and a consequent dabbling interest in Catholicism, he ended up an agnostic dissatisfied both with religion and with the abstractions of philosophy. Intrigued by the radical social ideas that were circulating Europe in the late nineteenth century, he became convinced by the new evolutionary view of human nature and sought to support it in a comparative study of society. Because of his resulting work, he is considered (along with Max Weber) the founder of sociology. But he was a student of social evolution and so could not stay away from religion or his fascination with it. Convinced of its importance, but unwilling to accept its doctrines, Durkheim worked hard to find a way to explain religion in terms other than its own revelatory claims. The last major work of his life, published in 1922, was a closely argued (if questionably researched) treatise on the origins of religion, in which he concluded that the contents of all religions are wholly fabricated in the social sphere for the maintenance of social meaning and order.

Durkheim developed functionalism as a necessary feature of the study of religion. He pushed past Marx's and Feuerbach's simplistic claims that theological assertions are mere charades of human invention or forms of false consciousness. Like them, he argued for a theory of religion that roots itself in the skeptical notion that religious ideas arise out of and serve social purposes, a reductive functionalism that makes them mere projections of imagination motivated by collective human processes and goals. Unlike Marx who viewed religion as a detrimental social irritant, or Feuerbach who saw it as a useful tool for human betterment, Durkheim asserted the utter necessity and foundational position of religion and theological ideas in culture. He felt that just because gods are the products of imagination does not mean that they are dispensable. If they were, he argued, we would have to dispense with all products of human imagining, like language or thought. In fact, Durkheim considered the imaginative products of religion, and particularly its deities, so important that he placed them prior to (and in some sense, ironically, more real than) all other human inventions. "It is admissible," he argued, "that systems of ideas like religions, which have held so considerable a place in history, and to which, in all times, men have come to receive the energy which they must have to live, should be made up of a tissue of illusions. Today we are beginning to realize that law, morals and even scientific thought itself were born of religion, were for a long time confounded with it, and have remained penetrated with its spirit."[13] In other words, religious ideas fund all others because religion is the first act of human communal consciousness.

To better understand this point and its importance for the later development of feminist theologies, we benefit by placing Durkheim in context. His theory of religion reflects indebtedness to Enlightenment innovation and particularly to nineteenth-century ideas of evolutionary human culture and the perfectibility of the human being. To religion's "cultured despisers," all ideas of God became, rather than ends in themselves, tools of human culture that were incidental (à la Marx or Feuerbach) or necessary (à la Durkheim) but essentially illusory with regard to their real content. The very idea, however, that the object of religion could be human culture itself instead of God constituted something new, breeding fresh doubts about the existence of God that lodged ever more firmly in Western consciousness.

Durkheim attempted to define religion by reducing it to an imagined first moment in the life of a society, identifying it with the most elementary collective act of group formation. He argued that the first moment of any society occurs in its original clustering of individuals into a self-identified group. The very moment a society comes into being as a society or clan is the moment its members recognize themselves as part of a group. The moment of self-conscious formation as a society requires the concept of "us," a notion transcending the individuals designated by the "us." Durkheim saw significance in this moment not in terms of social groups themselves, for it seemed possible to him that humans might function in groups by default, or in an ad hoc and temporary manner; rather, he saw religious significance in the consciousness entailed in the act of group formation.

Durkheim's influential functionalist critique of religion is born out of this insight. The moment a group sets itself up as a primary entity of identification for its members (such as a family, a clan, or a nation) and *names* itself thus is the first transcendent and therefore the first religious act. Since, he argues, the group or clan "cannot exist without a name and an emblem, and since this emblem is always before the eyes of men, it is upon this, and the objects whose image it is, that the sentiments which society arouses in its members are fixed."[14] The projection of a group identity is the creation of an abstract concept (the birth, he claims, of science and philosophy) and necessarily entails language and norms by which people can orient themselves and live. The group name, or totem, therefore takes on a *necessarily* sacred quality and becomes the very basis of the existence and identity of the society. Once group identity has formed, ideas relevant to identity, orientation, world, and group can then come into being.

In one fell swoop, Durkheim sought to demolish the grounds for any substantive categories of thought or ideas apart from their collective social fabrication and function in the formation of society. The primacy of the social group as template for organization itself meant for him that "fundamental notions of the intellect, the essential categories of thought, may be the product of social factors. . . . Clearly this is the case with the very notion of category itself."[15] The idea of society makes possible all things collectively human, especially beliefs, traditions, and aspirations of the group. If this idea were eliminated, all transcendent categories would vanish, including, by definition, both gods and the human societies they represent.

Symbols, particularly in the form of totems and deities, therefore have central social significance and are critical to Durkheim's theory of society. At the grandest level, he argues, "social life, it seems, would not be possible without the monumental symbolism of the great sacred power that shelters, even celebrates, fractured lives."[16] According to Victoria Lee Erickson, Durkheim's formulation of the process that sacralizes society in symbols of divine being is crucial to understanding social formation as cosmic construction.[17]

Thus, religion and religious ideas, according to this scheme, are the necessary products of being human. This is the foundation upon which Durkheim builds his central argument. Social conformity of some kind is absolutely essential, not only for the existence of society—for that is a kind of tautology—but even more fundamentally for what is human about humans. The essential sociality of human beings lies in the necessity of shared meaning in the identity and life of individuals. Society, then, is the creator of human existence, not the other way around, and for society to "live there is not merely the need of a satisfactory moral conformity, but also there is a minimum of logical conformity beyond which it cannot safely go." Without logical agreement there is no society, and there is no human being. Our ability to identify ourselves and to orient ourselves in the cosmos makes us sane. The alternative is a questionable humanity: "Does a mind ostensibly free itself from these forms of thought? It is no longer considered a human mind in the full sense of the word, and is treated accordingly."[18]

Durkheim's reduction of the contents of religion to social function is his most basic, and compelling, argument about the substance of religion. It is radically reductive in the sense that it makes God the sum of society, and purely functional in the sense that within the realm of human consciousness and human being, God, deity, totem, or divinity serves human needs at the foundations and outer edges of identity, mirroring back, calling forth, and giving shape and recognition to the values and concepts that locate human beings meaningfully in the world. Sacred objects and beings based locally on clan identities are sufficient until commerce and imperialism require larger collective social groupings and thus larger, more unifying sacred ideas. When multiple groups, clans, tribes, or nations merge, local emblems and deities are subordinated to higher, unifying emblems, leading penultimately to universalized emblems and finally, probably, to monotheism.[19]

For Durkheim, social theory is therefore theology, and vice versa. "If religion has given birth to all that is essential in society," he argues, "it is because the idea of society is the soul of religion."[20] This is reductionism par excellence. He makes the content of theology a social construction aimed only symbolically at the heavens (or the hero or the deity), which in reality binds the community and is in reality the sum of its identity. Gods, or sacred principles, actually keep the world intact, and even more so they keep us human because they are the highest names we have for reality and for ourselves. Without them, we are lost. The religious is therefore utterly serious business, and our sanity is based on a bifurcation between a pure sacred realm and a messy profane one.[21] The human is the final arbiter of the real—this is Durkheim's version of modern subjectivity—and if the sacred principle is society itself and vice versa, then *both* divinity and society are "real only insofar as [they have] a place in human consciousnesses, and this place is whatever one may give them."[22]

In his final writings, Durkheim left behind ideas of social construction that neither ridicule nor eliminate the necessity of divinity in the work of being human. But his ideas strip all known sacred things of their independent existence and immunity from criticism. Like the writers of all such reductions, however, Durkheim did not succeed in proving the impossibility of independent divine existence outside human imagining and social construction. And it is not clear that he wanted to. He merely made it harder to speak of that divinity precisely because our words weave images that lead back inevitably to ourselves. He was in awe of the human capacity to cast fantasies into productive realities. But even in his most incisive reduction of gods to human manufacture and reduction of the sacred to the awkwardness of self-consciousness, there remains in Durkheim's functionalism an intriguing space of silence about otherwise independent and unknowable divine reality. He did articulate more clearly than anyone before him the critical scope of functionalism, which needed only a more nuanced elaboration of social ideology to become functional social constructionism.

Functional social constructionism is a mouthful. As a term it is as cumbersome and ugly as the lumbering machinery of the modern industrial age, and this somehow seems appropriate. The massive, belching earth excavators that scrape the rich green skin of mountains bare for coal and ore are no more relentless and final in their strip mining than this idea that denudes and humbles the sacred realm. In France, the agnostic philosopher named Emile Durkheim, whose early rabbinical training kept him coming back to the problem of God, took up the Enlightenment ideas spilling across Europe and forged them into a powerful critique of divinity using functionalism. For him, the ancient Hebrew dream of the rent Temple veil became a new story consonant with the mechanical hubris of modernity.

Functionalism makes possible the simple reduction of the Father God to an imaginative construct. This alone is a powerful insight for feminism, but it does not account fully for the mature political, economic, and ideological critique that feminist theologies inherit from social theory. A contemporary of Durkheim, an economist in Germany named Max Weber, helped to mature the theory that would eventually ground feminist criticisms of patriarchal religion. He was not even aware of Durkheim's work, but he understood the new philosophical insights of historicism and what they implied for the status of truth claims. He began to see important connections between religious belief and the evolution of political ideology. Religion, as a historical set of beliefs and requisite behaviors, shapes motivation and ideology, which in turn shape economic and political structures. Thus, social construction and function, he discovered, cut both ways. We wield words and ideas, but in turn, they also wield us.[23]

Unlike Durkheim or Feuerbach or most of his German forebears, Weber was not concerned with explaining the essence of religion. Instead, he was interested in its consequences. He studied religion to better explain social and political behavior, "particularly since even the ends of the religious and magical actions are predominantly economic."[24] He saw that religious ideas and institutions function not only in the collective ordering of the universe for purposes of group stability and identity, as Durkheim argued, and not only to legitimize existing structures of power, as Marx argued, but he saw that religious ideas and institutions also function at the level of individual motivation, both political and economic, for social change.[25]

For Weber, the meaning of a religion, of its contents, symbols, and rituals, is summed up in the motivation for action that it engenders in human beings. Religious ideas function insofar as they play a direct role in the "development . . . systematization and rationalization of a religious ethic," and religion itself is in turn determined by the needs and influences of social classes.[26] Even more than Durkheim, Weber's view of religion and religious ideas was fully informed by the new historicism. Religion, like all constellations of important ideas, is evolutionary, proceeding in linear fashion from mundane demands for so-called magic in tribal economies to the social rationalizations that flow from priestly structures and their theologies in massive imperial cultures. Religious ideas are important not because of any independent or "real" substance to which they may or may not refer, but because of the reality of belief associated with the ideas and the interests, both material and psychological, that they support. "To be sure," he argued, "the ancient political god of the locality, even where he was an ethical and universally powerful god, existed merely for the protection of the political interests of his followers' associations."[27]

Weber's contribution to the idea of functional social constructionism modified and nuanced Durkheim's exclusive focus on collective identity formation. His insights into the relationship between religious ideas, piety, and the motivations of individuals in society introduced the possibility that a closer relationship exists between theology and corporate political and economic behavior. Theology, in a Weberian scheme, could conceivably become a tool for social change and activism to the extent that it is concerned with ethics and articulates a normative worldview. Theology is fundamentally the scheme behind religiously motivated behaviors that can adapt to the persuasive insights of prophetic action. In this way, Weber makes clear the connection between political motivations and theological concepts, a connection that feminist theologians did not miss.

Religion for Weber is therefore a social institution with primarily social commitments. For him, religious ideas (or theology), far from being Durkheim's originating concept of society, are the intellectual subset of a social institution that functions to rationalize the political economy. And theology as a secondary function of religion is useful insofar as it inspires and legitimates a religious ethic, promoting a kind of false consciousness that religion is about something other than politics. But religion and theology also function socially insofar as they accommodate political change through the medium of prophetic legitimation. Hence the racist theology that motivated and legitimated Nazism, and the prophetic justice theology of Dr. Martin Luther King Jr. that motivated and legitimated the civil rights movement. Religion and religious ideas are therefore historically important because of their profound relationship to human motivation, interests, and related social action.

While Durkheim's functionalism is more or less rigid, reducing all religious ideas somewhat passively to the collective ideas of society and cosmos (without reference either to individuals or to questions of social change), Weber's functionalism is more organic and what Robert Merton would later call "permissive, rather than determinant, of specific social structures."[28] Weber leaves undetermined the question of the so-called real content of religious ideas and so is not concerned about reducing them to socially constructed processes. However, his overall scheme of evolutionary historicism allows for and even implies a reduction of the status of divinity to the symbolized interests of social classes. In effect this does reduce divinity to its social function.[29]

Together, Durkheim and Weber created a mechanical means by which the motivations, beliefs, myths, and behaviors of human societies could be dissected. By the mid-twentieth century, when the intellectual centers of Europe lay exhausted in rubble, the idea of functional social constructionism jumped the Atlantic and found voice in the United States, a nation conceived in modernity. So functional social constructionism came into maturity just as the seeds of twentieth-century feminism began to sprout.

Theoretical sociology and phenomenology in the United States attempted to explain functional social constructionism in everyday life through the concept of "life-world"—an internally coherent (though not necessarily singular) set of interpreted experiences that individuals inhabit.[30] The life-world presents itself continuously and seamlessly to us as everyday, taken-for-granted, "paramount" reality, as "worldview." It is intersubjective; it is a world of meanings shared by its inhabitants, meanings that order and typify experience based on a common stock of knowledge. Different cultures, to the extent that their social meanings do not overlap, are truly different worlds.

Peter Berger, a young sociologist in postwar United States, took these insights to suggest that what lies at the heart of the life-world (and thus, functionally, at the heart of the real world) is socially constructed meaning. He then added a Durkheimian understanding of symbolic function and a Weberian understanding of meaning and motivation to make the argument that culture hinges on the creation and re-creation of a socially constructed symbolic infrastructure—a sacred canopy of shared meanings—that orders and gives coherence to human life. Meaning and "order" are linked; both are necessary for human life, and both must be constructed out of the whole cloth of collective experience and symbolically communicated. Identity and human understanding, in other words, do not just happen; they are made. And especially, following Durkheim, they are made through the production of sacred symbols. Thus, Berger argues that "symbolic universes are social products with a history. If one is to understand their meaning, one has to understand the history of their production. This is all the more important because these products of human consciousness, by their very nature, present themselves as full-blown and inevitable totalities."[31] Robert Wuthnow suggests that, for Berger, social order exists only under the sacred canopy, an organization of symbols that provides a meaningful world in which individuals can live: "A personal sense of order hinges on an appropriation of an identity or set of identities that, whether 'deviant' or 'normal', is reckoned with the larger social world."[32]

For Berger, as for Weber, the commonsense everyday exchanges of life form the material for what he calls world construction and world maintenance. He posits three interrelated, concurrent "moments" in world construction, which is the primary task of human society and of religion. The first moment is externalization: the natural, irresistible outpouring of human activity into communal projects; the raw materials of experience that becomes the world. The second moment of world construction is objectification, in which the created world takes on an autonomous status shared by others—it is really there, out there, perceived and affirmed in agreement with others. The third moment reabsorbs the objectified world back into subjective status so that it becomes the expected world, the pattern upon which recognition can occur even in isolation. It becomes the familiar world, the world that in turn determines subjective consciousness.[33]

World construction and world maintenance, being rooted in human ideas, depend directly on words and their symbolic power. From this insight, feminist theologies take off. Linguistic activity is the primary symbolic tool of world construction, and it is thoroughly a product of social imagination. Through the symbolism of language, human beings construct social "shields against terror" by establishing and sharing meaning through shared language and the power of names. Words of belonging and identity form mental walls against chaos and meaninglessness because the distinction between socially constructed names and the things to which they refer becomes blurred. If I cannot name something, it does not fit, and it poses something of a threat to the seamlessness of reality. If I can name it, not only does it have a place, but my position in relation to it and the world is clarified. So, according to Berger, "whenever the socially established nomos (names for things) attains the quality of being taken for granted, there occurs a merging of its meanings with what are considered to be the fundamental meanings inherent in the universe. Nomos and cosmos appear to be co-extensive."[34]

Since religion is the human activity of making the whole universe meaningful and not terrifyingly random, it is "cosmization in a sacred mode."[35] Effective cosmization, however, requires general acceptance of cosmic ideas (stories of origin, understandings of cause and effect, schematic geographies of the universe, the identity and place of human beings, etc.) as real. But how can we accept as real what is now revealed to be made up? According to Berger, we can accept the names for things and the schemes in which we place them as real because we are good at forgetting that we made up the schemes. Indeed, he argues, we must forget in order to be sane and apply ourselves to our daily routines.

Remembering that we made up the ultimate scheme and the meaning it gives us would do us no good. Our survival instinct allows us, compassionately perhaps, to forget. In this way Berger appropriates and puts to a slightly different use Marx's concept of alienation to describe this forgetfulness as the necessary slippage from consciousness of the human construction of all, and especially of symbolic, meaning. We basically, collectively, agree more or less to take for granted the "truth" of science, of a governing deity, of the "nature" of things like men and women, or of some meaning-producing scheme offered out of the common knowledge stockpile, and so consent to a sacred canopy that overarches and limits everyday life. In fact, we forget its origins in our collective imaginations so thoroughly that we go to war repeatedly over competing truths that we mistakenly think hold true outside social construction.

A few years after Berger published his notion of the sacred canopy, another American named Clifford Geertz picked it up for anthropology and added a dimension of psychological necessity that he had learned from Sigmund Freud and Bronislaw Malinowski. We need religion for meaning, but we need meaning because of suffering. Cosmic ordering and the sacred canopy give important answers to otherwise paralyzing ambiguities and help individuals endure pain for the sake of future goals and others.

Anyone who has suffered intensely knows that there is a desperate hunger for meaning and sometimes a limit to its ability to deliver. "The strange opacity of certain empirical events, the dumb senselessness of intense or inexorable pain, and the enigmatic unaccountability of gross iniquity all raise the uncomfortable suspicion that perhaps the world, and hence [human] life in the world, has no genuine order at all—no empirical regularity, no emotional form, no moral coherence." This, Geertz recognizes, is the deep-rooted, insanity-producing fear, and "the religious response to this

suspicion in each case is the same: the formulation, by means of symbols of
an image of such a genuine order of the world which will account for, and
even celebrate, the perceived ambiguities, puzzles, and paradoxes in human
experience."[36] Thus, we actually need to be alienated from the machinations of social construction, to forget our own authorship. We need, psy-
chologically, to deny randomness in the face of pain more than we need to
smooth out any underlying contradictions in the taken-for-grantedness of
the world. "The effort," Geertz argues, "is not to deny the undeniable—
that there are unexplained events, that life hurts, or that rain falls on the
just—but to deny that there are inexplicable events, that life is unendurable,
and that justice is a mirage."[37] Either way, without the functional alienation
of forgetfulness about the social constructedness of the world, both Geertz
and Berger agree that the efficacy of religion in the work of world construction would collapse. This is the mature functionalist reduction of religion and theology to social processes, and the explanation for why we did
not think of it earlier.

Beyond the creative process of construction and reconstruction of the
world and of individual psychological needs, religious ideas that make up
the sacred canopy also provide symbolic governance and maintenance of
the world they have helped to construct. "All socially constructed worlds,"
Berger contends, by virtue of their dependence upon social agreement, are
"inherently precarious . . . constantly threatened by the human facts of self-
interest and stupidity."[38] So Berger combines the strengths of Durkheim
and Weber to identify legitimation as the principal contribution of religious
ideas to the maintenance of the socially constructed world. My identity, my
place, my role, and my subsequent behavior toward others are judged and
legitimated within the sacred canopy of socially constructed meaning. Religion is particularly effective "because it relates the precarious reality constructions of empirical societies with ultimate reality."[39]

Ideas of ultimate reality are therefore touchstones and filters for the random barrage of empirical experience. These ideas are, more or less, preformed
molds into which experience can fit and make sense, or not fit and be discarded, or not fit but not go away and so trigger a social crisis and a scramble
for a new ultimate religious meaning. So Weber's ideas of meaning merge
with Durkheim's ideas of identity and order to produce, through Berger's
idea of the sacred canopy, an understanding of religion, religious ideas, deities,
and theologies as articulations "writ large" of a most basic human need for
coherence and *order*.[40] Geertz agrees with Durkheim's and Berger's emphasis
on order in the formulation of religious ideas. The ethos, or way the world
should be, emerges out of worldview, or way the world is constructed *to* be.[41]
Ethics follows nomos in world construction and maintenance.

The sacred canopy of meaning, which religion and theological ideas support, also forms boundaries of meaning and rules for life under the canopy. Unbelievers in the sacred canopies of their times (from theistic religions to democracy) transgress the boundaries of the status quo and threaten to expose its social constructedness. They are freaks, naysayers, heretics. These are categories with which feminist theologies are quite familiar.

FEMINIST THEOLOGIES TRANSGRESSING BOUNDARIES OF MEANING

Feminist theologies engage theories of social construction at every level. They depend upon the critical insight that language about divinity is socially constructed, and upon the critical insight that culturally accepted images of the divine function powerfully in the social sphere. Images of the divine as male are socially constructed, and they function powerfully to legitimate the status quo in which males are dominant. This kind of engagement with theories of social construction transgresses the immunity of scriptural traditions, church traditions, creeds, and rituals that hold up the sacred canopy. They engage questions about God and divine existence at the deepest, most taken-for-granted levels. They criticize texts and creeds that many church traditionalists believe are both directly revealed and universally normative. Feminist theologies transgress boundaries of propriety with regard to tradition, and they transgress the divine.

The so-called backlash against feminist theologies—concerted attempts by religious leaders and conservative religious groups to discredit feminist theologies as heresy—is a recognition of the fragility of traditional doctrines to withstand such deep criticism from within. Social theory and its assumptions of social constructionism strip immunity from the revealed tradition, but feminist theologies, as theology, cut closer to the religious bone by criticizing creed, tradition, and deity from the inside. In so doing they transgress boundaries that jeopardize the whole fabric of the sacred canopy and hence the basic orientation of the human-divine order. Feminist theologians tend to believe that their transgressions, often undertaken against the beliefs of their childhoods, are necessary to restore a more whole sacred canopy. They believe that they transgress boundaries that were not legitimate to begin with. Indeed, some hope to pitch entirely new canopies, if such a thing can be done.

But where does the notion of boundary transgression come from, and why is it important to understanding the skeletal structure of feminist theologies as transgressive? Boundary theory is part of the modernist stew of ideas. Mary Douglas, an anthropologist who has made the study of boundaries her life's work, illustrates their importance in the social construction of

reality with her ideas about dirt. She suggests that the best way to understand boundaries and boundary transgression (which directly affects feminist theologies) is to look at dirt. Dirtiness always reveals ideas of cleanliness
or purity since dirt is the opposite of purity. And dirt is, she argues, by
definition the product of purity.

As a social constructionist, Douglas understands culture as the product of
human invention based in routinized behaviors. The importance of her
contribution to functional social constructionism and to feminist theologies lies in her understanding of meaning and coherence as a system of
exclusion. The world maintenance activity of religious ideas is a kind of
border patrol between order and the chaos it excludes. It is a kind of negative sociology—what is rejected indicates the outlines of the acceptable and
recognized.[42] This makes sense to feminists who argue that the absence of
the female in the sacred order illustrates and illuminates the collusion of the
sacred with masculinity in patriarchal culture.

The idea of dirt, which Douglas defines as matter out of place, is particularly productive for feminist theologians since it maps the outlines, what she
calls the margins, of the socially constructed order, giving the social order
shape by embodying what is without shape or what contravenes order.
"Where there is dirt," Douglas claims with disarming simplicity, "there is a
system."[43] It is infinitely malleable (the same thing can be dirty or clean
depending on where it is placed) and thus attaches usefully at the symbolic
level to ideas and persons who threaten to stumble "out of place." She
claims that social order *of any kind* possesses a strong energy of repulsion.
Identity is born in this energy of exclusion. Backlash of any kind is the
energy of repulsion—the impulse of purity (masculinist transcendence) to
define itself by repulsing transgressive and therefore dirty otherness (female
embodiment).

To illustrate the social construction of pollution, Douglas focuses on the
idea of place and location in the order of things. Mundane examples provide a helpful lens for the larger understanding of systemic exclusion and
meaning construction. She argues that soil, for example, is really dirty only
when it transgresses the threshold of a house, when it is located on clothes
or in a pile on the kitchen floor, only, in other words, when it is not in the
garden under the grass. Food is not dirty on a plate on the table during the
time set aside for dinner. The *very same* food on a shirt sleeve, in the bed-
room, or on the plate stacked in the sink *becomes* dirt. It disrupts the idea of
order. So, femininity is not dirty in its proper place. It becomes dirty and
pollutes the clean when it threatens, theoretically, to get "out of place."

Order, in Douglas's understanding, *necessitates* the idea of boundary just
as it necessitates the idea of dirt and transgression. Things that are ordered

(like gods in heaven and human societies conforming to divine laws) have clear places for everything and everyone. As matter out of place, dirt reaffirms order by its very inappropriateness, by the repulsive reaction that it inspires. The ritual of cleaning (purifying, confessing, baptizing, fasting), which is the expulsion of things deemed dirty, is boundary reaffirmation. Mundane boundaries are blurred when things that have places get out of place. The idea of kitchen, for example, loses its internal coherence, or at least its internal coherence is threatened, when clothes are stacked in the cupboards or tossed over the counters. Is it still a kitchen at all? Mundane dirt is removed with mundane rituals of cleaning that reaffirm and sometimes reestablish boundaries of meaning between functionally different spaces.

The everydayness of dirt is interesting to Douglas as a cultural anthropologist because of its symbolic pointing beyond itself to the larger concept of pollution. Purity and pollution are cleanliness and dirt writ large. Perhaps it is fair to say that dirt implicates individuals or groups within larger societies even as its very presence reaffirms the social order, and pollution implicates the social order itself. Pollution is a transgression of symbolic, sacred order and has implications for the whole social system.

The social idea of boundaries illustrates dynamism in social orders that requires response and maintenance from the most menial to the most grand scale in human society. Divisions between purity and pollution structure experience and determine appropriate action, and rituals enact social relations by giving them visible expression. The idea of transgression is as important to the maintenance of meaning as is the idea of order because "defilement is never an isolated event.... The only way in which pollution ideas make sense is in reference to a total structure of thought whose keystone, boundaries, margins and internal lines are held in relation by rituals of separation."[44] For feminist theologies the significance of boundary theory is clear: rituals of separation, of purity and pollution, are especially and most powerfully embodied in religion.

God is powerful as a marginal idea. The margins, or boundaries, of reality are where power and danger lie because ambiguities of meaning and shifting edges of reality become explicit there. The idea of divinity establishes both what is most pure (and therefore ordered) in society and what is most powerful and able to expunge disorder. No matter how arbitrary, violent, or neglectful deities may be, they are never without internal consistency and never without purpose, even if the consistency and purpose are opaque to all but themselves. Feminist theologies threaten the order (purity) of revealed tradition and their proposals for new and different language and images become thereby a kind of dirt (pollution) in the religious sphere.

Resistance, even when it is pictured in terms of a wrathful deity, is consistent to the nature of the boundary between order and disorder.

The very word "sacred" or "divine" designates meaning, which disorder, or incoherence, spoils. The sacred therefore also constitutes the energy of exclusion (through which order is defined). In other words, the sacred, in boundary theory, is a dual force of marginal power and danger that is socially constructed to control and to provide for cultural dissonance. Because all margins are dangerous, ritual reaffirmations of meaning at the boundaries are vital to cultural cohesion and agreements about what is acceptable and what is not. If the margins, the boundary lines of the social order, the foundations of the sacred cosmos, "are pulled this way or that the shape of fundamental experience is altered. Any structure of ideas," Douglas suggests, "is vulnerable at its margins." But ironically, by its very repulsiveness, disorder has a "place." It snuffles and rumbles at the edges of meaning, threatening to expose meaning as the fabrication that it is. So disorder, dirt, and pollution, too, are religious ideas because while they "spoil pattern [they] also provide the material of pattern."[45] A prevalent theme in contemporary social theory and theology is the construction of otherness at the margins, and the threats the "other" (the feminine, the nonwhite skin, the non-Eurocentric thought) poses to the presumed center in which reside sanctity and solidity of meaning and order.

PATRIARCHY AS A FEMINIST CONSTRUCT OF ORDER

The concept of patriarchy and patriarchal order with all of its historical and symbolic content is probably the clearest example of the debt feminist theologies owe to social theory and boundary concepts of otherness. Patriarchy is a powerful boundary concept. It is the name for the sacred canopy that legitimates and produces male dominance, emerging with the first feminist voices in theology. We might even say that the concept enabled feminist theologies to emerge and became itself a notion to be debated and revised. Before publicly declaring herself a post-Christian feminist, Mary Daly drew a line in the sand when, in 1971, she wrote that as "the women's revolution begins to have its effect upon the fabric of society, transforming it from patriarchy into something that never existed before . . . it will, I believe, become the greatest single challenge to Christianity to rid itself of its oppressive tendencies or go out of business."[46]

These "oppressive tendencies" are consistently summed up by the term "patriarchy" and more recently by the term "kyriarchy" in feminist theological literature.[47] Both names refer to socially manufactured cultural structures that systematically and generally (if not always particularly) place women and others belonging beyond the boundaries of social power in positions of sub-ordination to dominant men. From patriarchy's early currency in the women's movement as the constellation of institutions and beliefs that benefit men and in which all men theoretically find a home, the word itself has become some-what less frequent in feminist literature, particularly as feminists broaden the base of their critique from sexism to interlocking issues of privilege and op-pression. Indeed for some, the term begins to sound too simplistically refer-ential, and sometimes just too inflammatory, to remain useful.

More recently, to avoid reductionist dismissals of patriarchy as evidence of a bloated conspiracy theory or ad hominem reproach of all things (and persons) male, Rebecca Chopp represents the more cautionary use that some contemporary feminists tend to make of the term. She argues that "the task we have as feminists in a large sense is the critique of all the specific acts of patriarchy as well as the critique of patriarchy as the domi-nant form of life, a form which I have suggested we can only speak of in heuristic fashion."[48] Rather than argue for patriarchy as a "thing out there," she suggests that the word refers to complicities and socially constructed beliefs that support, in sacred canopy fashion, the recurrent problems of sexism, racism, and other institutional violence.

Daly, never much concerned with such methodological (or what she might call "methodolatrous") caution, consistently has argued that patriar-chy refers universally to whatever harms women or nondominant men any-where. Playing with the nuances of Aristotelian causality, she defines femi-nism broadly and explicitly as the "Cause of causes, which alone of all revo-lutionary causes exposes the basic model and source of all forms of oppres-sion—patriarchy—and thus can open up consciousness to active participa-tion in Movement, Transcendence, and Happiness." This ontological vision leads her to claim that feminism is, therefore, "be-ing *for* all women and all Elemental life."[49]

The social concept of patriarchy is inseparable in much feminist litera-ture from contested and complicated definitions of the terms "woman" and "feminist," whether the terms are cast in metaphysical terms such as Daly's or in heuristic terms as suggested by Rebecca Chopp, Sheila Davaney, Ada María Isasi-Díaz, and others. Regardless of definitions, however, the argument that feminism is a critique of patriarchy as cultural or metaphysi-cal construct *and* a politically oriented advocacy for women is clear. It is structured at its roots by the insights of the social theories it has inherited. The systemic structure of domination that oppresses classes or castes of people based on sex, race, ethnicity, or social location that goes by the labels "patriarchy" and "kyriarchy" is the force that feminism generally opposes, and so the concepts are thematically linked.

Daly calls patriarchy the prevailing religion of the entire planet,[50] and Delores Williams claims that as a term inclusive of black women's experience, it "leaves too much out."[51] Some feminist theologians continue to find it a useful shorthand term for the problem of institutional and taken-for-granted dimensions of domination in the history of religion symbolized by the "Father," and others opt for the newer, more monarchical rather than paternal concepts to denote the sacred canopy of social domination by a few. In any case, the idea of patriarchy as a subject of conversation and analysis in feminist theological discourses has cleared the way for deeper feminist discussion of traditionally theological questions of sources, hermeneutics, and goals.

The majority of feminist theological writings from the mid-1980s to the present are less concerned with new elaborations of the evils of patriarchal abuses along the lines of older works such as Daly's *Gyn/Ecology*, Ruether's *New Woman/New Earth*, and Cannon's *Black Womanist Ethics*. Instead, they deal increasingly with constructive elaborations of divinity and doctrine in the face of postmodern criticism and multicultural theory; with internal critiques of method and authority; with issues of difference, essence, and communal accountability; and with definitional problems of gender construction, social location (experience), and theological construction. These latter theological and theoretical debates are built upon and nourished by the critical foundation feminist theologians have laid in social theory. Skeptical theories that posit the sacred canopy as a social construction allow feminist theologies to delegitimize patriarchal claims and to engage in the task of suggesting new ones. Without it, they could not even begin.

The idea of patriarchy as the overarching social system of meaning that supports male domination cleared the path for feminist theologians to apply this critical tool directly to patriarchal ideas of the divine. In 1979, when editors Carol Christ and Judith Plaskow introduced their new feminist reader in religion, *Womanspirit Rising*, with the claim that "feminists have charged that Judaism and Christianity are sexist religions with a male God and traditions of male leadership that legitimate the superiority of men in family and society,"[52] they associated the idea of the male Christian and Jewish deity directly with socially constructed systems of domination. The early feminist theological arguments were wide and vigorous in scope, built upon massive claims about relationships between religious ideas and cultural formation. Rosemary Ruether, for example, argued that the traditional Christian, Jewish, and Muslim idea of the one transcendent deity is largely responsible for the social, political, and ecological ills of Western society:

> The emphasis upon the transcendent consciousness *has literally created the urban earth*, and both abstract science and revolution are ultimate products of this will to transcend and dominate the natural and social world that gave birth to the rebellious spirit. The exclusively male God who creates out of nothing, transcending nature and dominating history, and upon whose all-powerful wrath and grace man hangs as a miserable, crestfallen sinner, is the theological self-image and guilty conscience of this self-infinitizing spirit. [53]

Mary Daly made the link quite blunt with her now famous claim that "when God is male, then the male is God." [54] Because they describe God as the product of social history, these theologians are primarily concerned with the consequences of particular images and ideas *about* God rather than with the ontological status of the divine. Feminist biblical scholar Elisabeth Schüssler Fiorenza has also taken the position that the status of God per se is not so pressing as the status of interpretation about and interpreted images of God. History, she argues, is a matter of social construction, and so feminist biblical scholarship and historical theology must begin from the standpoint that ideological issues are at stake in scriptural and ecclesial traditions that support sexist images and language about God.

The idea of functional social constructionism and the historicity of doctrine therefore grounds Schüssler Fiorenza's feminism as it does Ruether's and Daly's, and it determines her hermeneutical approach to theology. And they all argue that the only way that the historically conditioned endeavor of theology can be exposed and its mystification undone is through the construction and ritual adoption of "new theological structures and language" about God that explicitly include female images. Only then will women "be able to recognize themselves in the image and likeness of God." [55]

The constructionist argument that female images of God are necessary for the spiritual well-being of women, articulated by numerous feminist theologians in a variety of ways (harking back to Valerie Saiving's argument that classical ideas of sin are gendered and do not address women), is perhaps the most powerfully and widely accepted tenet of feminist theologies outside the academy. It is *the* crossover idea, meaning that it is the basis upon which most of the feminist theologies that actually get enacted in traditional worship and other spiritually focused settings happen. From inclusive language lectionaries to WomanChurch, and from women's ordination to Sophiology and rituals, the argument is made on behalf of new feminist theologies, sermons, liturgies, eucharists, ceremonies, and hymnals that, as Elizabeth Johnson puts it so succinctly, "the symbol of God functions." [56] And, the argument goes, because it has functioned so long on behalf of patriarchal social structures and to the detriment of women and other outsiders, the only responsible thing to do is to come up with better symbols.

After Ruether, Daly, and Schüssler Fiorenza began to use this social constructionist argument in defense of female images for God as a means toward postpatriarchal ends, the whole structure of classical Christian theistic doctrines, particularly those related to divine transcendence, independence, and noncorporeality, became fodder for feminist theological criticism. For example, Carter Heyward, Sharon Welch, Kelly Brown Douglas, and Rita Nakashima Brock began to question transcendence (in terms of its traditional association with God's separation from the world) as a meaningful and accurate representation of the divine and to focus on various ideas of immanental relationality. Heyward uses Martin Buber's mystical articulation of the divine I-Thou encounter to describe what she considers central to the Christian story, making it incompatible with patriarchal triumphalist and monarchical images. Welch finds in the communicative theory of Jürgen Habermas a resource for replacing the hierarchical transcendence of the Christian deity with a radically immanent (and some have argued atheological) idea of beloved community. Brown Douglas focuses on the immanental importance of Christ, particularly through the idea of the black Christ, to her liberationist theology. Focusing also on the Christological construct, Brock makes use of Whiteheadian process philosophy, which roots all of reality (especially divinity) in structures and processes of relationality.

All of these theologians see their formulations as profoundly feminist, extolling a virtue (relational commitment) long associated with women, though they do not claim to lift it up necessarily, or solely, for that reason. Their arguments are both functional and social constructionist. They see in traditional theological constructions a valorization of independence and separation that they believe hurts women particularly, but all of the earth and its inhabitants generally. By reconstructing this most basic theological image (which, as Ruether had proclaimed, "literally created the urban earth"), a new earth can, they believe, be brought into being. "I search," Brock says, "for theological images and ideas that will help us embrace the fullest possible life through the ultimate claim relationships make on our very being."[57]

In part, ideas of relationality are strong in feminist formulations because these ideas oppose ancient dualisms based on radical separations of spirit and body. They are also strong because they appeal to a liberal feminism rooted in ideals of civil rights, forged in an era of struggle against segregations and atrocities based on ideas of "nature." The God, Goddess, or divinity of various feminist theologies is, by definition, very much a part of this struggle. A primary criterion for feminist theological construction is that the symbol, image, or metaphor must first of all demystify the patriarchal, kyriarchal deity, pulling back the curtain to reveal the shriveled, fully human manipulator of the great projection of man. Another is that feminist ideas of deity or divinity must also serve the purposes of a new vision, one that, Brock says simply, "will help us."

According to the feminist reading, therefore, any understanding of divinity is clothed in social construction and functions to social ends. Feminist theologies make functional social constructionism one of their two fundamental starting points, as they must do if they are to demystify the overwhelmingly masculinist bias in Christian and Jewish tradition. Whether or not they agree on the status of absolute claims, on the veracity or revelatory capacity of the Bible, on the possibilities of metaphor for biblical reconstruction or postbiblical construction, feminist theologians, a/theologians, and thealogians share the claim that ideas about divinity are socially constructed and that they function in the world in powerful ways. (The term "thealogian" began to appear in some feminist writings and discussions in the early 1980s to specifically change the masculine Greek root "theo-" to a feminized "thea-." Goddess, not God, is thereby implied in a thealogian's work.) They share a conviction that any idea about the divine or revelation that models or functionally supports the domination of one group over others is neither absolute nor divinely inspired. Social theory is the strongest, and at times the only, tool white feminists, womanists, and others have had to establish a foundation from which first to deconstruct the powerful web-of-belief systems that support patriarchal ideologies (a process Daly calls the courage to see) and second to imagine other possibilities (what she calls the courage to sin).

In Conclusion: The Dichotomy That Has Plagued Theology Since the Enlightenment

Because feminist theologies root themselves in the modernist idea that the social and symbolic construction and maintenance of society are fundamentally real and true, they must somehow account for the deep skepticism this secular social theory imposes upon theological claims. The problem is that such profoundly functional arguments about the content of religious ideas require a methodological dichotomy between religious institutions (as social phenomena) and normative theological claims about reality (as true and real independent of social phenomena). Functional social constructionism as a theory builds on the assumption that the social phenomenon of religious institutions is separable from the substantive claims about ultimate reality (the theology) that the institutions themselves seek to make. Religious institutions, regardless of the shape and constellation of their creeds, have their social roles in society in common. Their different claims about divinity or ultimate reality merely give consistency to their institutional and to their members' actions. Social theory, in other words, does not adjudicate between competing claims about ultimate reality or divinity because it has already adopted a rationalist stance that places divine ideas secondary to social organization. Theologians are faced with the tricky problem of *this* reality claim when they adopt the critical insights that the history of social theory offers.

To clarify, the theoretical separation of religious institutions and their related activities from articulated beliefs and theology has served the emergent fields of anthropology and sociology well by modeling the distinctions these disciplines seek to make between functional and substantive meaning in the realm of religious practice. The methodological dichotomy between religion-as-institution and theology enables the spokespersons for the sciences of anthropology and sociology to exempt from their field of inquiry questions of real belief except insofar as the beliefs function in the "larger" realm of politics, economics, and social organization. It enables them to posit universal, transcultural theories of religion and religion's relationship to culture *under which* the specific theological claims of specific cultures fall. Durkheim then is right — religious ideas merely symbolize and concretize in sacred form society itself; there is nothing greater than that. Theology, insofar as it attempts to make claims about divine realities that are somehow independent of social manufacture (even if they are unknowable), cannot fully accept this most basic premise.

However, the dichotomy that sets religious institutions against theological content is both powerful and attractive in a pluralistic age. It makes possible comparative studies of religion and culture without specific reference to religious truth claims except as the claims articulate the particular forms and means by which a culture structures its identity, membership, commerce, and arts. Questions about *actual* divine things, or theology, fall under the category of colorful cultural expression, of relevance to believers at more or less face value, and of relevance to cultural theorists in terms of comparative solutions to universal problems of meaning, coherence, and sociality.

Revelation of any kind is untreatable by sociology and anthropology except in terms outside itself. Revelatory experiences that claim direct knowledge of independent divine realities can never be "true" in the sense that they may contradict social theory's claims about universal patterns of cultural construction. So revelation is explained in terms of social psychology, historical fabrication, cultural adaptation to the arrival of newcomers, or economics.[58] For example, Joachim Wach, a sociologist concerned with the role of religion in social "grouping, fellowship and association," is so invested in this dichotomy that he begins his massive volume on the sociology of religion with it, distinguishing between theology and "the science of religion" in claiming the importance of the distinction for sociological method. "Theology," he argues, is "a normative discipline . . . concerned with the analysis, interpretation, and exposition of one particular faith. The general science of religion," however, "which reckons within its province phenomenology, history, psychology, and sociology of religion, is essentially descriptive, aiming to *understand the nature of all religions*."[59]

The real meanings and interests of culture, whether the meanings and interests are understood in material, hermeneutic, or existential terms,[60] are—from the perspective of social theory—cloaked and served by the dominant religious ideas, not the other way around. Normative religious claims are therefore always socially constructed. The substantive content of the ideas can change from culture to culture, depending upon the particular constellation of interests and traditions that they serve, but the idea of social function allows the sociologist and anthropologist to speak of "the nature of all religions" as a subject of study and an object of understanding without reference to the actual beliefs of those they study, except as illustrations *of* belief.

The difficulty for theologians who engage social and cultural theory in their work is that what matters in this theory is the meaning imputed to a thing, experience, or idea, not the veracity or the so-called real truth of thing, experience, or idea itself. For example, God can never speak directly and unambiguously, break through interpretive lenses, or appear without guise. Social theory says "impossible" because interpretive guise is all we humans have. Indeed, it may be all there is, period.

There are good reasons for this skepticism, despite the rather limited assertions it allows about ultimate reality. Functional social constructionism depends upon the idea of meaning as fluid, constructed, and culture-bound so that we can account for similar objects, experiences, and ideas having different meanings and value in different times, places, and cultures. The overwhelming variety of creation accounts, for example, cannot all be *really* true, can they? If they were all true in some empirical, ahistorical, and acultural sense, the world as we know it would not only have a chaotic history, but it would have no history—as we understand narrative history, that is. One underlying assumption here is that not everyone can be right about the substantive particulars of religion because there is, then, too much contradiction. The assumption underlying *this* assumption is the ahistorical and transcultural notion that history—and reality—is ultimately coherent and noncontradictory; that it ultimately transcends the error-ridden constructions of human meaning in some rational scheme; that there is such a thing as "the nature of all religions," which has meaning wholly apart from the incommensurate theologies of the religions.

So social theory relativizes and historicizes the claims of theology regarding divinity and the world, and this relativization is itself based on ahistorical truth claims regarding human nature and culture formation. Social theory has accepted the historical nature of theological ideas and of religious experience by founding its own methods in substantive beliefs about the unity of prelinguistic or transcultural reality—namely, the social. According to functional social constructionism, theology as a function of religious activity concerns itself with coloring inside the lines, prettifying prefabbed sacred things, but it does not address the more fundamental reality of social construction—indeed ought not do so, lest theology tear the veil of forgetfulness or false consciousness that it ostensibly supports. Rather, from the theoretical perspective, theology need concern itself only with internal consistency and hence maintain its function both in symbolic world building and in religious institutional maintenance.

For feminist theologians, the insights of social theory are indispensable to their deep criticism of misogynist, racist, and triumphalist doctrines and traditions. Functional social constructionism enables their concept of historical and institutional racism, sexism, and ethnocentric dominance to have meaning and coherence. Perhaps like any good tool, functional social constructionism is also dangerous and deeply problematic for the theological task of articulating clearly the contents of religious belief in any true and real sense. But secular theories of social constructionism do not stand alone at the foundation of feminism's critical skepticism. Contemporary feminist theologies are also indebted to the work of early-twentieth-century neoorthodox theologians who struggled with the problem of functional social construction as they attempted to make coherent theological claims about divine reality. They bequeathed to feminist theologians a creative and important strategy for coping with functional social constructionism's deep criticism of substance in their work. Before turning to feminism's other theological foundation in experiential confession then, we need to complete the picture of historicist foundation by outlining the specifically theological strategy of the metaphoric exemption.

CHAPTER THREE

Can Feminist Theologies
Have Both Metaphor and Substance?

FEMINIST THEOLOGIES ARE NOT just social theory. They are not just a revolt against the patriarchal Father God. They are also a profound attempt at faithfulness to basic claims about divine reality. Insofar as they are feminist and concern themselves with the problems of gender, race, and cultural criticism in religion, feminist theologies are fundamentally shaped by the historical development of functional social constructionism and are a form of social theory. But insofar as they attempt to make claims about the shape and meaning of ultimate reality and divine relationship to the world, they are theology, and they are also fundamentally shaped by the historical development of modern theological discourse. Indeed, feminist theologies are particularly indebted to the modern theological voices that most powerfully responded to the acid reductions of functional social construction in the first half of the twentieth century. So, even though feminist theological propositions about language, images, ritual, and ontology have at times challenged or even moved beyond what appear to be basic Christian or Jewish claims, they still emerged out of the very questions and concerns with which modern theologians in the past century have grappled.

To say that feminist theologies are a progressive outgrowth of mainstream theology means that the contemporary contributions of feminist theologians, in both their critical and their constructive aspects, are part of the modern (which includes the related postmodern) era. This is not merely a circular argument of correspondence referring to the fact that feminist theologies have emerged mostly in the latter half of this century and therefore can be classified as such. It is rather a statement *about* this particular period in the history of Christian thought, which suggests that a movement as strong and apparently influential as what goes by the name "feminist theologies" has appeared and flourished. Feminist theologies started as a kind of metacriticism (although they did not rest there) in an era I have already characterized as omnicompetently critical. They emerge out of the challenges and ideas of early-twentieth-century Christian theology that specifically addressed itself to the skepticism of social theory. This contradicts some of the early, but persistent arguments of feminists such as Mary Daly who see in feminist theologies not only a new development along an older theme (of Christian doctrine, liberation, etc.), but also a "diarchal situation that is radically new"—an eschatological break with the overwhelmingly patriarchal past and present.[1]

Sheila Greeve Davaney, on the other hand, supports an evolutionary view, arguing that white feminist, womanist, *mujerista,* and other woman-oriented theological projects are "a thoroughly modern expression of the Enlightenment struggle insofar as [their] major proponents have denied that norms for adjudication and evaluation reside either in the past, in some deposit or residue of special revelation, or in a supposedly universal, neutral reason accessible to all."[2] She agrees with Daly that feminist theologies represent a revolutionary vision, but a vision within the context of modern theological discourse that is not content with fundamentalist claims. In a similar vein, Rebecca Chopp locates the activist push of feminist theologies in the context of historical U.S. concerns with politics and public discourse, claiming that feminism's place in the history of U.S. pragmatism fundamentally influences its strategies and priorities of political and social transformation.[3]

I agree with Davaney and Chopp that contemporary feminist theologies share an important heritage in modernist theological strategies for coping with Enlightenment skepticism. Although there are contemporary theologians who choose to dismiss modern sources of knowledge and theories of knowledge and who regress to a nostalgic fundamentalism in the hopes of attaining certainty, this option is not acceptable to persons who see the progress of human knowledge as inevitable or as necessary to religious integrity. And feminist theologies not only accept historicism, but I have argued, they depend on historicism as a means of criticizing the patriarchal sacred canopy. Feminist theologies accept the epistemological insight of functional social constructionism, which tells the story of human imagination as a world-building and reality-weaving genius. They also recognize the limits of this insight when it comes to divinity. Just because some gods are imagined is no proof that all of them are. Just because human beings need notions of divinity to reflect our hopes to us does not mean that real divine forces cannot take up that role once in a while. And just because we grasp at understanding ultimate truths through imaginative means does not eliminate the possibility that we might, sometimes, get part of it right.

In other words, theologians trained in the liberal arts and conversant with disciplines of study and philosophical inquiries outside narrowly confessional discourses increasingly struggle to articulate clearly and helpfully the contents of religious belief in full view of functional social constructionism. The suspicion that there may be no God to which the word points is certainly not new in the history of religion, but it is possible that there has never been a time when the suspicion was so well grounded and so widespread as it is now. But I do not doubt that throughout history in the West, many people have seen their religious belief as a hedged bet, like the medieval philosopher Pascal who preferred to wager faith in God over against the consequences of being wrong "in the end."[4] Skepticism is not new to theology, but the persuasive power of modernist skepticism is. The genius of feminist theologies is that they turn this modernist skepticism into a foundational strength, using it to mount their criticisms against the patriarchal God.

How have feminist theologies come by this opportunity to use skeptical insights to specifically theological ends? Functional social constructionism as a secular theory makes the move to deconstruction obvious. But theology cannot stand on that shifting ground alone if it wants to speak of God. Theological possibilities for feminism come from early-twentieth-century theologians who grappled with modern skepticism and who laid the groundwork for affirmations of divinity in light of functional social constructionism. Karl Barth may seem an unlikely candidate for grandfather and source of feminist theological strategies, but his neo-orthodox battles against the humanist optimism of his nineteenth-century teachers provide feminist theologies with a basis for using modern skepticism as a way of clearing space for theological thinking to occur. His total dismissal of cultural products as means toward theological understanding ended up exempting and relativizing all language and images for God while retaining a theological and ontological claim for divine being. In one sense, Barth defined the start of the twentieth century in theological terms. He framed his negative system so vigorously and persuasively that much of twentieth-century theological discourse has been, in one form or another, a reaction to his work.

Paul Tillich is another theologian whose work became a strategic source for feminist theologies. He attempted to account for social constructionism by making culture itself a site for ongoing human response to divine being. Unlike Barth, Tillich insisted upon constructing new metaphors and images that might be theologically acceptable in light of modern skepticism. Although they were contemporaries, Tillich represents more of a midcentury position in theology than Barth does. Tillich's work reflects this later era to the extent that, in the United States at least, theology was concerned with issues of inclusion and synthesis. The start of feminist discourses in theology is, in many ways, most directly due to Tillich's systematic reformulation of what he called the "theological circle."[5]

Barth and Tillich are by no means exhaustively representative of the twentieth-century theological response to the functional social constructionist problem. They are, however, emblematic in their different approaches. They are theologians, important in different ways to feminist theologies, whose two responses provide the basis of the metaphoric exemption that is the genius of feminist theological skepticism. They both attempt to address the contemporary question succinctly and poignantly posed thus by Edward Farley: "How does the coming forth of God as God evoke the beliefful conviction that God is actual? Neither a historical account of the origin of the communal symbols and doctrines nor a foundational 'rational' inquiry describes that coming forth."[6]

Despite a philosophical antipathy that Barth and Tillich held for each other, their work together provides a creative theological basis for taking social theory seriously. One exempts all language, religion, images, and anything humanly conceivable from correspondence to real divine existence. The other makes metaphors an important and even necessary means of being theological and being religious. Feminist theologies, as we shall see, take hold of both.

Barth's Exemption

It is overly simplistic to suggest (but remains revealing enough to bear repeating) that Karl Barth's theology from start to finish was a reaction against the Enlightenment humanism of Schleiermacher, Ritschl, Harnack, and their ilk. Another way to say the same thing in a more psychological tone is to suggest that his theology from start to finish was a kind of devastated disillusionment with "the works of man" and constituted a return of sorts to a more orthodox Calvinism that asserts first and foremost the aseity and agency of God. The extreme parochialism and nationalism swirling throughout Europe established the context and social material from which Barth, a man intensely engaged and interested in political life, would work. "In a world of Nazis," Peter Berger later wrote, "one can be forgiven for being a Barthian."[7]

The social problem, as he saw it consistently from the first decade of the twentieth century onward, was that the humanist social theory of nineteenth-century optimism made God through religion into a tool of human desires. He sought to strip away the polish of confidence and anthropocentrism that reduced God to a human construct by raising human agency to the level of god-maker, accepting the new sociology that suggested that religion is a necessary product of human social organization but rejecting its veracity regarding God. "Religion exists," Barth wrote. "Religion is possible and necessary. But it is humanity which is the beginning, middle, and the end of religion—humanity and only humanity."[8] Reflecting on his early acceptance and then rejection of the humanistic leanings of his teachers, Barth tried to locate the point at which he turned away from the Christian glorification of human potential:

> Had the pious human being, had religion of whose history and present state we had at the university heard so much that was glorious and afterwards tried to say it ourselves, become in our own person, problematical? Was it the encounter with socialism as interpreted by Kutter and Ragaz that opened our eyes to the fact that God might want to be God and to speak quite otherwise than in the fusty shrine of the Christian self-consciousness?[9]

From the sharp polemics of his early and revised writing in *The Epistle to the Romans* in the 1920s through the vast midlife exposition of the *Church Dogmatics* to the more moderate assertions of his late writing in 1956 in *The Humanity of God*, it is perhaps not too simplistic to say that Barth was concerned throughout with the utter divinity of God as absolutely free from the intellectual, political, religious, artistic, and historical (in other words, from the socially constructed) endeavors and constraints of "real human beings."[10] This, he argued again and again throughout his life, leaves for God the absolute freedom to be *for* human beings in (and in spite of) these endeavors and constraints. Like Luther with whom he quarreled, Barth never lost sight of this divine freedom, and he saw its defense to be a primary task of the theologian. Apart from the humanity of God in Jesus, God was, for Barth, "the overwhelmingly high and distant, the strange, the totally other, with which people find themselves dealing when they take the name of God upon their lips, when God confronts them, when they have to do with God."[11]

How then is Barth, a theologian who has been described by Tillich as "God-intoxicated" and indifferent to the "historical research of the liberals,"[12] implicated in the twentieth-century theological concern with cultural theory and the reductive critique of functional social constructionism? It is certainly correct to describe his theological life as a consistent elaboration of a central insight about the freedom dependent upon the aseity of God, an insight forged in reaction to the traumas and disappointments of human (and especially religious) potential in the first, violent decades of a horrendously violent century and outlined so dramatically in

The Epistle to the Romans. We can, however, also discern in this profoundly creative reaction a proactive acceptance and development of the functional aspect of theological language and ideas.

Barth was well aware that the experiences of human distress, the posturing of political states, and the ascension of parochial ideologies all flew in the face of the optimism of late-nineteenth-century humanism in the form of Schleiermacher's turn to the self. He also perceived that these modern experiences raised the ancient theodical problem in ever more pressing terms. The problem for Barth was not that the human world, after Schleiermacher's and Harnack's confidence in it, turned traitor and became violent and decidedly unenlightened. Barth did not pretend to be the first to deal with the tenacity of human perversity. He was well versed in Augustine, Luther, and especially Calvin to whom he returned most consciously. But Augustine, Luther, and Calvin did not have to deal with the stunning critique of the Enlightenment, with the possibility that reality itself is a product of culture, with Feuerbach and what Barth would come to call his "anti-theology."[13]

Barth faced the devastating tenacity of human perversity in the cultural context of profound and growing suspicion that the God to whom the word points is not really out there and is a functional projection of human desire only. This suspicion of social construction fueled Barth's rejection of liberal humanism and gave him his deepest insights. He credited Feuerbach with helping him to identify his problem with Schleiermacher and with all theologies that elevate the human being or that locate revelation in human or existential terms. While Feuerbach himself was drunk on the prospects of humanistic progress through the imaginative projection idea, Barth saw the very heart of the problem to which he would devote his career—the idolatrous self-aggrandizement of the human being into the realm of divinity with disastrous consequences for the world. His problem was that he agreed with Feuerbach, though not toward the same ends.

Feuerbach's insight about human abilities to project ideas of itself onto an imagined God does not give rise to optimism about infinite self-improvement, according to Barth, but instead to the complete bankruptcy of human endeavors to reach God. Barth agrees that we do have the imaginative capability that Feuerbach suggests, but it is a capability that reveals only the paucity of our abilities and the profound aseity of God to whom even the name God cannot refer. Feuerbach's skeptical claim is accurate, according to Barth, and the only hope that human beings have for letting God be truly and independently divine is a radical intellectual iconoclasm claiming that "all religion is unbelief."[14] There is, he claimed, "no such thing as a theological pictorial art."[15]

The point is that Barth fully agreed with the socially constructed nature both of theology and of religious speech and action in human culture and society. He did not doubt Feuerbach's claim that "the name of 'God' in which all the highest, worthiest, and most beloved human names are concentrated" could inspire human beings to higher, worthier, and more lovable beings. Barth had no quarrel with this as anthropology. But this historicist argument makes of all constructions, in Barth's thinking, anti-theology. The problem as he saw it was that the name of God, understood in Feuerbach's terms, necessarily can also function to opposite ends, concentrating all the lowest, vilest, and meanest human names, inspiring the same in human beings. From Barth's perspective, this is precisely what occurred in Nazi Europe with such devastating consequences for humanistic theology.

An interesting tension in Barth's theology regarding his appropriation of the historicist legacy of skepticism is that in his attempt to divorce theology from anthropology (from the functional and socially constructed aspects of religion and speech about God), he enacts a kind of functionalist appreciation of theological language. If he were not convinced that the manner in which God is understood has practical import in the ordering of social life, commerce, politics, and so forth, he could not have been at such pains to reassert the absolute otherness of God so that the parochial concerns and claims of would-be tyrants and Führers might be kept from attaching themselves to divinity and to divinely ordained orders of nature.

The flourishing of natural theology in the racist nationalism of Germany in the 1930s alarmed Barth. In the Barmen Declaration of 1934, he asserted, along with a number of other pastors and theologians, that the Nazi trinity of racism, nationalism, and militarism was a heresy, and he rejected "the false doctrine that the church could have permission to hand over the form of its message and of its order to whatever it itself might wish or to the vicissitudes of the prevailing ideological and political convictions of the day."[16]

This argument, for Barth, was perfectly consistent with his understanding of functional social constructionism in religion and theology. The independence of the church's message was necessitated by the corrupt synthesis of theology and politics in fascism, leading him to "regard the German Christians as the 'last, fullest, and worst monstrosity of neo-Protestantism.'"[17] On the other hand, he defended German Christians as members of a larger idolatrous Christianity. The "transformation of the Christian church into the temple of the German nature- and history-myth" was merely one more, albeit particularly loathsome, step in a two-hundred-year Enlightenment history of humanism and social invention.[18]

Barth took for granted the idea that human beings construct reality through religion. He was fully persuaded by functional social constructionism at this point, and it is this point that he drives home repeatedly in his writings. Agreeing with this social constructionist insight allowed him to assert the absolute otherness of God who relativizes all human endeavors, on the one hand, and the absolute humanity of God in Jesus Christ as the means to this knowledge, on the other. Precisely because he understood the functional social constructionist argument and was persuaded by it, Barth strove to drive a wedge between what human beings can and do conceive religiously, and the real God who is beyond all such conceptions.

He sought to exempt God from all human attempts to imagine, create, image, or ritually invoke because he recognized the vulnerability of language and images, innocently affirmed in Christianity, to misappropriation and idolatry. Even more than that, however, he was concerned with the mistaken appropriation of human speaking and imagining as revelatory source. Barth had no patience with natural theology for this same reason. To give an inch to the human capacity to imagine God's being is to become, in Barth's eyes, an idolater, for the line between the *analogia entis* (analogies from existence itself) and the blasphemous claims of emperor or Führer is, in his reckoning, too vague and too easily crossed: "Wherever the qualitative distinction between humanity and the final Omega is overlooked or misunderstood, that fetishism is bound to appear in which God is experienced . . . primarily in the likeness of corruptible man—'personality,' the 'child,' the 'woman'—and in the half-spiritual, half-material creations, exhibitions, and representations of his creative ability—Family, Nation, State, Church, Fatherland." That was the case, Barth believed, in all religious attempts to imagine divine being. As a result, he claimed, "the 'No-God' is set up, idols are erected and God, who dwells beyond all this and that, is 'given up.'"[19]

Barth's means of dealing with the Enlightenment problem of historicism and functional social constructionism was radical exemption, but it is important to see how much his theological system was grounded in an acceptance both of the critique borne by that theory and of the ever constricting status of theological claims in the cultural marketplace. By accepting the insight that religion is a cultural artifact among others (religion as unbelief, as humanity and only humanity) and that images and language about God serve political and sociological functions, he thought that he could make an even stronger argument for God's greatness and power unfettered by the nagging problems of natural theology and its contradictions or by the relativizing acids of social constructionism and historical criticism.

The scriptural revelation of incarnation in Jesus Christ is, for Barth, sufficient referent against the petty, shifting tides of culture and history. Theological substance matters to him more than culture, and it negates entirely the reduction of God to society embedded in functional social construction. This reduction is true, according to Barth, only insofar as it reveals the "No-Gods." What Barth could not acknowledge in this scheme was his appropriation of functional social constructionism in the idea of divine otherness, forged out of horror at the power of theological language about God to support the greatest human evils. If falsely constructed ideas of God could operate to such perverse ends in the imaginations of whole peoples, then presumably otherness must also function as corrective. His own resolution is not completely free of the functionalism he abhors.

It is still human behavior with which Barth is fundamentally concerned in the working out of his theology, and this concern sets the direction and drives the course he takes toward his conception of God. His insistence on God's absolute otherness in service of human humility and the relativization of all human constructs is as much a functional concept as Feuerbach's projection of human potential. Karl Barth asserts that the way out of the historicist trap of functional social constructionism is through radical renunciation and exemption of its capacity to reveal the smallest iota of God's existence, intentions, or actions.

There are two ways to argue that Barth's whole theology is built on the grounds of functional social constructionism. First, there is the somewhat circular argument based on the historicist assumption that since all theological claims necessarily are grounded in functional social constructionism, Barth's ideas are no different. On the other hand, we can argue that Barth was so troubled by the antitheistic doctrine implied in functional social constructionism and was so fully persuaded by its humanist claims that he could see no other way to reinstate divine independence and antifascist humility than through constructing the radically relativizing Wholly Other. His love for the God who would still be God is principally a love and a gratitude concerning human freedom from the onus of final causes, from the burden of ultimate reality construction, and from the house of mirrors behind the door of historicity.

In this way, Barth forged a neoorthodox theological claim that exempts divinity from human imagining. What is remarkable about his theology is that it is based not on traditional negative theology (although it is a strong form of negative theology) but on the very historicist claims of the Enlightenment. He used the skepticism of modernist thought to undermine any claims it could finally make about divine being and to reassert orthodox claims about divine greatness and independence. Feminist theologies, and contemporary constructive theology as a whole, depend heavily on this formulation of skepticism to affirm their own orthodoxy and consistency within the Christian, or Jewish, circle.

The systematic assault against the patriarchal authority of traditional theology, begun in the 1970s by Mary Daly, Rosemary Radford Ruether, Carol Christ, Judith Plaskow, and a few others, was possible as an exercise of modern faith precisely because of the Barthian idea that all human imagining, all language, rituals, traditions, indeed all religion, is fundamentally, as Barth suggested, "unbelief." The abuses and excesses of traditional, monarchical, authoritative ideas of divine will that reduced whole classes of people to subservient status were, in feminist eyes, wholly the fabrication of human will, not divine will, and could be criticized as such. Barth's exemption of human religious and theological enterprises from correspondence to divine existence meant that feminists could use skepticism to criticize the theological tradition without slipping into a complete Feuerbachian or Marxian reduction of God to human projection.

Echoing Barth's exemption, Sallie McFague argues for a metaphoric theology that recognizes divine independence from "the constructive character of all human activities."[20] To discuss the violent nature of the patriarchal family as it is symbolized in religious imagination, Rita Nakashima Brock characterizes Christianity as "deeply infected" with a social-historical product, and that "analysis of the social, political, and psychological roots of doctrinal claims is crucial to demystifying nonliberating theological concepts and modern defenses of these concepts."[21] Drawing more on traditional Jewish iconoclasm than on Barth and the Christian tradition of negative theology, Judith Plaskow identifies the same idea when she argues that the comfort and familiarity of male imagery for God do not mitigate its problematic contributions to an overall "system that consigns women to the margins." Echoing Feuerbach and a neoorthodox contemporary of Tillich named H. Richard Niebuhr, she makes the thoroughly modernist claim that "to speak of God is to speak of what we most value."[22] But unlike Feuerbach and like Barth, Plaskow uses this claim to indicate the need for criticism precisely because divine existence is not bound by human images and language. Womanist writers such as Jacquelyn Grant insist that in doctrine, history, interpretation, and religious expression black women must "speak out for themselves"[23] and they depend upon prior black liberationist and historicist dismissals of theological and doctrinal claims that support racism. As James Cone puts it, "that our language about God is inseparably bound with our own historicity seems so obvious that to deny it is to become enslaved to our own ideology."[24] That was precisely Barth's concern, and it made possible a dramatic and far-reaching cultural critique in liberation-oriented terms.

The central skeptical insight of modernist epistemology—that all attempts to speak of divinity backfire and illustrate only the speaker or the speaking community and its complex wishes, needs, and imaginative ways of being in the world—is transformed by Barth into a theological strategy that protects divine greatness. This theological strategy allows historicism its say because historicism can undermine only what is known and what is accessible to human interpretation. It cannot therefore, according to the Barthian strategy of exemption, ever touch true divinity since true divinity resides outside the known and is inaccessible to human interpretation.

Barth gets himself into some trouble over his decision to exempt from his criticism one thing that is accessible to human interpretation, and that is perhaps the most interpreted thing in human history: the Bible. Feminist theologians cannot exempt the Bible to the extent that Barth does because of its complicated misogyny, slave holding, violence, and ethnic triumphalism. For all women and nondominant men, the varieties of demands in the Bible that they keep silent, stay put, behave, follow the rules, and above all remain invisible are hermeneutical thorns. The suffering that they often endure when they do not keep silent, stay put, behave, or follow the rules does not ease the interpretive problem. The "texts of terror," which refer to particularly nasty stories of women's treatment as chattel, as sacrifice, as object of rape, and so forth, can be interpreted as lessons from hell or at least as examples of very bad judgment, but their inclusion in a revelatory Scripture is problematic to say the least.[25]

Without the leaven of historicism and the Barthian response that exempts divinity from the products of culture, such stories of violence and women's silence are bizarre and more vulnerable to misuse, while stories of their courage and of Jesus' treatment of them are less remarkable. Because of historicist insight, Delores Williams critically deconstructs the violent story of Sarah and Hagar with devastating clarity, and Elisabeth Schüssler Fiorenza untangles misogynist Christian texts to reveal their underlying position in the social and political culture of early Christianity and to reveal Jesus' noncompliance in that culture as all the more amazing. These scholars are able to apply functional social constructionist criticism to the revealed tradition, but retain claims for divine realities that are "not that." Elizabeth Johnson sums up the importance of strategic exemption in feminist theological analysis because of its ability to illustrate the socially constructed character of language for divine existence, and because of its ability to retain necessary mystery and independence to that existence. "In sum," she writes, "exclusive, literal patriarchal speech about God is both oppressive and idolatrous. It functions to justify social structures of dominance/subordination and an androcentric worldview inimical to the genuine and equal human dignity of women, while it simultaneously restricts the mystery of God."[26] This is because, Barth would argue, people mistake their own ideas, the no-gods of their imaginations, for the wholly other God.

TILLICH'S METAPHORIC INCLUSION

It was against the Barthian fortress of unassailable revelation and renunciation of historicity, however, that Paul Tillich developed his theological response to the Enlightenment view of culture. He did not directly address Feuerbach's charge that all ideas of the divine are human projections, but he spent his life grappling with the resulting question of the relationship of theology to religion and culture and the capacity of human beings to make and remake their worlds. His solution of metaphoric inclusion enabled the work of feminist theologies to apply the Barthian exemption to the task of constructing new images and language for the divine. Metaphoric inclusion, stemming from what he called the method of correlation, was Tillich's creative theological response to the deep skeptical challenge of functional social constructionism.

Where Barth was intoxicated by the wholly other God, Tillich was intoxicated by culture. The direct influence of functional social constructionism is therefore more immediately evident and at the same time much more difficult to adequately trace in Tillich's thought because he considered the revelatory possibilities of human culture to be both real and deeply problematic. Like Barth, Tillich fundamentally agreed with the theological problem posed by the social constructionist argument that religion and its theological accouterments are cultural products, but he was dissatisfied with Barth's answer, believing it to be philosophically and religiously untenable. Where Barth saw culture (including religion) as evidence only of human invention and therefore evidence of God's absence, Tillich saw culture with all of its flaws as the only evidence accessible to humans of God. Against Barth's conclusion that the earthliness of human-constructed culture indicates only the "not-that" and the heavenliness or otherness of God, Tillich wrote, "Certainly God is in heaven and man is on earth. But man can make this statement only in case heaven and earth have touched each other time and again, not only once, but in a process of history in which statements and then doubts have been expressed about gods who are thought to be on earth and men who are thought to be in heaven."[27]

Tillich attacked Barth at the point of method, claiming that Barth established his paradox of the "impossible possibility" of knowing God not through true dialectics as he claimed, but through a kind of supernaturalism that for Tillich required a retreat into absurdity. Tillich maintained "that the question about divine possibility is a human possibility, and that the divine answer is always already available."[28] Writing against liberal humanism and its thoroughly historicist assumptions, on the one hand, and also against what he considered to be Barth's supernaturalism, on the other, Tillich began early in his career to seek a middle path through the competing truth claims of skepticism and uncritical faith: "The liberal interpretation confuses history of religion with revelation; the supernatural interpretation makes them mutually exclusive; the dialectical interpretation finds in the history of religion answers, mistakes, and questions that lead to the ultimate answer and without which the ultimate answer would have to remain something unasked, unintelligible, and alien."[29]

Where Barth chose to take his agreement with the functional social constructionist critique to the conclusion of radical separation, making of all "erring human knowledge ignorance,"[30] Tillich chose in favor of human attempts at knowledge of God, mistakes and all, and based his entire ontological system on the idea that knowledge of divine being is accessible through the constructs of culture and through dialectical processes at the heart of human thought.

Tillich's public divergence from Barth occurred early in his theological career in the form of an essay entitled "What Is Wrong with the 'Dialectic' Theology?" which he first published in 1923. Even before that, however, he was attempting to develop a theology of culture that could account in meaningful ways for the profound impact of what he called "cultural science." The idea that culture in all of its structures and forms is the historical project and product of human creativity necessitated and gave rise, according to Tillich, to the three forms of cultural science, namely, "philosophy of culture, philosophy of the history of cultural values, and the normative science of culture."[31] He saw clearly that the relativization of knowledge accompanying the cultural sciences necessitated a new approach to the philosophy of religion that could take account of history and culture, a perspective he would later develop in his systematic theology in terms of the "theological circle."

The idea of cultural science enabled Tillich to account for the new historical criticism that nullified and relativized the traditional foundations of revealed knowledge. He was impressed with cultural science for exposing, for example, that "the Five Books of Moses stem from various sources and not from Moses himself."[32] Of greater importance to Tillich, foretelling by decades the arguments of Foucault, Wittgenstein, and Derrida, he argued that cultural science revealed in general that "the standpoint of the systematic thinker belongs to the heart of the matter itself."[33] That is, Tillich was persuaded by the social constructionist insight at its most basic level that the systematic thinker interprets a larger picture only from a partial view, making standpoint crucial to the interpretive results (an insight of vital significance to feminist and particularly womanist arguments about marginality a half century later). At a more complex level, he perceived that the systematic thinker creates as well as articulates horizons of reality. The angle of vision does not merely passively reveal a particular view, but the viewer brings to the angle of vision a notion of what the vista reveals. For feminist theologies, this insight would support their various arguments that exclusively male, exclusively white images of divine reality not only reflect exclusivist centers of value, but that narrow theological vision at the start (seminaries of all-male, all-white theologians) produces narrow results.

Tillich saw the limitations that social theory now placed on normative universals of any kind. "Here," he argued, "the alternative 'right or wrong' loses its validity, for there is no limit to the number of attitudes which the spirit can adopt toward reality. There is a Gothic and a baroque style in aesthetics; a Catholic and a modern Protestant dogmatic theology; a romantic and a puritanical code of ethics; but in none of these pairs of alternatives is it possible to form useful universal concepts of cultural ideas."[34] Universal concepts of cultural ideas are now empty, he contended, because all such concepts reveal ultimately only the standpoint of their human originators and, to the extent that universal concepts (such as justice, art, or Catholic systematics) are posited, they are not actually universal cultural ideas in their content but "normative concepts in disguise."

In other words, the reality of competing truth claims, such as Protestant or Catholic dogmatics, nullifies the possibility of real content when the claims are universalized unless one of them is truly right and the other truly wrong, a "supernaturalist" standpoint he believed to be no longer tenable in the milieu of cultural science. It is precisely on this basis that women of color have argued that white feminists mistakenly and with typically privileged erasures equated feminism with white middle-class women's concerns. What Sandra Harding calls standpoint epistemology is Tillich's argument here that no universal is without an originating standpoint, or perspective, that ultimately nullifies its universality.[35] While human beings will continue to create and enact new cultural forms and generate shared normative ideas within the parameters of particular cultures and even try to continue to universalize them, the theologian dissatisfied with a retreat to supernaturalism and unwilling to cede all to functional social constructionism is left to find a place for the particular universals of religious ideas, only after deciding that *those* ideas are not now also empty.

In his systematic theology, Tillich sought to make a distinction between culture and theology that allows culture and history a social constructionist status as world-making activity, but that gives to theology something of a prehistoricist claim to truth and hence a revelatory content that survives the vicissitudes of changing cultures, worldviews, or eras. This revelatory content is necessary to Tillich precisely because human beings live in a context of having been "shaped" by the particular and infinitely variable combinations of practice and theory that make up their particular cultural situation. No theory, in other words, will ultimately explain in any complete sense human experiences and human practices since theory is as conditioned by history and culture as is experience. Tillich is clear that human life and meaning are a social process of construction. He also realized that social construction implies an infinite regress all the way to and beyond divinity. Social theory's inability to offer certainty or cohesion to claims about divinity drove him to seek out a revelatory, explanatory, existential core that subsumes all practice, all theory, and all social construction under a larger, more coherent meaning:

> The infinite horizons of thinking cannot supply the basis for any concrete decision with certainty. Except in the technical realm where an existential decision is not involved, one must make decisions on the basis of limited or distorted or incomplete insights. Neither theory nor practice in isolation can solve the problem of their conflict with each other. Only a truth which is present in spite of the infinity of theoretical possibilities and only a good which is present in spite of the infinite risk implied in every action *can overcome the disruption between the grasping and shaping functions of reason.* The quest for such a truth and such a good is the quest for revelation.[36]

To Tillich, the truth that is present despite the infinity of theoretical possibilities can only be a principle of existence that encompasses all of the possibilities. Being-itself becomes that principle and becomes, therefore, the reality behind the symbol we call God. Culture and other human inventions can then carry important traces of the divine and possess infinite possibilities for divine action and revelation.

Persuaded that culture and knowledge are human constructs, Tillich views theology as the means by which the ahistorical "truth" of the gospel as revelation (of being-itself in the face of human finitude) can be applied to the widening cacophony of human cultural expressions without idolizing or reifying any individual expression. It accepts historicism's acid dissolution of any knowledge in the relativizing bath of human construction, but reserves a philosophical claim on ontology as the revelation of existence—Tillich's gospel—that will not succumb to social construction. All

of historicized reality is what existence, in the form of theology, must encounter and address. In other words, "the 'situation' theology must consider," according to Tillich, "is the creative interpretation of existence, an
interpretation which is carried on in every period of history under all
kinds of psychological and sociological conditions. . . . The 'situation' to
which theology must respond is the totality of man's creative self-interpre-
tation in a special period. Fundamentalism and orthodoxy reject this task,
and, in doing so, they miss the meaning of theology."[37] Culture is the stuff
with which theology must work. It provides the images, metaphors, pas-
sions, and inklings through which divine existence, as being–itself, glim-
mers. Culture is all we have of the divine, though it is not the divine. What
we make of culture is the concern of theology.

In essence, then, Tillich responded to the same critical barb of functional social constructionism that Barth did, but he chose a nearly opposite
path of resistance. Like Barth, he was concerned with restoring to theology
and to the various claims of Christian faith a real content, but Tillich sought
a content that did not have to rest on what seemed to him to be the
arbitrary exclusions favored by Barth. Tillich perceived that the seriousness
with which Barth took the social constructionist critique led the latter to
an unwavering nullification of real content in all human endeavors, a vigorous acceptance of the emptiness of cultural ideas, whether they are expressed in political, aesthetic, or religious terms. This approach, in Tillich's
mind, ended up nullifying itself by refusing to posit a more substantial
universal idea of reality that makes possible both sides of the equation—the
absolute and the relative.

A theology of culture became Tillich's response to the dilemma posed
by the humanistic hubris of functional social constructionism generated
out of the Enlightenment. He began to formulate a triadic view of culture
to account for and resolve the tension between functional social constructionism (which breeds "autonomous" culture) and supernaturalism (which
breeds "heteronomous culture") into a dialectical third, which he called
"theonomous culture."[38] His allegiances to social theory and to an independent divine existence meant that theology as the "science of religion"
would have to find its place in dynamic and critical relationship to both.

Theology is therefore deeply implicated, Tillich argued, in the task of
"cultural science," or social theory. He understood this to be the human
necessity to generate culture and the human ability to create and become
enmeshed in religious systems and ideas—including ideas of God—that are
constructions and artifacts that emerge, mature, age, fall into disrepair, and in
every way function. Standing alone, however, social theory becomes the
backbone of autonomous culture asserting "that man as the bearer of uni-

versal reason is the source and measure of culture and religion—that he is his own law."[39] Were theology to ally itself completely with this standpoint it would, as Feuerbach claimed, become anthropology. Moreover, it would lose any real claim on human life. Tillich believed along with Hegel that any real claim on human life is possible only through some idea of ultimacy.

The problem, as Tillich saw it, was the articulation of this ultimacy in terms that did not revert to arbitrary (supernatural) foundations. He believed that supernaturalism in any form gives rise to heteronomous culture, which places thinking and acting and governing under the "authoritative criteria of an ecclesiastical religion or a political quasi-religion, even at the price of destroying the structures of rationality."[40] The only way out of the supernaturalist dilemma for theology that he could see was through a hybrid Neoplatonic existentialism, positing being-itself as the ultimate referent for social theory and for supernatural claims about God. The culture founded on this ultimate referent is theonomous; that is, for Tillich, "it expresses in its creations an ultimate concern and a transcending meaning not as something strange but as its own spiritual ground . . . rooted in the divine ground which is man's own ground."[41]

Tillich believed that the development of an existential ontology allowed him to free his concept of the divine from the alleged irrationality of supernaturalism and from the negation of independent divinity accompanying functional social constructionism by making his concept synonymous with ontology itself and therefore necessarily prior to every critical or confessional standpoint, able to indulge and to relativize either one. The divine, as the ground of being, or being-itself, becomes the referent for human existence and thought, but even more than that it becomes the possibility of meaning in human life. In other words, it becomes the very possibility of social construction prior to the imaginative social acts that give orientation to specific cultural forms and worldviews. He argued that his concept of God as being-itself resolves the problem of reducing divinity to social function because "as being-itself God is beyond the contrast of essential and existential being."[42]

Tillich's ontological concept of being-itself makes the theory of functional social constructionism an important moment in human history and in the history of philosophy, but a moment nonetheless resulting from what he calls the fundamental "power inherent in everything."[43] This argument rooted in existentialism is, for him, the resolution of the dialectical and sometimes paradoxical predicament of the twentieth century, an era faced with the ramifications of social constructionism. For systematic theology to be real theology, it becomes a part of the necessary cultural expressions that can make sense of the new knowledge that the world is made, not given.

For his unifying theory of being–itself to work, Tillich realized that he would have to account for the vast diversity of religious expression and belief in such a way that the content of those beliefs not fall prey to the reductionist trap set by historicism. The cynical persuasion of the modern world, growing stronger all the time, was Feuerbachian and Freudian in nature, concluding from the incommensurate variety of beliefs that *all* religious beliefs are delusional. Tillich's attempts in this milieu to provide a solid ground for theology (no pun intended) led him, to the horror of Barth, closer to Rudolph Bultmann, who argued for a demythologized gospel and for an understanding of the symbolic nature of Christian religious ideas. Symbols became a means for Tillich to account for revelatory content in culture and to allow for the possibility of any religious connection to divine existence at all.[44]

The task of theology, for Tillich, is to articulate with philosophical precision the absolute status of God-the-ground-of-being—the only statement about God, he declared with no apparent irony, that is *not* symbolic. All other images and ideas concerning God are incomplete and symbolic, "directed toward the infinite which they symbolize and toward the finite through which they symbolize it." It is up to theologians to make this process plain, to work out its consequences, and to strengthen the rational bases of religious symbols within the fabric of existential ontology. Theology, he argued, "has neither the duty nor the power to confirm or to negate religious symbols. Its task is to interpret them according to theological principles and methods."[45]

Tillich used the idea of symbol to account for religious plurality and for the problem of religious social construction. In his systematic theology, but also in his sermons, Tillich took pains to articulate the function of religious ideas about God in social and political life. The rise of the Third Reich particularly honed his understanding of the immediate political functioning of religious symbols and quasi-religious functioning of political symbols. He wrote a document opposing National Socialism with ten theses arguing for Protestant theology's independence from "certain political movements." He did this not because he wanted to protect religious ideas from political roles but because, like Barth, he believed that the power of religious ideas to redirect "National Socialism to a goal that is true, just, and appropriate for their social needs" could happen only if the religious symbols and allegiances of Protestantism pointed beyond the narrowly chauvinistic political movement of Nazism to some greater reality.[46]

It is, no doubt, from his experiences of fascism and the ideological tides in Europe that he discerned the power of religious symbols to inspire and to distort. It is not only the capacity of religious (and pseudoreligious or political) symbols to function as finite references for the infinite that make them so important to the work of theology, but also their capacity to function as false referents for the ultimate. This capacity for false reference is, in Tillich's scheme, demonic. Heteronomy as the religio-political state and autonomy as the thoroughly secular state more easily foster the demonic, he argued, because both allow for the misapprehension of proximate referents (the state, race, church, images of the divine, science, society, nation) as the ultimate referent, the ground of being to which the symbol God points.[47]

This clear link that Tillich makes between the construction of symbols and political life became a powerful insight for feminist theologies. While Barth's exemption allows only for the radical deconstruction of all traditional patriarchal authority as "unbelief," Tillich's ontology of being-itself and of culture as means of discernment allows feminist theologies their constructive impulse. All things can be symbols for divine existence according to Tillich because all things participate in being-itself. And all things can become demonic insofar as they can be mistaken for divine being or absolute truth. This suggests that feminine or nontraditional images of the divine are warranted inasmuch as the image can point beyond itself to the larger, deeper reality of being-itself, and so long as we remember that divine existence, as the ground of being, is not the image. "We see," McFague writes, "through pictures. We do not see directly: the pictures of a king and his realm and of the world as God's body are ways of speaking, ways of imagining the God-world relationship. The one pictures a vast distance between God and the world; the other imagines them as intrinsically related. At the close of the day, one asks which distortion (assuming that all pictures are false in some respects) is better, by asking what attitudes each encourages."[48] Because we see through pictures (and Tillich would agree with McFague), we need pictures to discern in even the smallest way the reality to which the pictures point, in which they participate but which they can never encompass. This is metaphoric inclusion, the possibility that human imagination need not work entirely against the purposes of divine revelation and presence. Metaphoric inclusion is another, more culture-intoxicated means of dealing with the acids of functional social construction. Everything is socially constructed, but even socially constructed things exist, and the existence that grounds all social construction is divine being itself. So culture is not exclusive of divine reality, as Barth would have it. Culture includes divine reality because divine reality grounds culture in existence.

Thus, although his theory of symbols is a central feature of Tillich's discussion of the actuality of the divine and gives feminist theologies their greatest permission for constructive re-imagining, Tillich's answer in existential ontology speaks most clearly to the challenge of functional social constructionism. His concept of nonbeing, for example, is an ontological description of the threat that social theory brings to the divine, namely, it negates the reality of the divine outside human construction. This nonbeing of divinity, which in Tillich's scheme would necessitate the nonbeing of everything else, might be cast as the cynical possibility that there is no ultimate reality, that everything is only a word game or the product of a biological/evolutionary quirk that makes human beings both the authors and the dupes of an obsessive creativity. To manufacture illusions—and then happily or unhappily fall for them—bespeaks a terrifying human loneliness in the universe. This interpretation of nonbeing suggests that there is no "there" there, only artifice, fantasy, creative intellection that makes living possible in the angst-ridden face of nonbeing.

Being-itself becomes, therefore, Tillich's necessary ontological answer, the "power inherent in everything" that makes possible even the question of its own nonexistence. It is a somewhat circular argument, one that allows Tillich to embrace the necessity of reductive reasoning without losing God. He uses social theory against itself, suggesting that it is a product of God since skepticism is a necessary part of thinking existence. And the necessity of an ontological principle of being is all that Tillich believes he needs to bring in the content of Christian faith. The Christian event, he tries to argue, is the only place where the revelatory truth of being-itself as power over nonbeing truly occurs. The Gospel accounts of Jesus' life, death, and resurrection illustrate, for Tillich, the power of being-itself concretely and courageously to *live* as "bearer of New Being."[49] His defense of Christian content as exclusively real does not hold up in his larger, more inclusive system. As a Christian theologian devoted ultimately to the exclusive truths of his tradition, however, he had to try.

More important, Tillich's theology is fundamentally and explicitly concerned with the function of religious symbols in human life, and thus, he must account for the fact that "if a segment of reality is used as a symbol for God, the realm of reality from which it is taken is, so to speak, elevated into the realm of the holy."[50] Like Barth, however, Tillich's concern with the social function of theological ideas is that he account for them in such a way that the idea of function does not disrupt too much the possibility of speaking of Christian symbols as having substance, as referring to what is impossibly possible (Barth) or possibly impossible, namely, to what has existence and agency outside human construction and political ideas.

Tillich's reliance on ideas and assumptions of functional social constructionism led him to develop an elaborate and systematic understanding of the structure and function of symbols in theology to account for the constructionist impulse in human being and thinking. He also considered it fruitless and overly simplistic to retreat from revelatory possibility resident in the functionalist viewpoint of social theory, or cultural science as he called it. Consequently, he devoted his prodigious career and writing to the problem of articulating an inclusive metaphoric theology in which the acid of functionalist skepticism could be neutralized by the larger undergirding principle of being-itself. Put together, Barth's strategy of radical exemption and Tillich's strategy of metaphoric inclusion become, in feminist theologies, the metaphoric exemption that turns social theory to theological effect.

FEMINIST THEOLOGIES AND THE METAPHORIC EXEMPTION

The metaphoric exemption is therefore the modern theological strategy that feminist theologians use to make their claims against the distortions of the patriarchal/kyriarchal tradition by exempting those traditions from correspondence to real divinity. The insights of functional social constructionism, which threaten to fold divine realities entirely into the batter of human imagination, are limited by the exemption. As Barth realized, social theory cannot deconstruct what is not accessible to human thought, and so he posited divine reality in perfectly orthodox terms of inaccessibility. But feminist theologies have not stopped there. The metaphoric exemption, through Tillich's philosophical retrievals of culture, exempts the products of culture (including all thought) from any direct correspondence to divine existence, but allows for participation in that existence. Theologians could begin to tend to culture for its life-giving, full humanity-affirming possibilities. Mary Daly offers "spirals" and "Verbs" for divine being; Sharon Welch contemplates the metaphor of beloved community; Delores Williams re-imagines black church and incarnation in women's bodies; Johnson envisions Christ as Sophia; Brock looks to the metaphor of the heart; Brown Douglas looks to the black Christ; Plaskow considers inclusive monotheism; and McFague explores the metaphor of world as God's body.

The metaphoric exemption enables metaphoric creativity in these feminist theologies to take place without idolatry because all language, images, metaphors, and ideas for divine reality remain exempt from true correspondence to actual divine being. It clears the table by delegitimizing and demythologizing all human constructions through exemption, but allows for religious consideration of new metaphors (or old ones) because imaginative construction is necessary to human life. Metaphoric, symbolic communication is an epistemological necessity. The metaphoric exemption has therefore led to an explosion of creativity particularly from feminist theologians seeking to interpret religious ideas in more liberating and transformative terms. For them, the metaphoric exemption is the ticket to radical re-imagining and restoration, a gift of modern skepticism to theology.

The metaphoric exemption, as a creative response to critical historicism, has also contributed to important tensions in feminist theological discourse. Not only does it support the question of "whose reality, whose images?"—a question of cultural dominance relevant to communities of women with overlapping and sometimes divergent allegiances to other communities—but it supports other questions as well. As a predominantly skeptical strategy, the metaphoric exemption does not necessitate claims for independent divine existence, and so it supports theologians who are not convinced that theological ontology is a good thing. These theologians are not interested in the strategy of reclaiming divinity by renaming and re-imagining the God of Abraham and Sarah, of Jesus and the disciples. They tend instead to see the metaphoric exemption out to its logical conclusion of complete exemption, complete dissolution of a basis upon which to claim divine being.

In 1987, Sheila Davaney suggested to feminist theologians that ontological bases for their arguments are fundamentally untenable.[51] Sharon Welch added a strong argument for understanding divinity apart from the monolithic ontologies of the Christian tradition, and Kathleen Sands has argued against ontological absolutes. A methodological division has therefore begun to emerge between the feminist theologians presupposing an ontological base for their arguments and those questioning the status of ontological claims altogether. None have resolved the question of whether ontology and the monolithic claims of absolutism are inseparably linked or whether ontology can be presupposed in nonmonolithic terms.

Davaney is suspicious of the tendency in feminist theologies to associate metaphors with ontological reality, despite the qualification of the metaphoric exemption. When white theologians in particular suggest that their experience resonates "with ontological reality and divine purpose, the message, at least covertly, is that these women, and not others, know 'the way things really are' and that their visions, and not those of other women, carry the weight of divine authority."[52] She suggests that the fundamentally deconstructionist stance that most feminist theologians take toward patriarchal institutions and theological systems contradicts an equally widely shared reliance upon "referential models of knowledge" for constructive claims about women, experience, and divinity. The metaphoric exemption, in other words, cannot be applied selectively. Revealing the influence of her teacher Gordon Kaufman, Davaney argues for "a feminist theology that carries through the insights of historical consciousness more consistently," a suggestion that has grown in importance in the ten years or so since she made the suggestion.[53]

Kathleen Sands is one for whom the metaphoric exemption does not preserve a residual divine reality after the reductions of social construction. Instead, she makes use of feminist literary and psychoanalytic theory to argue against notions of divine being altogether, identifying ontological claims as nostalgic regressions to the dominance of the One. Feminist theology, she says, is floundering "on the ruins of the Absolute."[54] The heuristic scheme that Sands uses to classify feminist theology draws on classical philosophy and distinguishes the feminist theologians who fall into the rationalist tradition (represented by Rosemary Ruether) and the ones who, she claims, fall into the dualist tradition (represented by Carol Christ). The rationalists attempt to establish systems large enough to engulf all differences, while the dualists work out oppositional strategies. Both types depend on foundational, metaphysical assertions of the One, the Other, and the Absolute. Because her concern is with theodicy, ethics, and postmodernism, Sands (like Davaney) is critical of the often ahistorical foundations underlying conceptions of women's experience and nature that she perceives at work in the dominant feminist theological literature, both rationalist and dualist. She does not want (nor does she believe it possible) to completely evade either rational or dualist propositions, but she argues strongly against absolutist claims of any kind. Like Sharon Welch, she uses a variety of literary sources to explore a fragmentary landscape (it is this that she calls the ruins of the Absolute) upon which a radically historicized, feminist vision can be built.

Much like Davaney, Sands argues that theological ontologies in feminism are contradictory and serve predominantly escapist functions and can no longer be intellectually—and she adds morally—justified. On the other hand, she suggests that nihilism, the often supposed consequence of contemporary postmodernism in feminist academic circles, is not the necessary consequence of this critique. She does acknowledge, however, that nihilism is a possible consequence of such radical skepticism.[55] Reminiscent of Daly's deft biophilic criticism of Tillich's fundamental angst, Sands suspects that postmodern nihilism can result *only* from a certain kind of consciousness and commitment that is not reflected in feminism, a privileged consciousness that cannot or does not "breathe in the deep waters of tragedy."[56]

> Why would the death of the One leave only nihilistic truthlessness in its wake, unless truth is still secretly assumed to be one and transcendent? Why would the critique of power aim at sociality as such rather than at social

injustice, unless a human nature quarantined from the defiling effects of social power is still imagined?[57]

The two theological strategies that produced the metaphoric exemption: Barth's neoorthodox rescue of the traditionally distant God from the clutches of modern skepticism and Tillich's embedding of God in being-itself to be able to claim a higher ground than modern skepticism, do not wash in thoroughgoing historicist approaches to theology. Sands places herself into the company of feminist scholars like Davaney, Welch, Chopp, and Isasi-Díaz who see the basic feminist theological issue to be the question of ontology and the social consequences of foundational retreats. She might agree wholeheartedly with Isasi-Díaz, who argues that theology itself is "acceptable only as a heuristic device that provides a 'space' in which different theologians can meet to discuss their commonalities and differences in order to deepen their understanding."[58] It is itself so radically a historical endeavor that questions of revelation and truth cannot help taking a backseat to hermeneutical preoccupations.

The benefit of hermeneutical preoccupations is that feminist theologies in all their diversity can be understood more along methodological than doctrinal or political lines. Unlike divisions between theologians that are characterized by basically essentialized communal commitments, the methodological question of ontological foundations does not set feminist theologians committed to traditional religious communities over against those working in post-Christian, pagan, or Jewish settings, as if loyalty to tradition is a question that can be answered once and for all.

The metaphoric exemption does not necessitate a resolution to the ontological/historicist debate. In large part, the radical critique that Sands offers is a kind of honesty meter for feminist theologies beyond their commitments to particular communities and particular ideas of justice. For example, she points out that even theologies attempting to answer charges of racism and of incorrectly universalized ideas of "woman" are often unproblematically reliant on other universal assertions for the purposes of "expanded critique": "In general it can be said that religious feminists who rely on the transcendence of the biblical God have not been entirely alert to the rationalistic and anti-tragic patterns within their thought. Their critical scrutiny has focused instead on ancient metaphysical dualism, and they tacitly blame this metaphysical dualism for the hierarchical thinking of Western patriarchy."[59]

Sands wants to argue that both the rationalist tradition, which seeks to make sense of evil, and the dualist tradition, which seeks to demonize it, are caught up and implicated in each other, and depend upon ontological arguments for the good. Underlying both rationalist and dualist feminist theological arguments, then, is an assumed and coherent One, the One upon which feminist theological claims are unproblematically built. They use, as Davaney says, the "language of ontology and metaphysics, long in dispute in other arenas, as a way of contributing to the validity of the feminist vision."[60]

In many ways, the question of foundations is becoming increasingly crucial for feminist theologies that maintain conversations with feminist theory, philosophy, and sociology. The skeptical idea that the idea of God functions and the theological strategy of exempting real divinity from the final reductions of social construction gave birth to the very possibility of feminist theology in all of its forms, to the possibility of a postpatriarchal vision, and to the possibility of a reinterpreted biblical tradition, but it also poses one of the greatest challenges to these imaginative possibilities.

PART 2

Challenges from Experience

CHAPTER FOUR

Multiple Claims of Divine Presence

I remember when I was holy.
When the shimmer of golden light
bid me sit in its presence.
When in silence,
my cells soaked up swoon and ecstasy
and my mind wrote up
name tags for the experience.

I remember when I was holy
and each incense-scented morning
wrestled with muscles in
cross-legged pain,
spinal column held ever more erect
following the prescription of
Your rules and I never questioned.

Now I think I am made of
mud and doubt.
I rarely feel holy,
I rarely remember feeling holy,
I rarely contemplate what holy is, yet,
sometimes I am caught
by a passing wave of joy—
so full of light
I am breathless.

It does not come at properly prescribed moments,
but unbidden while hauling bricks
or laughing over bouillabaisse with Chris
or seeing the sun glow
green through tree leaves.

I look down
. and see both feet
standing firm
on everyday ground.

I did not know
this was possible.

—Donna S. Gates[1]

I suggested earlier that feminist theologies are a river with two source springs; a tree with two taproots. I have traced the one root growing out of social theory. Through the strategies of neoorthodox theology, it matured in feminist theologies into the finely turned tool that is the metaphoric exemption. The metaphoric exemption is a philosophically, theologically, and intellectually coherent strategy with beauty in its well-drawn edges and in its artistic simplicity. It gives to feminist theologies their critical architecture.

I now turn to the other source—lived experience—that gives rise to the feminist theological river. Lived experience is a complicated category that has preoccupied contemporary feminist theologians for many years. It is not easy to define without inappropriately limiting its scope and without naively glossing its vulnerability to interpretation. Nevertheless, experience does occur. Women and men continue to experience real discrimination, real structural inequities, real pain and suffering, and what they understand to be real spiritual life. If they are to address these dimensions of human life and history, and offer any meaningful prescriptions for correcting injustices, feminist theologies must account for experience in some way, however different and incommensurate particular experiences may be.

Lived experience opposes the thoroughgoing skepticism of the metaphoric exemption. It is a tumbling, vibrant source; it is resistant to theory and vulnerable to the vagaries of autobiography, impression, dream, and even delusion. It is, without irony, the essence of difference. But experience, theorized in some way, makes theology that is concerned with oppression and liberation possible. Feminist theologies stem from the problematic and concrete particularities of real women's lives in real cultural contexts with real communal commitments. Beyond their origins in lived experience, however, feminist theologies are intimately and irrevocably shaped by the ongoingness of such experience. They continue to drink deeply from that well.

For this reason I suggest that feminist theologies cannot afford to side-step the experiential claims that women and men make of divine presence, even when those experiences imply heretical multiplicity, uncompromising embodiment, traditional oneness, unlimitedness, profound everydayness, finite particularity, resilient absurdity, magnificent otherness, alarming intimacy, shape, coherence, transience, or even imaginative play.[2] Experiences of this sort do occur, and sometimes they occur in relation to the proposals and ideas that feminist theologians put forward. Theological proposals do not create experiences of divine presence, but they are also in no position to refute them entirely, however contrary or untheorizable such experiences may turn out to be.

> By the sapling with its burlap wrap
> Tishku and I line up to board.
> The train wheezes
> in the icy fog. There is a
> clearing of throats.
>   There are kisses,
> promises to call, and a silence
> in the form of the gentleman
> who falls in behind us,
> who folds his scarf before us
> in an opposite seat.
>   One lurch
> and we're rolling.
>   One glance sneaked
> at Tishku, and the gentleman feels disarmed.
> An accidental touch, a discreet whiff. . . .
> A sunbeam lights her streaming locks:
> he's ready to crawl.
>   Oh well. One kiss
> blown through a little fog, and she'd
> created light, which she gathered
> in a scarf, to shape the sun.
> With that warmth
> plus a pound
> of her mucky flesh,
> she molded the earth.
> An hour of wishful thinking
> produced him. Not his looks—
> she let his parents make those—
> but the tree of him,
> the promise.

And look at Tishku,
dressed in her best mortal clothes:
cashmere coat, silk sheath, and pearls.
I gave her all these for days like this
when she crawls from under a rotting log,
longing to follow me through civilization.
I said when I must travel on business—
business with gentlemen—I expect
she'll wash the worms and slugs
out of that hair.

—Marjorie Power[3]

Women and men profess to experience divine presence in multiple ways and under myriad circumstances. I am confident that human experiences of sacred realities brought clearly into consciousness and imaginatively expressed are not the sole purview of a particular group, religion, or culture, nor do they take place in limited settings. The history of religions strongly suggests otherwise. A person does not have to be a feminist to experience divine presence. I am, however, interested in feminist religious experiences because of their apparent vitality, insistence on multiple embodiments, and the challenges they raise for theological reflection. More to the point, I am interested in the fact of feminist religious experiences in their vitality and multiplicity because of the philosophical weight that feminism necessarily places on the category of experience. Barring blanket dismissals of religious experience as fundamentally delusional—which most, though not all, theologians are generally loath to do—stories and accounts of divine presence and activity that do not fit the metaphoric exemption pose some important challenges for feminist theological tasks. Like the representational and sometimes abrupt presence of descriptive narratives and poems in this chapter, divine presence seems simply to be there from time to time, to become coherent, to take on meaning (an epistemological claim in itself, to be sure), and to pass on. The general robustness of feminist spiritualities, which I will discuss in greater depth in the next chapter, is related to the strong nourishment they receive from the sometimes disruptive importance of experience in feminist theologies.

Although it is now clear how foundational the evolutionary ideas of modernist skepticism are for feminist projects and theological propositions, skepticism is only one part of the story. The other part of the story is experience in all of its difficult resistance to theory and all of its epistemological challenge. Feminism is rooted in categories of experience, but it does not yet know what to do with spiritually focused or religious experiences.[4] Spiritually focused experience is a particular kind of experience, stemming from or generating interpretive moves that emphasize the untheorizable space between language and encounter; moves that recognize liminality even when it is romanticized and glossed. Poetry and the outlines of story are sometimes the only ways that words can approach the profound and sometimes unreasonable impact that spiritual or religious experiences can have on mind and identity. It is not surprising therefore that in the process of thinking about this work, poetry and stories poured out from the individuals familiar with feminist theologies who responded to my unsystematic request that they try to describe their experiences of divine presence. What I have begun to notice among persons who are open to such things is that divine presence seems, quite simply, to occur. And the least that we can do, as Annie Dillard says, is be there.

To experience some kind of "real" or "direct" encounter with the divine is one thing. To put it into words that convey its impact is wholly another. That is the beautiful conundrum of divinity in the world. We can talk about it but not ever fully reenact it, and our talking is a whisper of what has already passed by. It is hope, nostalgia, and challenge.

> I think they told us to forget Yoruba.
> Ogun He definitely cut out.
> Guess he only like winning.
> But She didn't.
> Followed us till her feet and hands bled.
> Why She stick around nobodies?
> Nobody nobody She say Anyway
> you mine.
>
> Shhhh She say in the night.
> Stay strong She say.
> She rip her gold red black yellow royal
> headcloth so the baby have a wrap.
> She slink around the night
> keep the singing in the pot.
> Her breath sexy and free
> like moss in the right places.
>
> Jesus okay She say. You gotta live.
> But She don't go away.
> Dream me She say. You mine still
> to the ends of the earth.

> She still there, I can see her
> leaning on that sister's new Grand Am,
> butt up on that door but no alarm ringing.
>
> Shhhh baby She whisper
> in the moss.
>
> —Janie M.[5]

Women and men profess to experience in profound ways what they understand to be divine presence. Jerome Gellman notes that even the most ardent skeptics are hard-pressed to defend blanket declarations against such experiences.[6] People claim, over and over again, to experience divine presence in myriad immediate and ongoing ways. I suggest that feminist theologies must account for this perception in a more rigorous and serious way than they have in the past. This does not mean that feminist theologies must document or account for every individual alleged event of sacred coming forth in the world. Rather, because they grant some important authority to experiences of other kinds, feminist theologies must account for the fact that feminist women and men perceive divine reality in innumerable concrete presences, and evaluate their theological claims in light of this fact.

The metaphoric exemption, being an expression of skeptical caution, lobbies for dismissal. There is no way to adjudicate between incommensurate experiences, and so, according to the metaphoric exemption, experiences of divine presence cannot reveal anything concrete about divine realities. To the extent that people think otherwise about their own experiences, they are deluded. At the very least, the metaphoric exemption suggests, theologians should not engage in the chaotic realm of immediate impression, suggestive encounter, or imaginative dialogue with imagined spirits. Feminist theologies have a hard enough time with credibility as it is.

There is good reasoning behind the metaphoric exemption's dismissal. But the point here is that feminist theologies are not only founded on the metaphoric exemption nor do they take their only sustenance from that clear, cool source. Feminist theologies are also founded on the richly dense and sometimes disruptive claims of living histories, concrete communities, and real people encountering one another across great gulfs of belief, culture, and circumstance. These theologies take shape and form, or perhaps more eloquently they receive soul and flesh, from the lived experiences of real women and men in a great variety of concrete settings. Problematic as the category of experience is (and it is problematic), notions of experience and claims from experience are foundational to feminism, particularly so to feminist theologies in all their resilient variety.

Increasingly, feminist women's and men's religious experiences of divine presence are told, shared, written down, and retold with vigor. It seems plausible that feminist theologies can and should address these experiences as well as experiences of systematic abuse or communal liberation. The quantity and vitality of feminist experiences of spirituality and divine presence are not, however, the most pressing warrant for feminist theological attention to the question of experience and divine presence, although I have chosen to include anecdotal examples here as reminders of their existence. The most pressing warrant for theological attention to feminist experiences of divinity comes from within feminist theologies themselves, from their prior commitments to the category of women's various experiences as source and leaven for their work. The lived experiences of women in circumstances of sexism, racism, mothering, daughtering, peacemaking, lamenting, protesting, poverty, wealth, slavery, removal, ownership, ritualizing, triple jeopardy and complex privilege, loving men and loving women, threats of violence, standing up for children and outcasts and animals and bits of earth, learning to speak for the first time, making solidarity and failing at solidarity are only some of the experiences that are foundational to feminist theological core concerns and to dialogical work across boundaries of community and culture.

But what about experiences of divine presence? What do these experiences in particular have to offer feminist theologies? In general, experiences of any intense or momentous account are highly untheorizable (like divine realities themselves). Thus, poetry, art, music, dance, story, and even silence so often seem the best means to capture and tell of an experience of divinity, to express something of its quality and its pressing importance. Despite the difficulties involved with theorizing the resilient and incommensurate "thereness" that lurks in particularized feminist accounts of divine encounter and the abundance of poetic and impressionistic stories of sacred reality, feminist theologies must somehow account for the multiplicity and concrete facticity of divinity in experience. They must do so particularly for women and men who agree with feminist theologians that they should pay better attention to the world and to immanental possibilities for more embodied divinity. There are, however, consequences that come with taking the facticity of experiential confession more seriously.

At first glance, the image is of two aging trees in a field. Gnarled, faintly suggesting a treehouse that once inhabited the tired branches. I turn the postcard over to learn that these are two of the Little Big Horn burial trees.

The image changes . . . ribbons, buckskin, beaded saddle blankets, flesh and bones and strands of hair. I hear ancient drums.

I feel my own red blood coursing. I remember learning that "mulatto" on my grandfathers' birth records was code for "Muscogees who hid in Cherokee caves" a few hundred feet from the Natchez Trace section of the Trail of Tears in northwest Alabama. My grandparents' farmhouse still stands only a few miles from there.

I hear modern drums beating ancient rhythms accompanied by the shake of the turtle shells of the women dancers. I see ribbon shirts, shawls and broad smiles. Eldermens and elderwomens, young people, childrens. I hear Joe Tarpaleechee softly say, "What tribe are you?" I respond shyly, "Muscogee—from Alabama." Joe shakes my hand Creek style and welcomes me.

I begin a journey—nokusē (bear), tvklikē (bread), blood quantum, cvmbē (sweet), tribal town, removal, estē-hvtkē (white man), estē-catē (Indian), Five Civilized Tribes, Hē sáketvmesē (God, Master of Breath), sovereignty, mvtó (thank you). I hear drums.

—Cindy Davenport[7]

The difficulties of theorizing the ultimately untheorizable have not stopped theology from attempting to speak of divinity in the past, so experiences of divine presence, untheorizable as they seem to be, should hardly pose an insurmountable problem. But the issue is not whether theology can address the challenges of incommensurate experiences in its own more generalized attempts to understand divinity in the world. The issue is what doing so will mean for traditional and doctrinal understandings of divine being as One, separate, perfect, and pure. Feminist descriptions of divine presence do not tend to emphasize these things, even in their many particular differences. Individual feminist experiences of divine presence tend to fundamentally challenge monotheistic uniformity, transcendent otherness, and traditional doctrinal images altogether.

Of course, not all feminist women and men experience the same thing. That is part of the point. The apparent fact that many women and men experience divine presence in ways that fundamentally challenge doctrinal claims about God is also part of the point. Are they heretics? Are they delusional? What can, and what should, feminist theologies say about these experiences, especially given their foundational claims about the importance of lived experience in the formulation of theory? That is the issue. But before I can take up the problem of beginning to define and describe a way of speaking about feminist religious experience and spirituality, I must evaluate the so-called warrants for discussing experience as a foundational root in feminist theologies in the first place.

THE QUESTION OF FEMINIST EXPERIENCE

The idea of experience is not simple for feminists or theologians. Feminist theologies especially have grappled with the problem of defining the category of experience in such a way that it does not "leave out too much" as Delores Williams says, particularly the experiences of nonmainstream women: Asian American, African American, Hispanic, Native American, lesbian, fundamentalist, Jewish, and so on. Honoring the particularity and facticity of lived experiences without making the error of what Mary McClintock Fulkerson calls "false universals" is a significant challenge because warrants from experience slide easily into normative claims for others.[8]

The taproot of experience comes from feminism's overall concern with real-life ethical problems of systematic oppression, with justice, and with liberation. Oppression can be accurately identified only by the experiential claims of the oppressed. Justice is verified only by the experiential claims of its recipients. And liberation is available to common knowledge only through the testimony of the liberated. Thus, like Latin American liberation theologies, feminist theologies tend to rely on modified correlational and analogical methods that link pressing ethical and existential concerns from experience with theological answers (although they also criticize the principal architects of these methods for flaws of cultural nearsightedness).[9]

Feminist theologians strive to define these motivating concerns in ways that make sense (if not find agreement) across cultural divides and that, at the same time, make the theological and ethical conditions of their work clear. Thus, many of them have found common ground in liberation theology, from Rosemary Ruether's and Dorothee Sölle's explicit linking of feminism to Latin American liberation theologies,[10] to Elisabeth Schüssler Fiorenza's articulation of "critical feminist liberation hermeneutics,"[11] and Kelly Brown Douglas's, Sharon Welch's, Katie Cannon's, and Kathleen Sands's attempts to formulate feminist liberationist ideas in ethical terms. At root, articulated experiences of systemic subjugation, theories of political action, and a concern for the complicity of religious ideas in these experiences tend to be the elements that feminist and other liberationist theologies share. Catholic theologian Lisa Sowle Cahill sums up nicely the connection many make between liberation and feminist theological methods when she suggests that these theologies "arise out of an experienced situation of oppression and have as a primary aim the deconstruction of unjust social structures and institutions."[12]

The experience of oppression, related personally through sociological studies or through historical documentation, is part of what makes feminist theologies feminist. In fact, it is on the basis of this foundation in experience that internal criticism within mainstream feminist theologies first emerged. Generalized, unproblematized, and universalized notions of white women's experience in early feminist theologies generated strong critiques by many others who argued that white feminist writings misrepresent or inadequately account for multivalent layers of oppression (or other experiences that generate different theories and different conclusions) that are overlooked by the white privileged eye.

No longer willing to universalize women's experience from the basis of a taken-for-granted white, middle-class, heterosexual ideal, Marjorie Hewitt Suchocki, for example, attempts to place the category of experience into a wider, more nuanced frame, arguing that the "feminist approach to redevelopment of doctrine maintains that all theology is rooted in experience and that the structure of experience is mediated through socially constructed language, which in turn is affected by one's embodiment as male or female"[13] and presumably by one's embodiment also as black, white, Hispanic, Asian, and so forth. Elizabeth Johnson puts the importance of experience into a more traditionally Christian language of rational piety, arguing that the "lens of women's flourishing focuses faith's search for understanding in feminist theology,"[14] while Delores Williams argues that experience is the very source of the "female-stuff" needed to "craft a world of meaning. Womanist words and descriptions must be true to the reality they claim to represent—black women's lived experience in the everyday world."[15]

Sheila Greeve Davaney, primarily addressing white feminists, has argued for caution and greater analytical suspicion concerning the status of women's experience as source for theological reflection. She is aware that all theology is informed by experience and history, but she argues that while women's personal experiences are important sources of information for individual women, white feminist theology continues to suffer from its own forms of cultural blindness brought on by the universalizing tendencies of white feminists about *their* experiences.[16] Sharon Welch, on the other hand, has countered Davaney's critique with the argument that so-called appeals to white women's experience are only normatively universal if they are then applied that way in abstraction (precisely the way, she suggests, that white men's experience has been used in traditional theological formulations). She argues that the very nature of practical, everyday experience is that it resists universalization because of its partiality and transient character, and the growing explicitness with which even white feminists tend to use the category of experience makes it available for critique in more accountable and fruitful ways.[17] Experience in all of its particularity, she asserts, continues to be vital to feminist theological tasks, so long as it is not abstracted into universal claims for all women everywhere.

Mary McClintock Fulkerson suggests that both Davaney and Welch are right, but that any appeal to women's experience (or experiences) still raises difficult issues for epistemology because of the ease with which particular experiences can be treated in universal terms. She therefore builds on Welch's argument for retaining particular experiences by suggesting a distinction between women's experience in general as a universalizing norm and feminist women's experience as a heuristic tool for further exploration:

> When women's experience [in general] is used as a warrant for a claim, this implicitly grants that experience the status of a universal shared consciousness. It can thereby sponsor the accounts of oppressive and liberating texts and traditions as what women should/will find liberating and oppressive. This claim is at odds with the use of feminist women's experience, which could at least claim the located character of its judgment regarding sexist texts and go on to explore the conflicts and desire that are inextricable with power and meaning.[18]

At the heart of these discussions of experience is the problematic issue of epistemology and reference. It is the question of whether individual or collective experiences somehow disclose real things and relations, or whether they are too implicated in social construction to disclose anything other than the social imagination at work. Wilhelm Dilthey argues that "our knowledge of what is given in experience is extended through the interpretation of the objectifications of life and their interpretation, in turn, is only made possible by plumbing the depths of subjective experience."[19] What he means is that the content of particular experiences, such as the presence of the divine, is not accessible to consciousness except through the many filters of social construction. This implies a self-referencing hermeneutical circle that may not allow for resolution. It is like the old game of telephone where the original message becomes distorted beyond recognition. As Victor Turner suggests, the depths of subjective experience risk incoherence because in the process of coming to consciousness and expression, experience of any so-called real becomes ever more implicated and embedded in the social constructions out of which it emerges if "it" exists at all.[20]

Despite, or perhaps because of, the important questions that cling to it, the category of experience in feminist theologies continues to play a pivotal role in the foundational warrants even of feminist theologies that attempt to complicate experience as a category. The term "experience" in these writings tends to refer to the constitutive character of group identities that are related to communally shared experiences based on race privilege or oppression, gender, economic status, family or cultural tradition, sexuality, and so on.[21] These are experiences abstracted out of the particular autobiographical and essentially untheorizable status of event and cast into the generalized frame of historical experience that gives culture its definitive shape and texture. Epistemological concerns about the status of experience in its "subjective depths" and in its infinite particularity remain backgrounded to the more readily available generalizations about "women," "culture," "race," "privilege," and "oppression."

So when Delores Williams argues that womanist theology must be fundamentally "true to the reality they claim to represent—black women's lived experience in the everyday world"—she is referring to a generalized shape of experience with which she assumes the untheorizable singularities of individual black American women's experiences will substantially agree. Elizabeth Johnson asserts a generalized experience for women in Christianity that, like Williams, she argues is an "essential element in the theological task." Although she eschews what she calls stereotypical norms, she does not give up a claim to such experience in its most general shape because the shared experience of "living within patriarchal systems," she states, "does forge among women recognizable experiences of suffering along with typical patterns of coping and victoriously resisting, strategies that enable women to survive."[22] She, too, is referring to a generalized shape with which she assumes the untheorizable singularities of individual Christian women's experiences will substantially agree. If, for example, the particularities of a black American woman's experiences of any religion substantially do not agree with Williams's notions of womanist experience, or if the particular experiences of a Christian woman of any ethnicity substantially do not agree with Johnson's generalized notions of women's experiences in Christianity, then the delicate matter of hegemonic claims of experience as definitive for group identity emerges. Experience as a generalized category with specific content is highly vulnerable to hegemonic readings, even within specific groups and communities.

Anne Carr represents a mainstream understanding of white feminist theology that tends to take for granted shared terms such as "woman" and "feminist" and attempts at the same time to account for differences emerging in feminist and womanist literature concerning normative proposals. She states the issue in terms of vision, arguing that although "different theologians offer different ways of understanding what serves as a norm in their proposals, the distinctive character of feminist theology is not a norm but the perspective of women, a specifically feminist angle of vision."[23] Just *what* is the perspective of "women" that can be identified and interrogated is not clearly established. Neither is a specifically feminist angle of vision that does not gloss the particular features of ethnicity, class, and the other cultural manifestations of difference that, in Susan Thistlethwaite's terms, "make a difference" between women, differences that shape feminist discourses.[24]

The problem of defining so-called feminist experience is by no means resolved despite its continued importance in feminist theologies, particularly feminist theological projects hoping to get past topics of difference alone to other shared concerns of doctrine or theological construction. It is, nevertheless, still possible to talk about feminist experience in features general enough to say that sexism exists, and racism exists, and other socially malicious ideas that implicate women exist. This simple claim is warrant enough for feminist theologies to engage in the next step, which is to find ways of talking about experience that bring to light the particularities of concrete communities and that do not shove differences under the rug.

Feminist theologies therefore constitute a school of thought and practice that is ineradicably rooted in generalized and particular experiences of racism and sexism, particularly as the experiences implicate religious institutions and theological ideas. They are also, on the basis of such experiences, concerned with the development of new institutional structures and theological ideas that affirm women (however defined). Not all feminist theologies have concerned themselves with traditional theological concepts, and not all have focused directly on issues traditionally associated with mainstream religion, but all feminist theologies do presume basic—though different—"experiences of suffering along with typical patterns of coping and victoriously resisting." Most of what goes by the name feminist theology builds upon or directly addresses assumptions about concepts of God and divinity and the relationship of these concepts to cultural (in this case patriarchal or postpatriarchal) ends. The ways in which various feminist theologians have drawn upon this taproot of experience to address central concepts of the divine are central to what makes their work both theological and feminist.

THE QUESTION OF EXPERIENCE IN THEOLOGY

Because the issue of religious experience is not simple, feminist theologians have been ambivalent about it in their constructive work. The slippery and contested status of individual experience in philosophy leads to a theological tendency to sidestep it altogether, as though its status is resolved. Certainly, as Edward Farley suggests, "the term, experience, especially when used in connection with theology, invites serious confusions." To avoid such confusion, he makes a distinction between idiosyncratic or "momentary" experiences (plural) that are more or less individual, and a deeper, communal form of experience (singular) that he describes as tacit, enduring, and that therefore exemplifies "experiential theology."[25] It is not that individual experiences are by definition invalid in Farley's understanding; it is that validity is also individual and therefore problematic for the more general work of theological reflection. In principle, individual or momentary religious experiences are neither enduring nor historically communal enough to provide a basis for theology that can be applied in enduring and communal ways.

There is no question that the general intellectual task of constructive theology is, for the most part, one of coherence in ideas of ultimacy that can be translated beyond the individual, beyond the autobiographical, into meaning and orientation for human life in general. Gordon Kaufman justifies his dismissal of religious experiences of divine presence altogether as essentially delusional by arguing that the central responsibility of the theologian is "to deal seriously and critically with the question of God" apart from those experiences.[26] On the other hand, Paul Tillich makes the question of experience important to his systematic method, claiming it "has been a central question whenever the nature and method of theology have been discussed."[27] His resolution, similar to Farley's, is an attempt to stretch the concept of experience out of its simple association or identity with reality and ontology. Unlike Farley, however, Tillich sidesteps the problem of autobiographical variance by narrowing experience to the scriptural source, making the only experience relevant to theology the Christ event in the Bible. He is able to make experience important, but to control it, claiming that "experience is called the medium through which the objective sources are received, this excludes the reliance of the theologian on a possibly post-Christian experience. But it also denies the assertion that experience is a theological source. And finally, it denies the belief in experiences which, although remaining in the Christian circle, add some new material to the other sources."[28]

The so-called question of experience, then, is typically treated in modern Christian theology as foundational or constitutive in terms of its capacity to yield up basic and generic human conditions, a thematic approach that attempts to take history and historicism seriously. This would reflect Farley's distinction of experience from experiences. It provides for theology a working space that is not held hostage to the vagaries of autobiography and competing accounts of the same events. Individual experiences are notoriously unreliable in philosophical or thematic terms. They are disruptive and often uncanny and therefore confuse the philosophical and theological task. David Burrell argues:

[A] sane epistemology will normally presuppose that our range of knowing is coextensive with the kinds of beings we are in such a way as to deflate pretensions to knowledge of things quite beyond us. That range cannot be equated with "our experience," however, and not simply because the term "experience" is notoriously protean. It is rather that our knowledge must extend to things presupposed to our experiencing anything at all, which might be called "the structures" of our experience.[29]

Despite the illuminating progress that existentialism and phenomenology have made toward thematic treatments of experience, the basic importance of experience (even understood thematically rather than autobiographically) in feminist projects raises the issue of the "real" more directly than in any other discursive context. Even feminist theologians who raise important questions about the status of "women's experience" do not want to completely subsume its particularity and vulnerability under more universalistic structures and themes. Rather, their criticism concerns unreflective, static, and inappropriately applied *versions* of women's experience, limiting the possibilities of that experience in all of its complexity and *instability* to deepen and strengthen feminist reflection.[30] Dorothee Sölle argues that precisely because feminism is concerned with the historical and contemporary status and identity of women in cultures still predominantly hostile to their advancement, experience understood categorically and experience understood in its unsystematic particularity are necessary to the root justifications for feminism itself:

> Although it is sometimes exaggerated within the religious women's movement so that there is virtually no subsequent reflection on it, [experience] is fundamental to the critical capacity of women and others who are oppressed, who appeal against a dominant theology, opinion, or ideology on the basis of their own experience. The most important criterion for this concept [of experience] is intersubjectivity, in other words the communicability of experience. So, again in connection with the question of God, it is not a matter of my having this God and your having that God, but of the communication of experiences in which we find ourselves together again.[31]

Experiential confession is therefore an essential strength in feminist theologies. Indeed, for most white, womanist, *mujerista*, and other feminist theologians, theology is meaningless unless it articulates a clear relationship between the contents of religious faith and concrete experiences of divine encounter, which in turn shape just human relations. Elsa Tamez, for example, writes that liberation theology done by women in Latin America *"does not remove the experience of oppression from the experience of God*, or the life of faith; it has demonstrated another methodology in making its point of departure the practice of liberation within this context."[32] Ursula King notes that although "Third World feminist theology is diverse and different from feminist theology in the First World, it also shares a number of similar characteristics. Feminist theology is deeply rooted in women's experiences; it is marked by commitment and oriented toward personal and social transformation, toward praxis, and in turn *much theological reflection arises out of such praxis*."[33]

Some, like Ada María Isasi-Díaz, suggest that the academic practice of theology in its tendencies to look past the particularities of discrete experience is "frankly irrelevant" to nonwhite or, in Isasi-Díaz's case, Hispanic women. "This is made evident," she says, "by the fact that many Hispanic women have lived their religion mostly outside the official churches with which academic theology deals and that they have ignored the language of such a theology."[34] It is important to avoid understanding Isasi-Díaz's point simplistically (and I believe erroneously) as an attack on academic theology's concerns with concepts of divinity. *Mujerista* writers argue that the reflective work of feminist theologies with their concern with women's experience *and* with more theoretical concepts of God is significant to Hispanic feminists.[35] In addition, there is a growing range of womanist, Asian, African, and white North American writers concerned with the concept of God in theology and in liturgical practice.[36] Isasi-Díaz's point is not to circumscribe or essentialize the abilities and interests of Hispanic women as a simplistic reading might suggest. Rather, it is to indicate some of the typical failings in academic theology, mainstream white feminist theology in particular, to address adequately the *range* of social and religious experiences of women in various communities, and to be shaped by those experiences in the process of theological reflection.

Despite the various emphases on shared experiences of oppression, however, feminist theologies are still faced with the modernist skepticism that makes all but the most generic experiences of divinity vulnerable to dismissal, falsification, or claims of delusion. And even the most generic and communal experiences of divine presence are prone to what Marx called false consciousness, a concern of great importance to feminists given the millennia of women's complicity in their own subjugation. If experiences of the divine are to become a part of feminist discourse, what experiences are trustworthy for the theological task? Is the best route the one taken by theologians such as Edward Farley and Gordon Kaufman, who recommend treating experience phenomenologically, trimming off the idiosyncrasies of individual expression and illuminating the deeper, shared structures? Or is it better to stick with the politics of identity, distilling shared meanings for experience along lines of allegiance, tradition, or community, as is the case with many or most feminist theologians? Either route discourages attention to the individual, the transient, and the particularly embodied experience. Both routes appreciate the colonizing errors that ride shotgun with any parochial or temporary claim to truth or with any culture-bound experience. But neither fully addresses the stubborn persistence of the autobiographical, the particular, the hard-to-theorize "thereness" of feminist spiritual experiences.

Generalized experience, moreover, is theorizable experience. It lends itself to the work of antisexist and antiracist theory because as generalization it is not complicated by the basic incommensurability of singular experience. Generalizations are themselves theories and so lend themselves to theory. Generalized themes in women's experiences are essential to the political work of feminist theologies, vulnerable as they always are to the erasures of difference. It is not that the individual and the autobiographical have no place in feminist theologies. The space has been cleared, by the work of womanists, lesbian feminists, white feminists, *mujeristas*, Asian feminists, and other feminists, for narratives, stories, images, and accounts of individual suffering and individual triumph to have a place, to find resonance in the generalized context of feminist theological work.

What remains relatively untheorized and underdeveloped, though, is the place of subjective, sometimes noncollective experiences that relate specifically to divinity, to constructs and concepts of sacred realities. The idea that collective experiences drawn along certain gender, class, race, or sexuality lines may influence possibilities and meanings for theological construction—and may provide avenues for divine revelatory activity—is well articulated in feminist theological literature. Possibilities for other kinds of experiences, particularly visionary or religious experiences related to feminist theological constructs, are not as well articulated, despite the vitality and apparent abundance of these experiences within feminist circles. The problems facing this latter kind of analysis are many, but I do not believe that they are insurmountable.

HOPPY HAD NEVER BEEN a nice cat. When Michael found him in the back alley he was a little grey ball of fur smaller than Mike's hand. "Can I keep him please?" It was Michael's ninth birthday.

Hoppy bit deliberately and unpredictably all his life. He would have nothing to do with people. We named him "Hoppy" for the funny way he walked. We should have named him "Curmudgeon."

Thirteen years later Hoppy lay stretched out across a floor register, thin, ragged, sick. He had not eaten in three days, except for a few licks of half-and-half which he couldn't resist under any circumstances. He was not in pain, but it seemed he was dying. I had a decision to make. Would I take him to the vet, via the car trip which always terrorized him, possibly only to have him euthanized at the end of the terror—or possibly to bring him home well? Or would I leave him alone, soaking up the warmth from the register, and let nature take its course, possibly to die unnecessarily—but certainly to do so in peace and relative dignity?

I decided to leave him alone.

A few months later, my father lay stretched out on his couch, very ill. He was depressed, sallow, coughing, bone thin, refusing to eat, refusing to seek medical help. I had a decision to make. Would I force him to go to the doctor, probably to be sent to the hospital which was more frightening to him than anything else in the world—and possibly to be made well again? Or would I leave him alone, in the familiarity of his apartment, possibly to die there—but certainly to do so in relative peace and with at least as much dignity as I had allowed my curmudgeon cat?

I decided to leave him alone.

The cat lived.

My father died.

Both decisions were good.

Four years later, Hoppy lay dying. There was no doubt about it this time. He lay at the edge of the kitchen floor, unable to move any farther. He'd been there for two days, watching us with his usual resentful stare. I put a towel between the linoleum and his bony body. He hadn't enough life left to bite me for it.

I sat with Hoppy as he died. Even while he still breathed, he died from the outside in—his tail, his ears, his paws became cold though his heart still beat. Then finally he made a small sound, a single mew.

I went out to the back yard to dig a grave for Hoppy. I lined the grave with fresh wild catnip. I wrapped his body in the towel, placed it in the damp brown, dusky hole, and covered it with flowers and dirt. I brought out my deerhide drum, sat beside the fresh grave, and began to beat whichever rhythms came to my hand. I said to the dead cat, "You have been a lousy cat all your life, you damned curmudgeon. So I ask of your spirit, now, one favor, which you surely owe me. I ask your spirit to help me grieve well."

I do not know how much time passed before I was next aware. My first awareness was of needing to breathe. I had not inhaled for an eternity. My sobs were so intense they were silent, too deep to find any audible expression at all. The only sound was my drumming, which seemed to be disembodied, coming from another place and time.

I grieved well. I grieved for the cat. I grieved for my father. I grieved for the many losses of my life, named and unnamed. I had entered a timeless, mystical realm.

This was confirmed for me by another four-legged creature. Hannah, the black Labrador who lived next door, who usually greeted me with overwhelming enthusiasm, sat without moving at the base of the maple tree, a few yards from me and Hoppy's grave. How long she had been there I don't know. She was still, silent, guarding the mysterious time I had entered with the spirit of the cat. When I could function again, she came over and sat down quietly beside me, laying her head on my knee. This was indeed sacred space, and we both knew it.

—Cynthia Trenshaw[37]

How can feminist theologies take account of experiences like this without making them normative or without slipping into dismissive neglect that traditional theology has often visited upon women's accounts of revelatory presence (from the disciples' refusal to believe the women running back from the tomb, to Anne Hutchinson's banishment from the Massachusetts Bay Colony, to contemporary dismissals after the Minneapolis Re-Imagining Conference in 1993)? Such revelatory, sacred experiences do seem to occur to women and men who step into the possibilities that feminist theologies offer, with infinitely variable particulars, and they demand attention.

Revelatory experiences of divine presence stick like a burr to feminist and other constructive theologies, however. Their very existence raises the question of the authority and place of everyday claims to practical, mystical, and communal experiences of divinity that challenge the safety of the metaphoric exemption (the criterion that all referential language about God in fact not reveal divine being but refer to the human imagination). Contemporary feminist theologies, particularly in their Christian manifestations, have grounded themselves in the coherent deferrals of the metaphoric exemption—on the shores of what Gordon Kaufman calls "the imaginative project" of theology—in order to relativize and decenter the exclusivist and idolatrous claims of traditional theological and ecclesial systems, and to posit new, more inclusive, and arguably more defensible propositions.

What is more, participants in both Christian and post-Christian feminist ritual and worship settings often rely on the work of feminist constructive theologians for guidance, on the one hand, and for theological justification, a kind of permission to proceed, on the other. But the metaphoric exemption is decidedly muted and sometimes missing altogether in contexts where feminist theologies are understood and enacted. According to Lesley Northup, "When women gather intentionally to worship, what they are doing is rarely static or passive; most often, it is a vital process, not always successful but always creative—that is, it is ritualizing, rather than observing or participating in a fixed, received ritual."[38] The metaphoric exemption reminds that divinity cannot be seen, touched, comprehended, or reduced to the present in any real way. Often women's experiences of divine presence do not conform to these rules.

> The curves of Torah hold him like a woman, my son.
> I let him go now,
> into his manhood and see him
> for the first time trembling
> in the world of fringed white and blue
> I have lit the candles and remember
> his hungry mouth, his study of breast
>
> This Woman he holds, he and his God hold
> parade and kiss
> read with hungry lips
> holds him between
> the fat spirals
> the Woman he holds
> he worships.
> It is good.
>
> —Anonymous[39]

The muting of theological iconoclasm in the context of ritualizing (which, modifying Dilthey, I am calling lived feminist theology) poses a poignant sort of problem for feminist theologians. They are faced, on the one hand, with the political, philosophical, and doctrinal necessities of social constructionism as the starting point both for their critique of patriarchy and for their contribution to a postpatriarchal vision. They are faced, on the other hand, with real people in living worship or spiritually focused settings who make claims about experiences of divine presence or sacred activity partly as a result of this theology; who believe that the symbol or image or idea that they are experiencing or invoking is real, even when they also acknowledge its sources in imagination. Most of all, feminist theologies are faced with women and men who take seriously their theological ideas and who also believe that their spiritual experiences of sacred realities are not delusional or simply imagined.

Those days were lonesome. No, not just lonesome, but downright destitute, bereft of the familiar, of familial, of all that was until the wrenching moment when all that was, was life, banished to a small, remote House of Prayer, sixty miles from Montreal in the middle of nowhere. It was January, with its unrepenting subzero plight.

One Sunday afternoon, while trekking through the cathedraled forest, weighed down with feelings of abandonment, and dire loss, I pleaded with the Divine Presence around me, whoever She, He, It, was, were or will be, for a sign, please dear God, something to keep my chilled soul from despair.

Frozen tears on my cheeks, frozen sobs in my heart, I lifted up my eyes and saw in that dapple-colored sunset sky, two gigantic jet streams, crossed and forming the biggest X-kiss I have ever seen. Through my blurry-teared eyes, my seemingly absent, but now so-present God, had become a Skywriter! I was not abandoned, I was loved. The frozen winter turned to spring!

—Joann Heinritz, CSJ[40]

Whether or not what people say they experience really is divine is an impossible issue to resolve. But it is a false issue for feminist theologies unless all experiences of the divine are declared unreal. The fact that people perceive divinity as present in concrete ways is enough warrant for feminist theologies to confront the tension between experiential confession and metaphoric exemption because of their prior commitments to categories of lived experience. The inaccessibility of experience to objective testing and the vulnerability of experience to delusional interpretation do not pose strong enough objections to justify dismissal or disregard of the issues that such experiences raise.

Feminist theologies have matured past the simplistic ideas of the Enlightenment. David Hume and other Enlightenment philosophers who were converted to the new science of empiricism found experiences of divine activity objectionable because they could not be proven, and because those philosophers were as yet unaware of the profound limitations of empirical proof to address meaning and truth. They concluded that reason could not support testimonies that could not be subjected to empirical (repeatable) observation, and so they were content to discount any experiences to the contrary.[41] Two and three hundred years later, some theologians discount the possibility of direct experiences of divine presence, others assume such experiences but find them too unruly and ungeneralizable for their work of constructing concepts of the divine, and most theologians choose to ignore them altogether. Questions of proof and suspicion of experience remain in contemporary theology only because theologians make the mistake of assuming such experiences to be universally authoritative and normative if they are taken to be genuine. In addition, the fact that "religious experience" is almost impossible to define, as William James demonstrated, makes the theological deferral of experience that much easier to do.

Nevertheless, as Rudolf Otto suggested, there is a commonsense dimension to the idea that religious experiences, if they occur, somehow transform the boundaries of the ordinary; they reveal or indicate a sacred reality, and they place a demand on consciousness.[42] Whether outside observers choose to explain such experiences in terms other than the spiritual or religious (such as the social, cultural, neurological) is their prerogative. The experiences of divine or sacred presence that feminist women and men talk about are authoritative only in terms of themselves, normative only insofar as they are taken to be real, often full of detail, full of ordinary and domestic elements, concrete and plausible, even as they evoke wonder or profound emotion. It is no wonder that such events seem naturally more accessible to the rich nuance of poetry and story than to the overly descriptive prose of theory. They do not have to reveal normativity in any absolute sense to be ontologically real.

> Alder, willow, buckeye and blackberry
> riparian wood riffling the watershed
> a blighted barn, a shipwreck splintered
> now green tips swollen and whips reddening.
>
> Look there into the tangled frieze
> where a red pulse beats in the green rot:
> flourishing and perishing in each moment
> and in every part both living and dead
> weaving and unraveling Mobius growth strings
> armature of spring through silhouette of winter.
>
> Inside the stalk, inside the bark
> inside-out the spark in the rock
> leaps the living sap of living attention,
> only alive that jumps the gap
> only alive from pulse to pulse
> only alive in this precarious pounce;
> nothing leaping to nothing—
> stinging in the spine of the wood.

This tissue of the planet is the living thought of God.

Vine creeping to cover our roads
we chop it back, trim, prune and hack
the eager tendrils of her, the green
unruly God, and she grows back,

She will outgrow our axe.

—Inna Jane Ray[43]

The seemingly irrepressible vigor of feminist spiritual experiences in their variety and multiplicity cannot determine the content of feminist theologies without losing the very qualities of particularity, embodiment, and multiplicity that characterize them. Particular experiential claims cannot be authoritative in some ahistorical or referential sense, nor can they avoid the conditioning agent of interpretation and social construction. But feminist theologies must face the issue of whether experiences of divine presence ever can reveal more than human imagination. Are spiritual experiences of direct divine presence (so claimed) necessarily beyond the scope of theological discourse? They are not beyond the scope of words, of conversation between women, of storytelling, and of prayer; and this fact alone should give feminist theologians of all kinds pause.

When did I become a canyon?
When did I fill with rain?
When did you become a ladle dipping into me?
When did the canyon of your ladle
empty soaking the rocks all around?
When did the rocks dry?
When did the air become moist with their drying?
When did the moisture soak the clouds?
When did the clouds become a canyon?
When did I become a ladle dipping into clouds?
When are you coming back?

—Dianne Bilyak[44]

CONCLUSION

To put the various pieces of the question together, what are theologians who place an interpretive value on socially constructed ways of knowing to do with the variety and range of experiences of divine presence that are increasingly taken to be directly linked to changed metaphors, images, and language about God? Most thoughtful persons engaged in worship and spiritual reflection based on feminist theological constructions do not make simple associations of God and image. Those who do so are not, for the most part, the subject of this analysis. On the other hand, with James Fernandez, even the most thoughtful can recognize that "powerful images may repose in lexicon alone" and that at the same time there may be images important to the symbolic universe of meaning that do not have their source in language. He calls this the "argument of images that lie behind and accompany behavior."[45]

Religious and spiritually focused experience and revelation are themselves clearly caught up in the historicist web of social construction and function, and the complexity of religious experience cannot be reduced to an issue of simple reference or ahistorical authority even though my argument leads to the suggestion that alleged experiences of divinity demand allowances for divine substance even in the most carefully exempted metaphors. But just as the metaphoric exemption tells us that experience cannot be relied upon to yield simple, normative descriptions of divine being, exclusive emphases on metaphoric exemption risk simple denials of the possibility altogether that divinity might become present. Presumably, no theologian who accepts the ontological assumption that divine realities exist wants to deny completely a divine capacity for real presence in some comprehensible way. Even Barth clung to his gospel for this.

Ultimately at stake (ironically, perhaps) is an approach to theological construction that at the very least does not *disallow* divinity an agency and autonomy sufficient to break through distortions of social construction or, to use Farley's expression, to "come forth" into the human realm of consciousness. While Farley is closer here to Tillich than to theologians such as Kaufman (who disallow any experiential referent for divine coming forth), he cautiously resists the total denial implicit in the metaphoric exemption by assigning divine content in hindsight to what he calls the facticity of redemption. In other words, God's presence can be experienced as memory after it has left its shaping mark on the community or on the world—much like Moses is granted a view only of the divine backside after God has passed by. "On the other hand," Farley agrees with Kaufman, "this coming forth is clearly not an offering of God's being to the human act of meaning. . . . Whatever the power and eventfulness of redemptive transformation, human beings do not in fact 'experience' God or entertain God as a discretely meant reality." God does come forth into human knowing and experience, according to Farley, but only as the "one and only referent" for redemptive transformation. This is the paradox of what he calls the "designated and nonpresentational God."[46]

Where Farley argues that the coming forth of the divine is never discrete or specific but only traceable through the facticity of redemption, the coming forth that I want to suggest is the equally designate, but more discrete and specific, less traceable but more free divine that is capable of becoming at times concretely embodied in human fabrications of time and space, of myth and metaphor. The experiences of many feminist women and men tend to dispute Farley's deferral. They do claim to experience divine coming forth, and that the divine does so in concrete, confounding, and sometimes highly personal ways. But perhaps only the most radical skeptics and deconstructionists, though not so-called a/theologians, are able methodologically to assert a blanket negation of the very possibility of divine action that is independent of human intention or theory.[47] And certainly theologians like Farley and Kaufman who, like Barth, want to preserve essential divine otherness by limiting experiential claims must admit that if divine being is able theoretically to act independently of human intention or theory, it must be able to (though it may not always) act in ways that are comprehensible to the limits of human consciousness. Theologians who accept *at some level* an ontological premise of divine existence and divine independence are hard-pressed to deny this theoretical possibility.

What Farley and Kaufman avoid in their different assertions of nonpresentation is the error-ridden and complicated human web of meaning that can never satisfactorily (to the mind) comprehend an other, let alone a divine other. This incapacity on the part of the human being, however, does not necessarily negate the capacity of the divine to act freely in comprehensible terms, even if such terms do not translate into predictability or congeniality to intellectual demands for consistency. If divinity is free, it must in theory also be free in its relations with human beings and the world. If it is free in its relations with human beings, then experiential accounts of divine presence cannot be dismissed out of hand because they are not systematic enough for the limitations of theological discourse.

Feminist theologies, deeply dependent on the metaphoric exemption for their criticisms of tradition and for permission to construct new ideas, are burgeoning with experiential confessions of divine presences, times, and spaces. These experiences irritate and trouble the smooth, dismissive waters of the metaphoric exemption by standing in stark opposition to it. The metaphoric exemption as a taproot of feminist theologies claims that all language and images and ideas do not refer to real divinity since they are products of human imagination. Experiential confession as a taproot of feminist theologies insists on the freedom of divinity to take up those references or to become present in other forms altogether, regardless.

The moose stands at the edge of the river
knee deep, dipping her head
until it disappears entirely under water.
For a long time she stays there,
then slowly lifts her head and looks at me.
The river runs between us.
She is eating her evening meal.
I am learning how to dwell
in the tributaries of my dreams.
This is the season
for which I have yearned.
Fully myself now, I am weaned
from the church and absolved
even of that ache that followed amputation.
This world itself is temple:
the mourning dove—silken vestment;
the turtle—orthodoxy;
the rattlesnake—warning
at the doorway to the shrine.

—Pat Schneider[48]

CHAPTER FIVE

Lived Feminist Spirituality

W HAT ARE THESE FEMINIST CLAIMS of divine presence, substance, or
response that they should trouble the waters of constructive theology and threaten the fragile architecture of the metaphoric exemption?
Systematic research on the descriptive accounts of communities and individuals engaged in feminist spiritual life or worship is relatively new, and
few sources exist beyond the anecdotal, the local, and the preliminary.[1]
Indeed, almost as much literature denouncing feminist spirituality and religious experience exists as does literature documenting or supporting it.[2]
Clearly, however, the presence of both forms of commentary indicates a
current spiritual liveliness within and at the margins of feminist and other
progressive religious circles that seems connected to the liveliness of feminist theological discourses.

It is therefore important to illuminate, even in a preliminary and anecdotal way, the suggestive character and variety of feminist religious and
experiential claims, and the backlash against those claims, in order to make
a persuasive argument that new feminist experiences of divinity indicate a
more complex relationship between religious language and divinity than
constructive feminist theologies currently admit. Feminist spiritual life is
robust although it is not structured in institutional forms. It crosses the
spectrum of Jewish, Christian, and post-Christian ideologies, and it is focused both in communal and in individual forms ranging from so-called
mystical visions to interpretations of worship and ritual as theologically
relevant and powerfully "real" embodiments of "real" divinities.

I will not attempt here to provide a complete sociological survey of the
diffuse phenomena of feminist spirituality and feminist ritualizing. Fortu-
nately, others such as Cynthia Eller, Lesley Northup, and Charlotte Caron
have begun that work. Instead, I will suggest a descriptive characterization
that depends on the preliminary studies and surveys of these and other
scholars, putting their findings to use to serve my broader proposition about
the dual foundations of feminist theologies. As I suggested in the begin-

ning chapters of this book, generalizations of any kind are always limited because of their abstraction from context, but they can give shape to an argument. In this case, generalizations about feminist religious experience will serve my view that such experiences, being neither simple nor simple-minded, directly engage and challenge the metaphoric exemption of feminist theologies.

Although I argued in chapter 4 that the category of experience both founds and complicates feminist theologies in particular, theology in general has always existed in some tension with the enthusiasms, imaginings, and necessities of human experience, especially when that experience makes claims about God. Feminist theologies are facing this tension ever more profoundly as more and more people participate in and experience feminist worship and spiritual focus and out of such experiences make claims about divinity that resist or challenge the central metaphoric exemption of feminist constructive theologies. For example, in response to the Re-Imagining Conference, a worship-based ecumenical Christian gathering of women in 1993 that generated extensive and often vitriolic controversy in various mainline Protestant denominations, participant Carolyn Henderson wrote about her experience of the divine this way: "She was there in Fullest Presence when the doors of the convention center closed and a civic room became a Temple blessed with Holiness and filled with women seeking. . . . I finally heard the call in a woman's voice. She is with me every day. I turn and listen to Her. She sends me signs, messengers, words, paths, music, and Great Love. I sense Her. I hear Her. I am coming to know Her."[3]

The point here is not that the monotheistic object of Christian doctrine is "really" a She, although that might be the case, or that the monotheistic object of Christian doctrine is capable of revealing a gendered aspect to certain individuals, although that might also be the case. The point is that some persons who put into spiritual practice the constructive proposals of feminist theologies are professing experiences of divine presence that lend specificity and, to the worshipers at least, authenticity of a referential kind to their understandings of divinity. Feminist theologies, intent upon their metaphoric exemptions even as they allow for some referential validity,[4] must find a way to explain these revelatory claims by other means (i.e., in sociological, psychological, cultural, or biological terms) or to account for them in theological terms. Either path is fraught, and either path contains possible contradiction.

"Feminist spirituality" is the term that most often appears in literature about feminist religious experiences, although a broader reference to the "women's liturgical movement" has also appeared.[5] It is a concept that, in its widest sense, encompasses the ideas, beliefs, rituals, and sometimes lifestyles

of feminists engaged in religious activity related both to their understandings of divinity and to their understandings of feminism. The idea of feminist spirituality is a broad, nominal category referring to diffuse strains of
new, feminist-oriented religious beliefs and practices within and outside
organized religious institutions.[6] As a discernible movement, its features
first appeared in small worship groups, consciousness-raising groups, and
new age and counterculture communities in the early 1970s alongside the
grassroots political and social women's and civil rights movements of the
same period.

For the purposes of her study of the growth of feminist spirituality in
North America, Cynthia Eller has defined it as a "spontaneous, grass-roots
movement with no overarching organization, no system of leadership, and
no regularized form of membership."[7] Eller's research focuses predominantly on the emergence of feminist spirituality among white women, yet
the spiritual practices and beliefs of African American, Caribbean, Hispanic, Native American, and Asian women based on retrievals of traditional female images and ideas experienced rapid growth in the 1980s.

While all of the ideas and practices associated with feminist spirituality
are not uniformly shared by all spiritual feminists within or across cultural
lines, Eller suggests some shared general characteristics of feminist spirituality. They are values related to women's empowerment, ritual practice,
reverence for nature, use of gender as a primary mode of religious analysis,
and a revisionist view of history.[8] These characteristics are interdependent
and mutually explanatory. Values related to women's empowerment characterize feminism in its broadest sense, but spiritual feminism distinguishes
itself through a focus on sacred power, often expressed in ritualized form,
as a fundamental means toward empowerment. In addition, sacred power is
generally understood in terms that oppose it to the social dynamics of
racism, sexism, heterosexism, and ethnocentrism.

Reverence for nature follows from and incorporates this ritual focus, in
part because of traditional identifications of women and nature, in part
because of the overall growth in the popularity of environmental issues,
and in part because of a symmetry between ecological and feminist rhetoric. Furthermore, feminist writings in religion have significantly contributed to and depended upon gender analysis and theory. Regardless of
whether the analysis results in a social constructionist or an essentialist
view of women, gender as a category underlies the bulk of spiritual feminist speech and action. Finally, historical revisionism marks spiritual feminism in particular because of the importance of founding myths in religious life. Whether this revisionism occurs in the form of matriarchal
prehistories or in reconstructions of feminist traces of resistance, the im-

portance of history as a source of inspiration and strength in service to
future-oriented empowerment plays into spiritual feminist ritual practice
and theoretical analysis.

Feminist spirituality in the context of traditional religion tends to share
these basic characteristics with the posttraditional feminist spirituality movement. Although the boundaries that separate traditional from posttraditional
religious feminism are by no means rigid or always clear, the revisionist
view of history that traditional Christian and Jewish feminists are more
likely to espouse concerns biblical exegesis and hermeneutics rather than a
posttraditional tendency to espouse theories of prepatriarchal cultures.[9]
Traditional feminists also tend to support theological reconstructions of
foundational doctrines from their religious traditions rather than more trans-
parently syncretistic ideas and doctrines shared with New Age movements.
Like the spiritual feminism Eller describes, feminist Christianity and Judaism also often reflect a grassroots spontaneity in practice, sometimes dependent upon individual ministers and rabbis who incorporate feminist
theologies in liturgy and sermons, or sometimes dependent upon individuals who form study and prayer groups that incorporate ritual elements.
Unlike the posttraditional spiritual feminist movement, however, Christian
and Jewish feminism has emerged in more organized and institutional forms,
through congregational bodies, denominational offices, and extradenominational theological and spiritual centers.[10]

Referring to posttraditional spiritual feminists, Eller provides a curious
insight into the particular power of religious imagery and language when
she argues that "even those women who are consciously aware of having
invented the goddess to suit their spiritual needs are frequently surprised at
how well she fills them."[11] According to functional social constructionist
wisdom, it is obvious that the invented goddess often fills her creators'
needs quite well. That is her function, why she was invented in the first
place, and she would be discarded if once imaginatively evoked and clothed
in ritual garb, she did not perform. Within this framework, the analytical
task of the religious scholar, then, is to describe, catalogue, and assess the
many subtle layers of her social efficacy in the minds of the women who,
having invented her, then worship her and reap the social and psychological benefits of doing so. The invented goddess who surprises becomes first
and foremost the valuable raw material of collective human imagination, a
chance to see Durkheimian social construction at work at its most primal
level of identity formation. Her efficacy may surprise her worshipers, but
not the social scientist or cultural anthropologist.

There is, of course, another way to interpret Eller's observation. There is
a double edge to the theological imagination when it is put to work in the

context of spiritual focus and worship. Is the invented goddess merely an imaginative construct whose efficacy fully is explained by functional social constructionism? Or does Eller's observation reveal the possibility of occasional "direct hits" in theological language, a possibility of some real correspondence to something outside the self-referencing loop of social construction, something, moreover, that responds appropriately *to* that language? The experiences of some traditional and posttraditional feminists suggest the latter. As Donna Myhre writes in part of a poem thanking the religious leaders and theologians in the United Methodist Church who signed a statement of support for the Re-Imagining Conference, "Now I think: there is theological correctness, which can exist only in the minds of men. And there is Her-I-See."[12] After an extensive study of the growing feminist spirituality movement in the United States and the specific experiences, beliefs, and practices of the women she calls spiritual feminists, Eller concludes that "whatever problems feminist spirituality may have, clearly a lack of robust experience of the divine is not among them."[13] A robust experience of divine presence seems to be a hallmark of feminist spirituality.

> Though I never heard the word Goddess spoken when I was a child, I felt her power in the eerie calls of the peacocks that nested on the roof of my grandmother's house as my brother and I fell asleep in the yellow bedroom, in the waves that crashed over me as we played at Huntington Beach; in the oaks and scrub brush along hillside trails I hiked in the San Gabriel Mountains; in the liquid eyes of black-tailed deer as they turned to look at me in Calaveras State Park; in the pouring rain that filled my rubber boots as I walked home from school.[14]

COMMUNAL RELIGIOUS EXPERIENCE AND RITUAL

A robust experience of the divine in feminist spirituality coincides with the centrality of communal expression and the worship experience in both traditional and posttraditional lived feminist theology. In a Christian context, Heather Murray Elkins argues that while the "formality of liturgical theology" is important to understanding feminist religious experience, it is secondary to the "primary task of worship."[15] A woman interviewed by Charlotte Caron for her study of Christian feminist ritual says that rituals "give groundedness in our core—which I perceive to be connected to God. And once we've caught that vision, we are changed....It is a birthing."[16] From a posttraditional perspective, Eller suggests that the fundamental plurality of beliefs espoused by spiritual feminism makes worship and ritual enactment so important:

That practice should dominate faith in feminist spirituality is no doubt related in part to the great diversity of "faiths" present in the movement. Belief
is not likely to be central in a religion where there is little agreement on that
in which one is to believe. Conceptions of the goddess are so varied and
personal that they provide insubstantial common ground for spiritual feminists. If spiritual feminists are to come together to form covens or groups, or
to exhibit sufficient unity of purpose to form a socially recognizable movement, there must exist a stronger glue than theological doctrine—this glue
is ritual.[17]

Both traditional and posttraditional feminism share a concern with the
way that lived theology must occur, moving from theory into practice. This
places lived feminist theology in some tension with feminist theologians
such as Davaney and Sands who espouse radical historicism. These theologians tend to call into question the very possibility of revelatory experience of divine presence in ritual or spiritually focused settings by dismantling ontological claims to divine being. Carol Christ identifies this tension
at the heart of feminist social constructionism in the context of religious
practice when she argues that its "intellectual detachment, its side-stepping
of the question of the referential nature of religious symbols in the lives of
those for whom they have meaning, is its greatest weakness, and is a characteristic feminist theologians would do well not to emulate."[18] Indeed,
some Christian feminists engaged in organizing and leading communal
practice see the transparent functional social constructionism of many feminist theologies threatening the possibility of pragmatic theological contributions to feminist worship and also see abstractions overshadowing feminist commitments to concrete communities. Some go so far as to say that
Christian feminists "need to cease participating in this abstract, intellectual
debate and shift our faith commitments and energies into conversations
and actions focused on what it means to *participate* in the redemptive, sav-
ing work of Christ in the world."[19]

Excessive abstraction will always be the temptation of theologians and
simplistic rejections of abstraction the temptation of essentialist activists.
Ideally, however, feminist theologians attempt to bring together the important pragmatic and intellectual aspects of their work into a unified process so that the work of theological reflection is best understood in terms
of its practical applications. Yet it is possible that this can work coherently
only when the substance of the feminist theology in question does not
eliminate all bases for religious experience that give specificity to God or
for independent (actual) divine being. That is, feminist theologies are less
able to avoid the implications of their practical effects than schools of theo-

logical thought that are less tied to concrete communities. Traditional theology can more easily minimize the importance of sources and norms rooted in perceived experiences of divinity because it does not identify them as important in the first place. Feminist theologies do not have this luxury.

Mary Hunt, a Catholic feminist theologian and founding director of the Women's Alliance for Theology, Ethics and Ritual (WATER), takes the significance of ritual experience one step farther, arguing that, by definition, feminist theologies cannot be divorced in meaning from their ritual applications: "Feminist theology never stands alone, but always in the good company of ethics and ritual. No action-reflection model will be adequate that does not put real life questions to the fore. Nor can there be any adequate expression of feminist insights without the aid of the arts, prayer, movement, and silence. Thus we see theology as intimately connected with ethics and ritual so that to describe it in isolation is already to have violated our process."[20]

A problem here comes from the fact that feminist theologies primarily are engaged in a constructionist, rather than purely interpretive or doctrinal, task (notwithstanding the fact that doctrinal theology has always had its constructive elements). Moreover, their sources tend to be diffuse and accessible, rooted in concrete and communicable experience, and their norms encourage lay participation in the imaginative work of theological and liturgical construction. According to Caron, the criteria for rituals that "lead to justice and well-being for feminists" include "structuring the ritual to be just by nature; creating processes of involving all participants and sharing leadership; connecting ordinary events and experiences from women's lives; . . . inclusiveness; and embodiment."[21] These criteria are familiar, drawn from a common pool of feminist values, and can be found repeated throughout scores of feminist writings. The result in theological terms can be intensely creative, at times chaotic, often highly individualistic, and consequently difficult at times to translate into communal practice, even though community building is so often a stated, or valued, goal of feminist worship and spiritual life.

Joan Timmerman suggests that one of the most trying challenges of lived feminist theologies is the temptation toward quick fixes and an eagerness to participate in the fabrication of images for God: "Maybe it's an American thing—let's get an instant image for God, take it home, put water in, dilute it, drink it down, and we've got it—our religious experience. The hard work is constructing communities and sharing and working with those symbols until they die."[22] Thus, although rituals are "done to create results"[23] and "permit us to live a new myth, to experience its cosmogony, its symbols, its traditions, its modes of expression,"[24] they need rooting in communal life to be given the depth that only repetition and the evolution of founding traditions can provide. "Community rituals are about life and death, who we are, who is God."[25]

Elkins indicates that women preparing and leading feminist worship are faced with the task of what Claude Lévi-Strauss called *bricolage*, a collecting together of the bits and pieces, and that this process is the result of the peculiar but intimate exclusions women have experienced through the ages in Christian worship:

> Many of us are reared with an instinct to *bricolage*, formed by the limited means and meanings of women's participation in traditional worship patterns. There are few printed clues for a woman who prepares or presides at the Table. We keep each other alive by sharing a story here, a stole there. There are only precious fragments, hints of how a whole body of Christ might appear. . . . *Bricolage* is handed on, not handed down, but it offers an encounter with all that is human and holy.[26]

The impact of women taking on priestly roles, either publicly through church ordination or privately through the legitimation of ad hoc feminist worship groups, appears initially to be far more profound for the women involved than for the wider church community. Joy Bussart suggests that at heart the reason is pastoral. Not only is the performance of sacred tasks in ritual an enactment of the divine-human relationship, it is also, on some level, representational. Her point is that "there are women in the pews who are longing. There's a desire for a sense of being created in the image of God because women have been denied that access for so long."[27] The *purely* functional invented goddess is implied here. But Christians, like many other religious people, tend to have a peculiar investment in believing in the reality of the deity they worship in terms other than, or greater than, the reality of social construction. This investment counters Richard Rorty's claim that "it's words all the way down,"[28] and thus the "longing in the pews" (or outside them) translates beyond a real concern for social function into a longing for religious forms that mirror lived religious experience.

Traditional and posttraditional spiritual feminists often make the point that the norms of traditional worship do not provide forms for the real religious experiences of many women, especially if these experiences "reveal" or even "merely imagine" a deity as wholly or even partly not male. The implication here is that theology should at some level serve communal worship needs. But the context and requirements of worship and ritual make them, perhaps by functional necessity, hostile to the grating reminders of social construction. It is precisely in this context, however, that the theologian must be careful about discounting the *possibility* of a metamorphosis of metaphor into actual divinity.

INDIVIDUAL RELIGIOUS EXPERIENCE

Just as the communal religious life of most religious and spiritual communities builds upon assumptions of personal piety, the commonly stated communal goals of feminists in worship settings such as various WomanChurch communities, ritual groups, annual gatherings such as the Women's Ordination Conference, and the Re-Imagining Community tend to rest upon assumptions of individual experiences, beliefs, and commitments. At this individual level the richness, variety, and challenging "reality" of revelatory experience for constructive feminist theologies is most clearly delineated. All good theology, one might argue, must include at some level the inspiration of devotional experience, and although this experience does not dictate the rational explication of theological discourse, it gives life and shape to the enterprise, as any reading of Barth, Tillich, Teilhard de Chardin, Starhawk, Williams, Ruether, Cobb, Tamez, or countless other theologians demonstrates. For feminist theologies in general, the question of the place and shape that individual (and even at times idiosyncratic) experiences of divine presence that have specificity and above all reality for those who take feminist theological proposals seriously is a live one. An example might clarify this issue. My mother, a poet, wrote of a transformative experience that she had after rejecting patriarchal constructs and struggling with feminist alternatives. Her experience occurred during an annual trip to Ireland in terms so vivid that the bulk of her description is worth repeating here:

> I think a kind of divine humor touched me in the night. The same sense of musical laughter that woke me once, years ago on a silent retreat and I thought it was angels—and again here, last night, only this time it is my own laughter—but too beautiful, laughter beautiful beyond what my body could make—the feeling of it lingering in my own dark depths, like the spots and streaks of light we collected in dark rocks on Sligo beach: ancient fossils, crinoid stems, looking like stars falling through a black sky, caught in stone for a million years—laughter like that, timeless, in motion, motionless. And now, as I write, all at once there is a stillness in my mind, an absolute silence, in which I see the face of god!—I see the face of god—why not? Why not?

Who was it who ever said a mortal may not look on the face of god and live? How did he know?

I am sitting in this ordinary chair in this kitchen of Bríd, while Máire sits talking with their mother after a Mass I chose not to attend. I see the face of god and there is laughter behind the eyes and behind the grin (not smile, grin) and it is only one face of god who has many faces like the statue in the window of Michael Quirke the woodcarver of Sligo who was a butcher and carved wood and three years ago gave up butchering and carves and talks poetry and Irish mythology behind the window of his shop. . . .

What I forgot to say about the face of god was what surprised me most—not that the face was laughing—but that the face was a woman's face. And that beyond the woman's face, turned away, with just an edge of cheekline visible, another face looked toward shadow—not threatening, not problematic—a man's face. And I knew there was at least one more face—completely unseen, on the dark side of the moon/the head/the figure/the statue in the hand of the woodcarver Michael standing in the butcher shop turned carver shop . . . this world. . . . Another face which I could not see at all. All three faces moved me deeply, but it was the woman's face that was in the light, meeting me directly, and her laughter was ocean and all waters, and deep beyond what my ears could hear. Deeper. What my bones could feel. Rocked by it, rocked in it. . . .

For the first time, the word which rises is "goddess," but it doesn't matter. One face of god is a woman's face, and the face is laughing, and it is one of at least three faces and they are all faces that are carved by the hands of a man—no—they are not carved by the hands of any man or woman. And yet they are. Michael, the woodcarver, in the window of the world, carving with his knife. Myself, in the kitchen of the world, carving with my pen. A round, green child's marble softened by waves that I found on a beach once when my heart was hurting, and took the marble as a sign; the sound of gentle laughter in the silence of a retreat once, long ago.

Everything is a sign. I have seen one of the faces of god and it is a woman's face and it is a form I can hold—no—not hold—a form to make visible to me, this: *laughter.* Beautiful, unspeakably beautiful, laughter.[29]

As with accounts of mystics throughout the centuries, stories such as this suggest a question that is not easily dismissed: Is the invented, metaphorical goddess (or god) merely invented, or does she (or he) sometimes appear in response to prayer? Is she (or he) sometimes stumbled upon, revealed, found? The heart of this question is by no means new, and theologians have always struggled within a tension of acceptance and skepticism of the poetic and challenging accounts of persons who claim some kind of direct knowledge, visions, or experiences of God even when they also acknowledge their own imaginative contribution—"myself . . . carving with my pen."

In sacramental traditions such as Roman Catholicism, the tension between mystic and theologian is less marked than it is in iconoclastic Protestantism and Judaism. Protestants have historically affirmed, for example, a direct access to grace that implies the potential for similar access to knowledge and vision, but have radically tempered the liberties of pietism, on the other hand, by a synchronous opposition to Catholic sacramentalism that abhors mystically revealed images in favor of the abstract Word. In effect this allows the Roman images of patriarchal sovereignty so popular in medieval Catholicism and prevalent at the time of the Protestant Reformations to provide even iconoclastic Protestantism with a baseline against which all other imagistic language and visions would be deemed suspect or even idolatrous.

My mother's trinitarian vision, or any number of similar feminist "revelations," might be fitted into more or less traditional Christian clothing if necessary, and that may be important for theologians concerned with meshing the images of feminist spiritual experiences with the inherited communal images and doctrines of their religious traditions. That work depends, however, on a clear assumption of the importance of such visions and experiences as source material combined (in the case of theologians serving the church) with given sources of doctrine and church tradition. A significant percentage of women, like my mother sitting at the kitchen table, are engaged in spiritual and devotional practices; they read and discuss feminist theologies, but are no longer wedded to specific church traditions. Others still belong to specific church traditions or specific cultural contexts in which church doctrine and tradition play basic social roles. In either case, the question remains: What is the place of this kind of lived experience in the work of feminist theologies that seek to guide and inform these various communities and individuals in their spiritual explorations? The issue here is not whether the lived experiences of feminists can provide raw material for new theological constructions and metaphors, for they certainly do that already. The question is whether or not there is room for the glimpsed gods or goddesses of complex religious experience in their theologies. Feminist theologies cannot yet account for feminist spiritual experience (which is itself inspired by the work of womanist, *mujerista,* white feminist, and other feminist theologians) in such a way that the implications for some kind of carefully nuanced reference are not dismissed entirely.

FEMINIST RELIGIOUS EXPERIENCE AND DIVINITY(IES)

Some feminist theologians are writing for a church tradition to which they belong. Some are writing for a wider audience, many of whom are no longer engaged in the traditional congregation and its doctrines per se. In any context, however, religious investment in a divine "real" is not absurd or always simplistic or obvious. Spiritual feminists both within and outside traditional religious communities tend to assert that they are well aware of the limitations of language, symbol, and metaphor fully to address or reveal the divine. They are also aware of the socially constructed, interpretive, and manipulative potentials of experience itself and are often unsure how to interpret their experiences theologically. Even in the center of my mother's mystical vision, when she says, "The word which rises is 'goddess,'" her iconoclastic awareness remains strong enough that the specificity of "goddess" (to the extent, that is, that the word "goddess" reveals a specificity of gender formerly concealed in the masculine norm of "god") is discomforting to her, and so she dismisses the word, saying, "It doesn't matter."

Along with the feminist theologians whose work they study and discuss, North American spiritual feminists are for the most part well schooled in the iconoclastic principle of constructive theology, and they remind themselves often (primarily in print) of the partiality of the images they use. Timmerman, for example, reminds readers of the Re-Imagining Community newsletter that no metaphor or symbol for the divine is ever complete or adequate:

> We keep grieving that [symbols for God are] not adequate; we should be rejoicing that they're not adequate. . . . The only images that are going to deliver pastorally are ones that come out of our experience and that we care about enough to ritualize. You don't just throw them off in prayer and hope that you get zapped. After the experience comes the articulation of the symbol; that gets shared, the stories get told, but then the ritualization takes years to gather all the richness, and it can't be done all by oneself.[30]

Perhaps it is because, as James Evans claims, the "idea of God is rooted in concrete human experience [which] means that any discussion of God must begin with a people's recollection of their encounter with God,"[31] that spiritual feminists are so concerned with, anxious about, and aware of their experiences of divinity in feminist worship. Joern expresses awareness of the complex social constructedness of metaphors and the provocative importance of religious experience for theology when she says that "imaging God as female is not a quick cure for body/spirit dualism. Male images of God have not protected men from splitting off from their bodies. Furthermore, images are nothing more than they pretend to be—symbols of a reality we find difficult to apprehend. But when [during the Re-Imagining Conference] I sang 'Come My Mother,' I literally saw myself walk into the presence of God rather than floating in as a disembodied spirit."[32]

The experience of constructive feminist theologies put into ritual practice has the effect of confounding, or enriching in potentially challenging ways, the necessary skepticism of constructionist methods and claims. To say, for example, that "religious ritual is a way many people create, express, and enact connections with the holy"[33] means only that ritual and worship deal with the human *experience* of the divine whereas theology deals with ideas *about* the divine that perhaps can prepare people adequately for the experience or for life lived around the experience of divinity mediated through the manipulations of ritual, worship, and thought.[34]

Theology as an intellectual practice is always struggling to articulate understandings of the holy so that ritual itself might be more firmly rooted in prophetic reason and in doctrines that make sense, are justifiable, and are morally and socially legitimate. On the other hand, if religious ritual is a way many people create, express, and enact connections with the holy, theology also demands that, in principle at least, the holy have the final say, a demand that makes of ritual experience not only a well-nourished end point of good theology, but one of its important starting points as well.

This is not a problem for premodern theologians, whose work never deliberately raises the specter of functional social constructionism. Such theologians could assert the revelatory basis of doctrine and tradition to adjudicate errant visions and experiences verging too closely on concrete particularity. The double jeopardy of modernism's contribution to contemporary theology and contemporary theology's contribution to feminism is the investment feminist theologians make in the power of symbols and cultural enactments (as the means of culture formation), on the one hand, and the complexity of concrete particularity and experience, on the other, especially when the experience points to the possibility of an answer to prayer that yields up laughter and a certainty of face. Joern captures a sense of this investment and its complexity: "I thought of the passage in Isaiah where God says to the people of Israel, 'I will not forget you. I have carved you in the palms of my hands.' I thought about God as an embodied God and us as an embodied people and how little we understand about what it all means."[35]

Constructive feminist theologies that take seriously experiences of divine presence in specific, responsive, and particularistic terms are faced with the dual challenge of maintaining the metaphoric exemption in feminist worshiping communities without undermining the possibility either of experience as a means of divine communication or of divinities who can so communicate. At the same time they must help answer the charge made against their communities that feminist worship is idolatry. It is not clear that constructive feminist theologies have yet fully developed an adequate response to either challenge.

THE BACKLASH AND FEMINISM IN TRADITIONAL RELIGIOUS SETTINGS

What is so toxic about this reclaimed cup of milk and honey? Is it that laity offered it? Did it infringe on the sacramental authority of clergy? Was it because women dared to lay hands on its meaning and shape, confusing the line between sacrament and the holiness of all daily bread and prayer?[36]

The importance of *living* feminist theologies, a value and a goal espoused by the vast majority of feminist theologians, leads to the principal question of this project, namely, what feminist theologians are to do with the results of lived theology. The ease with which theologians throughout history have exhorted the faithful to remember the ineffability and inaccessibility of the divine was in part the result of the fact that they did not have to contend with the depth of modern skepticism internal to contemporary theology itself. Consequently, despite such exhortations, earlier theologians did not work seriously at cross-purposes with the ordained, who have the task of exhorting the faithful to fix their attention upon the true God. The modern paradox particularly of feminist theologies is the attention they must fix upon the embodiment of ritual expression, and the seriousness with which they must take the claims and experiences of those involved at the same time that they must insist on radical metaphoric exemption. Ironically, the contemporary resistance of the majority of Christian churches especially to lived feminist theologies, popularly called the backlash, indicates the seriousness with which many Christians take experiential claims of divine presence, and the profound depths of human self-understanding to which ritual can take theological ideas.

One contemporary example of lived feminist theology that illustrates the challenges of the modernist paradox is the experience and aftermath of the large worship-oriented gathering of women in 1993 called the Re-Imagining Conference. The Re-Imagining Community, a membership organization formed in the turbulent wake of the conference to provide information and support to the conference participants as well as to capitalize on its success, is explicitly Christian and intentionally reformist.[37] The intensity of backlash against the conference and its participants contributed to the formation of this membership community and provoked defensive claims by participants that their intentions and experiences of feminist worship at the conference were explicitly and consistently Christian. Nancy Berneking and Pamela Carter Joern, two organizers of the event and editors of a volume of participant writings, addressed the climate of suspicion following the conference and its resulting conspiracy fears that Re-Imagining was the result of anti-Christian insurgency. They attempted to distance Re-Imaginers from Christian feminist critics who question the enduring validity of central Christian traditions, and from their post-Christian and New Age spiritual feminist contemporaries. Berneking and Joern identify a conciliatory norm for the Christian feminists of Re-Imagining and describe those who make up the Re-Imagining Community as regular churchgoers whose faces are comfortably familiar in Sunday worship:

> The members of the Re-Imagining Community are not seeking a new religion. Most occupy pews every Sunday and have no intention of abandoning the traditions they claim. They serve on committees, sing in choirs, visit the sick, and pray for the community. Yet many feel isolated and undernourished. The three questions printed on the back of each *Re-Imagining Community Newsletter* reflect concerns we've heard again and again: How do we sustain hope? How do we stay connected? How do we nurture faith in God? Re-Imaginers are devoted Christians who feel exiled from their own tradition and are trying to find a way back home.[38]

Locating themselves within the fold of traditional practice has become increasingly important to some feminist Christians primarily for two reasons. The first is a real climate of fear generated out of highly publicized censures and in some cases institutional backlashes against feminist liturgical practices. The growing popularity and general accessibility of feminist theological literature over the past twenty years may have made the possibility of a serious backlash against a gathering like Re-Imagining seem remote to the bulk of participants used to traditional gatherings of such venerable organizations as United Methodist Women, making the attacks all the more disconcerting when they occur.

The second reason some feminist Christians seek to defend their position within traditional Christianity is the more contestable argument that the spiritual and liturgical practices inspired by constructive feminist theologies are not in fact heretical, that they do not ultimately contradict the most basic doctrinal claims of Christian faith. "In the very midst of their idolatry," Sally Nelson, writer for the conservative magazine *Good News,* claims, "the conference participants still resist being known as heretics or pagans. A heretic is one who distorts the gospel. A pagan is one who casts it aside in favor of an idol. Sadly, these people have done both, and it is time for the Church to discipline those who still claim to be its own."[39] Bishop Earl G. Hunt, president of the conservative Foundation for Evangelism, explicitly links feminist reconstructions with archaic apostasy, arguing that "no comparable heresy has appeared in the church in the last fifteen centuries."[40]

Constructive feminist theologians argue conversely that idolatry really lies with religious conservatives, such as Nelson and Hunt, who valorize both particular interpretations of the gospel and particularistic images of God coming from these interpretations.[41] The name-calling on both sides is strong. The disclaimer feminist Christians like those of the Re-Imagining Community are making, that they really belong within their traditions and long to return, constitutes a protest against conservative Christian attacks on feminist language for God and on feminist critiques of fundamental Christian doctrines of atonement, Christology, and theology. It is an argument that feminist reconstructions and the ritual enactments of goddess imagery in Christian settings do not in effect threaten these doctrines but strengthen and deepen them.[42]

Not all feminists, of course, agree. Catherine Wessinger argues, for example, that she "was not surprised that conservative Christians severely criticized the Re-Imagining Conference for being heretical. From the view of traditional Christianity, it *was* heretical. I would have been more surprised if there were not a backlash."[43] Wessinger's statement comes not from a position of sympathy with conservative Christianity, but from a non-Christian position of academic interest in new religious movements. She points out having "noted rhetoric in the backlash against Re-Imagining similar to accusations used against alternative religions that are pejoratively stigmatized as cults,"[44] and she identifies the source of these accusations to be the kind of boundary maintenance suggested by Mary Douglas's anthropology.

In another example, Heather Murray Elkins, assistant professor of worship and liturgical studies at Drew Divinity School, came under attack by Professor Thomas Oden in 1993 after a reference to Sophia as divine Wisdom was made in a Drew communion service led by Rev. Susan Cady. In articles Oden published in *Good News* (November–December 1993) and in the United Methodist *Newscope* (October 22, 1993), Cady was pilloried as "'an unworthy minister' who has 'driven out church members who challenged her authority.'"[45] Riley Case picked up this theme and enlarged it, providing a listing of examples of "paganism" in seminaries and a listing for Drew entitled "Drew University, the Theological School: Communion is offered in the name of Sophia, goddess of wisdom."[46] Elkins argues that the worship service in question was fully orthodox, and that it met "all sacramental standards of United Methodist worship."[47] The issue for Christian feminists, she claims, is one of signification and of prophetic risk:

> Where can a worshipping woman's ability "to signify" for a community receive confirmation instead of accusations of unorthodox behavior? Those who carry on "discourses of emancipatory transformation" cannot simply talk to one another. Nevertheless, the risk of ecclesiastical backlash for worship and preaching that presses against the confines of convention is real. Gospel is easily turned into gossip, and hearsay can become heresy.[48]

From the social constructionist point of view, conservative attacks on Christian feminism serve sociological purposes of identity coherence through explicit boundary constriction. Christian feminism, on the other hand, is similarly understandable as a response to a social crisis of legitimation through boundary expansion. Both conservatives and Christian feminists claim orthodoxy for the standards they employ and must do so to gain legitimacy for their equally reformist and change-oriented pursuits. Christian feminism is thus progressive and boundary oriented through inclusion, while Christian conservatism is regressive and boundary oriented through exclusion.

Interpreting the conservative backlash against lived feminist theologies in this way satisfies an explanation of cause and effect in sociological terms, but is comprehensive only if it likewise provides satisfactory accounting of religious experience in psychological terms (namely, as delusion). Religious experiences that individuals interpret as "real" indications of divine presence can only, from a purely sociological and psychological perspective, be understood in delusional and enthusiastic terms for the sociological argument to be complete. Otherwise, the functional social constructionist argument cannot account fully for the revelatory claims of feminist spiritual Christians or for the depth of their detractors' resistance. Without the explanation from boundary theory, the dispute boils down to competing claims and interpretations of ultimate matters at a level that is not accessible to interrogation and that cannot succumb to rational proof; in other words, it boils down to competing claims about so-called real divinity.

By way of illustrating this fundamental incommensurability, Eller found that one of the most common responses to her question "Do you believe in a goddess?" was "Believe in her? No. I experience her." She goes on to explain,

The fact that many spiritual feminists do not find it necessary to believe in the goddess does not mean that she is considered to be only a figment of the feminist imagination, a convenient construct of the mind. As Starhawk suggests, the reason one does not have to "believe" in the goddess is that she can be experienced directly.... But ..."believing" in goddess is more a matter of adopting a new term for an old experience to call attention to its sacredness and its femininity.[49]

More traditional feminists tend to avoid the term "goddess" in favor of pronouns (She Who Is or Her-I-See) or to minimize it in order to avoid the problem of gender specificity ("the word that rises is 'goddess,' but it doesn't matter"). That many shrink from the term "goddess" as evidence of paganism is connected to the fact that Christian cultures have long associated the term thus (notice that the reference to Sophia as goddess is alone sufficient explanation of heresy in Riley's attack on the Drew eucharist), to the fact that many are not sure what it means to their central beliefs to adopt the word "goddess," or to the fact that they are reluctant to trade one gender-specific designation for another gender-specific one for the divine presence that they pray to, see, or experience. Backlash highlights the social power of language and ritual enactments, and its heat also illuminates in relief the focus and energy of feminist worship and belief.

The interesting fact of the Christian backlash against Christian feminist theologies is that its target, namely, self-described Christian feminists, reveals the expansion of feminist spirituality into the institutional church. Practicing religious feminists have known about this expansion for a long time. The Re-Imagining Conference was, for many of its participants, nothing new. What was new was the growing mainstream awareness of and attention to the ritual dimension in feminist thinking. Conservative alarm testifies in some measure to the vitality of feminist worship even in its sporadic and occasional occurrences.

So if there is, as Joy Bussart claims, a "longing in the pews," it is manifested in a variety of ways when channeled into feminist worship practice. It is communal and individual; it is traditional, posttraditional, and sometimes a syncretistic combination of both. Most important, it results in transformative experiences of alleged divinity that confound traditional negations of referential association. The longing itself probably results in part from feminist theologies, and the religious activity it seems to engender constitutes in part a challenge to feminist theologies. The various religious experiences of women and men who take feminist metaphors as seriously as they are meant lead the theologian inexorably to the question of the divinity the metaphors purposely misrepresent.

The diffuse, powerfully imagined, and shared responses that sometimes emerge out of feminist religious experiences are both end products and by-products of the creative intellectual work of constructive theology. They are, on one level, socially mediated and conditioned responses to socially constructed goods since religious experiences, like all experience, are a process of modification and meaning-making, a filtering of events through sedimented stocks of knowledge and pressed into molds of the recognizable. And perhaps, as radical historicism suggests, nothing of any "real" residual divinity is ever left but an occasional, disconcerting, and shapeless certainty. Or perhaps this complicated mixture of history and interpretation suggests an Enlightenment foundation for a neo-Plotinian philosophy of emanation. Or perhaps divinity actually emerges into reality and shape *by* or in response to the material and intellectual constructive work of human attention, much as some spiritual feminists imaginatively "find" goddesses,[50] or much as the great Hopi Kachinas are guided into form, presence, and effectiveness by masks made for them, masks that "deceive" only children.[51] These and other possibilities for constructive theology are inspired by and respond to the variety and range of feminist religious practices and experiences. Whether communal and oriented to ritual and justice work, or whether individual and oriented to reflection, feminist spiritual experience is Christian and post-Christian, Jewish and pagan, sometimes this, sometimes that, but always taking up and engaging the products of constructive feminist theologies that re-imagine divinity with women in mind.

Given the argument that feminist spirituality exists and is robust, that religious experience is a part of the web of social construction, and that the general features of feminist religious experience may at times challenge the ultimacy of the metaphoric exemption, a final question remains. It concerns the implications for feminist theologies of religious claims to greater referential content in the metaphors they use. If there is any possibility that religious experience can have revelatory validity (as some persons quoted would argue), in what ways can constructive feminist theologies, cleaving to the metaphoric exemption, account for it? In other words, if the logical conclusion of the metaphoric exemption is the negation of substance in any tangible or knowable form, how can feminist theologies adequately respond to even the possibility of divinity being or acting otherwise? The answer is already implied. Their strategic underpinnings in the metaphoric exemption place feminist theologies in the awkward position of negating the referential validity of any but the most remote and shapeless kind to their metaphors, negating thereby any experience-based claims to the contrary as well. It is to this question and to possibilities for its resolution that part 3 turns.

PART 3

Confronting the Backlash

CHAPTER SIX

Re-Imagining the Divine

FEMINIST THEOLOGIES IN ALL THEIR DIVERSITY are fed and divided by the taproots of metaphoric exemption and experiential confession. How can these theologies proceed, pulled as they are at the roots in opposite directions, by social constructionist skepticism in one direction and experiential affirmation in the other? I have argued that both roots are indispensable. One results in healthy reminders of the fallibility of human ideas of the divine, and the other results in vigorous offerings of new ones. One demonstrates the limits of human perception, and the other emphasizes ongoing embodied revelation. Such an uneasy collaboration is fraught with tension, but it is unavoidable. Given this historically conditioned framework, there are two questions for feminist theologians: How should this internal tension be viewed and tended? And what images of divinity does it suggest for feminist theologies?

The first of these questions is methodological. The second is substantive and forms, in many ways, the conclusion to which this whole work is moving. But like the tips of icebergs, resilient conclusions rest on larger foundations, and so it is important to address the methodological question first. Because feminist constructive theologies do not limit themselves to one particular religious tradition, the question of methodology must leave aside for the moment the specific contents of religious traditions, doctrines, and mythologies. Tradition, in the form of scripture, doctrine, ritual, or cultural history, is vital, even necessary, to the complete work of theology, but for feminist theologies it is not foundational. This is not to say that the contents of, for example, the Christian or Jewish tradition and Scripture are irrelevant to the work of feminist theologians concerned with articulating Christian or Jewish theologies in liberating terms for women and men affected by the dynamics of social oppression. Rather, I suggest that the contents of particular traditions condition and adjudicate new mythic or metaphoric proposals. Sacred stories and doctrines set the horizon of possibilities, for example, for the articulation of an improved Christian mythos or new Jewish metaphors for divinity. But the specific tradition and its creeds, scriptures, or rituals do not determine the foundations of what is feminist or what is theological about feminist theologies, but what is Christian about them (or Jewish, Muslim, Wiccan, or some other tradition). It is ironic to place the hermeneutical task prior to, for example, accounts of creation. To do so should raise eyebrows. Nevertheless, there is a social constructionist logic to the idea of looking at the underlying structure of assumptions upon which sacred narratives meaningfully hang.

So I argue that methodology—the way we do theology—must draw equally from the two taproots of metaphoric exemption and experiential confession in order to offer stronger, more living constructions of divinity. What is more, a dialectical foundation such as this offers new resources for conceiving the important and historically problematic theological notions of transcendence and immanence, abstraction and embodiment, one and many. With a more clearly articulated structure or a skeletal frame, the colorful enactments of myth, revelation, tradition, and ritual can come to life, not as dispensable drapery, but as the living flesh of faith and spirituality.

I have argued that the uneasy collaboration between metaphoric exemption and experiential affirmation in feminism's theological foundations comes from twentieth-century responses to Enlightenment skepticism and historicism, on the one hand, and from the critical authority that feminist theologians place upon categories and claims of lived experience, on the other.[1] The tension resident in the foundations of feminist theologies between historicist skepticism about certainty—especially certainty about divinity—and commitments to categories of experience that profess a real divinity capable not only of "being" but of "being-there" can result in contradiction or radical agnosticism. If the metaphoric exemption always reminds us that God is not *that* (that face; that gift of food; that flame; that particular, delicate, terrible beauty; that touch; that death), then there can be only silence; there can be no divine embodiment, however fleeting, however real. If the metaphoric exemption exempts all human constructions from any correspondence to divine being, we can never say about the divine, "I have experienced (seen, witnessed, heard)" and mean it with utter, foolish certainty.

But if there is correspondence between human constructions and divine being, what is it? Where does so-called real divinity touch and enflesh the little, particular, and partial human attempts to name and visualize and, even more so, experience the presence of divine being? How can we elucidate and understand the correspondence without falling into the trap of idolatry and ontological confusion? Feminist theologies tend to run this risk more than most because they hold to notions of embodied wisdom and concrete, particular, and communal manifestations of divine activity at the same time that they criticize traditional theology. They also run this risk because feminist theologians strive to offer new language, metaphors, and images for the divine that reflect this notion of embodied wisdom and divine being.

The richest feminist theological proposals focus on replenishing the sacred store with new mythic content, imagining the divine clothed in metaphoric garb that uses discrete, comprehensible, and illuminating images relevant and meaningful in contemporary life. But theologies that seek to develop and defend new mythic content are more vulnerable to contradiction or confusion because at the same time they must employ the metaphoric exemption to retain for divinity otherness and independence. Most theologians still assert that divinity really exists and remains essentially beyond human construction, but new myths are obviously constructed and so reveal the constructedness of old myths, undermining confidence in both.

Feminist theologians do not pretend that their new offerings are anything but products of human imagination. Quite the contrary. But if the tension between exemption and confession is unavoidable, so is the risk of undermining any certainty or even possibility of reaching and touching divine being (assuming the desire to do so is not a nostalgic dream). It is a risk endemic to feminist theological pursuits. This is one difference between feminist theologies and other contemporary theologies that more cautiously focus on systematic cognitive frameworks while avoiding discussions of actual mythic content. Some of these other theologies intend to rehabilitate the mythic content of Christian doctrine on a contemporary foundation that they hope will hold it. Others work only on systematic frameworks for theology, leaving open the possibility for undescribed new contents without directly risking any contradiction of metaphoric exemption and confession.[2]

Feminist theologies are in an interesting spot, rooted as they are so deeply in the insights of the metaphoric exemption and in exuberant validation of the concrete. Because experience (itself such a complex concept) cannot be completely defined by the processes of social construction, the problem remains of the place of religious experiences that threaten to confound the metaphoric exemption. Although the vagaries of personal or even of communal experience do not and should not determine the final content of feminist theologies, the significance of women's and men's various and rich experiences of oppression, of solidarity, and of liberation still undergird the most basic feminist commitments. Feminist theologies are therefore not in a position to dismiss confessional experiences of divine presence and of divinity that become concrete in the images and metaphors of feminist constructions. If they do, a much more fundamental contradiction ensues.

Structured at the core by professed experiences of oppression, solidarity, liberation, and divine presence and by the metaphoric exemption that casts a jaundiced eye on any claims the former might make, feminist theologies can be fatally divided by this polarization or energized by the sparks it creates. Much is at stake at either pole. Constructive feminist theologies cannot do without the metaphoric exemption unless they are prepared to abandon their roots in skeptical historicism, which gives them the very tools they need for dismantling traditional authority (pulling back the curtain on Oz, so to speak). And without the metaphoric exemption, they must abandon their roots in iconoclastic caution that give feminist theologies the moral authority to denounce as idolatry the exclusivist images of patriarchal religion. Without the metaphoric exemption, constructive feminist theologies would have no critical ground from which to mount their deep critique of misogynist history and from which to offer alternatives. The metaphoric exemption is the ground on which feminist theologies stand.

However, the metaphoric exemption also exempts any claims about divinity that may come from personal experience. Constructive feminist theologies can ill afford this outright dismissal. To do so damages the credibility of feminist affirmations of women's interpretations of their own experience. More seriously, it undermines the credibility of other experiential claims related to oppression, sexuality, justice, memory, community, family, ethnicity, and so on that ultimately undergird and shape feminist constructive proposals.

A vital reintroduction of confessional experience into the fabric of feminist theologies does not have to mean that demands from individual experience are binding or normative for theological construction. Not all experiences are revelatory of divine presence, and not all experiences are lucid or available to the narrative of religious life. *But some are.* To say otherwise would lead theology into nihilistic nonsense and irrelevance for the personally lived religious life. Feminist constructive theologies must find a way to account for the possibility that the divine may sometimes contradict the metaphoric exemption by being there occasionally in the metaphor. Ironically, the issue here has less to do with *what* people experience of divine presence and more to do with the fact that they *do* sometimes experience it. If God, or some other name for the divine, is understood to possess being and substance beyond human imagination and to be active on its own behalf, feminist theologies cannot dismiss the possibility that God also responds to human imagination and construction, comes into presence in those constructions, and sometimes embodies them.

Until now, constructive feminist theologies have tended to navigate between the poles of metaphoric exemption and experiential confession by neglecting to treat claims related to direct religious experience. Feminist theologians, aware of the dangers inherent in dismissing all women's spiritual experiences as delusional, have chosen a strategy of benign neglect. Issues of religious experience, and particularly of experiences that suggest embodied presence, tend to be characterized as "feminist spirituality" and so do not muddy the cleaner lines of constructive theory. This tactic compromises the metaphoric exemption by means of oversight and allows feminist theologies in general to avoid contradiction until the issue is forced. But when the issue is forced from the outside by accusations of idolatry (as in the backlash), feminist theologies resort to the metaphoric exemption, applying it to themselves, reminding opponents that real divinity is neither compromised nor directly indicated by the new images. While effective to a point, this strategy has the unfortunate consequence of dismissing the actual experiential confessions of the very women it seeks to defend.

How can constructive feminist theologies invoke the metaphoric exemption without erasing yet again the voices of women and men who claim to "know what they know" from their own experience in defiance of oppressive norms? The answer may lie in how we view the basic interaction of metaphoric exemption and experiential confession. At their most basic level, constructive feminist theologies fit a condition that Edward Farley calls reflective ontology.[3] Farley suggests that human beings are fundamentally shaped by a need to distinguish what is real and true. Hence philosophy and science, and hence the child's insistent demand to know "why." Farley calls this need an elemental human passion for reality. This passion is both a pragmatic matter of biological survival and a more complex and rich matter of social thriving and meaning.[4] It is also a passion that is never fully satisfied. Human beings are constituted by this passion for reality and profoundly wounded by our inability ultimately to possess it. It is our greatest strength and our greatest vulnerability.

Feminist theologies pursue this passion for the real with both hands. They attempt clarity (and elimination of the unreal) through the metaphoric exemption with one hand and look for revelation through women's various experiences on the other. But neither hand yields up reality in any complete sense. Neither fully satisfies. This is both their strength and their greatest vulnerability.

I have discussed in depth how feminist theologies are rooted in two opposing impulses. The notion of passion for the real helps to clarify the dangers inherent in the collaboration. Passion does not breed caution or moderation, and so too much of one impulse can wholly negate the other.

The credulity of religious experience needs temperance by the skepticism of social theory. The skepticism of social theory needs life breathed into it by simple affirmation or acknowledgment of the numinous. The one constitutes the other, but it is also its most serious threat.

With the addition of Farley's idea of reflective ontology, the full skeletal structure of constructive feminist theologies as an organic and energetic relation between opposing poles is clear. The skepticism of the metaphoric exemption and the affirmation of experiential confession can be understood in lively relation as mutually corrective rather than as mutely opposed and merely contradictory. In mutual correction they are dynamically related, and this dynamism is also a vulnerability, especially given the underlying and elemental passion for reality that enlivens the whole.

Because in current feminist theologies the metaphoric exemption tends to overwhelm confessions of divine reality, this creative polarity is a normative rather than descriptive proposition. If feminist experiential claims of reference or correspondence are to have any corrective weight against the overwhelming skepticism of the metaphoric exemption, they must have a more consistently thematized place in constructive feminist theologies than they currently occupy. I have already articulated the dangers involved. The metaphoric exemption protects feminist theologies and their readers and practitioners from charges of idolatry and from confusion of human constructions with divine reality. However, *vulnerability* to these confusions is not itself the problem. Metaphoric exemption and religious experience, both necessary, make each other vulnerable. Vulnerability alone never determines the sufficiency or insufficiency of a thing, as human life itself attests. The structure of feminist theologies is therefore a dialectic between skepticism and confession that is both strength and vulnerability.

The Constitutive Strength and Vulnerability of the Metaphoric Exemption

As a theory of reality, functional social constructionism serves two important purposes in its constitutive founding of feminist theologies. First, it grounds their critique of patriarchal culture, and second, it establishes the legitimacy of theological construction through the metaphoric exemption. If reality is understood to be socially constructed, then the role of the theologian is also constituted by construction. The theologian, at this end of the dialectic, is primarily an architect, working pragmatically to influence human life through the symbolic materials that motivate that life. Within the constraints of context (cultural warrants, revealed tradition, church dogmatics, political and ethnic sensibilities, and so on) the theologian sketches out a symbolic system that gives shape and direction to living. The theological system's adequacy is judged first on its effectiveness in orienting human life toward better values and goals, and only second on its consistency with given doctrines. At the extremes of the metaphoric exemption, it is very difficult to speak of divine being apart from human imagining. Indeed, the defensibility and even desirability of ontological claims for divinity become increasingly suspect, as Kathleen Sands, Sheila Davaney, and Gordon Kaufman all suggest. Standing only on the metaphoric exemption, epistemology is agnosticism. Unmodified by experiential and ontic confessions of divine presence and existence, feminist theologies as constituted by the metaphoric exemption are only criticism, even of their own constructions. The metaphoric exemption is like an acid that, uncontrolled, can only indiscriminately dissolve the things it touches. Correctly channeled, however, it can etch and carve, serving well the task of construction.

Directed out toward history and culture, the critique carried by the metaphoric exemption has allowed feminist theologians to argue that the constructions of feminist theologies threaten far more than linguistic and liturgical customs because they undermine the legitimizing substructures of patriarchal culture itself. The Father God of traditional Christianity is the patriarch of traditional Western culture enacted as deity in liturgy, as political leader in government, as boss in industry, and as father in the home. All of these enactments are products of the legitimizing power of social persuasion through symbolic social construction and, as Weber would have it, through political and economic reinforcement of that symbolic construction. They are brought down by the metaphoric exemption that reveals them to be cultural artifacts rather than revealed truths.

In this way, the metaphoric exemption is the critical tool that provides feminist theologies with their corrective protest against what Mary Daly calls the "prevailing religion of the entire planet" and what Ruether calls "the transcendent consciousness [that] has literally created the urban earth."[5] It dissolves the sources of patriarchal religion's legitimacy in nature and revelation. "Nature" comes to signify an interpreted matrix of meanings distilled over time from human ideas. Dominant cultural invocations of nature, as an objectively real and divinely created order in which men, women, and all the rest have their respective places, lose their power when the metaphoric exemption reveals such interpretations of nature as social constructions. The metaphoric exemption also transforms the revelations of scriptural sources into the highly manipulated and politicized writings of a historical, all too human, tradition. Both nature and revelation turn, in the acid bath of the metaphoric exemption, from objective truths to political pawns. Nature and revelation, once sources of resolution in squabbles over questions of reality, become reality's most contested sites. No longer is anything what it seems. The "natural" threatens to emerge within the realm of what was "unnatural," and revelation turns out to be the realization that we made it all up. The core criticism that feminist theologies employ, what Elisabeth Schüssler Fiorenza dubs the "hermeneutic of suspicion," is rooted in this conceptual reorientation.[6]

Thus, functional social constructionism in the form of the metaphoric exemption gives feminist theologies their best tool for exposing the opportunistic underbelly of imperial religion and for delegitimizing tyrannical deities. And feminist theologies of all kinds have put the tool to use, leading some feminists such as Carol Christ, Starhawk, Mary Daly, and Emily Culpepper to adopt post-Christian or posttheistic stances that dispense entirely with the patriarchal divine order.[7] However, the metaphoric exemption is also integral to feminist theologies that attempt to remain within predominantly Christian religious spheres. It allows them not only to denounce patriarchal values and tendencies as idolatrous and even heretical, but also to claim core Christian values as consonant with feminist goals for justice. The Father God is no more real, according to the metaphoric exemption, than the Mother Goddess because both are merely metaphors for divine reality. If one image causes undue temptation to violence, prejudice, and idolatry, then it must be modified or replaced. This is the prevailing sentiment across the feminist theological spectrum.[8]

Feminist theologies lean heavily toward the metaphoric exemption precisely because the exclusiveness of masculine images and symbols for the divine has caused them to be deeply entrenched in religious imagination. The problem here is less with male images per se and more with their exclusive currency in dominant culture. The image of God as Father is not by itself the problem. Or to be precise, the image by itself is exactly the problem. McFague makes this point clearly in her constructive arguments for new metaphors as supplements, not replacements, for tradition. Paul Tillich identified the essential relationship between holy kinghood and unduly elevated kings, and Mary Daly identified the essential relationship between holy fatherhood and unduly elevated males. The metaphoric exemption, as the theological arm of social constructionism, illuminates such critical links. Herein is one of its great strengths.

In addition to its deconstructive role in criticism, the metaphoric exemption constitutes feminist theologies in their task of construction. As such, it is a contemporary form of negative theology. Because it demands that no human construction refer directly to divine being, it supports functional social constructionism's radical denial of divine being. But as negative theology, the metaphoric exemption does not eliminate the concept of divinity. Negative theology only conditions the divine as inconceivable and inaccessible. What is more, the history of negative theology in Western culture, known by the Latin *via negativa*, is far longer and denser than the modern history of functional social construction. It represents an intellectual tradition concerned with the task of letting God be God in the most awesome and absolute sense of the name. Traditionally, it is a form of ontological assertion that uses negation to say what God is not, thus obliquely referring to what God is. Filtered through the combined rivers of Hebrew iconoclasm and Hellenistic concerns with essence, the evolution of negative theology in the synthesis of these ancient traditions becomes the basis of the claim by a contemporary feminist scholar that "to speak of God is among the most difficult and audacious things that humans do."[9]

In its contemporary manifestation, negative theology as metaphoric exemption represents a more or less defensive response to the sweeping criticism of "modern science." Dorothee Sölle suggests that this *via negativa* is necessitated by context. "Living in a world in which modern science explains and dominates life," she argues, "it makes no sense to begin from God as a starting point if one wants to make oneself understood in context. What is to be taken for granted is not the supreme being once called 'God,' but the impossibility of associating anything at all with this word" resulting, she says, in a "situation . . . characterized by a pragmatic, unmilitant and painless atheism."[10] Whether it results in pragmatic atheism or in reminders of divine otherness and greatness, the metaphoric exemption as a response to modernity makes the claim that since all we know is socially conditioned, metaphors that remind us of their constructedness are more defensible than those assumed to be wholly "true."

Both classical and contemporary forms of negative theology operate in constructive feminist work. The classical form preserves divine greatness beyond human metaphoric imagining, necessitating *metaphoric* imagining. The contemporary form addresses the elemental human passion for reality, even in the context of "painless" atheism. Metaphors for God that bring about social goods are therefore valuable, even for atheists who recognize the social function of such symbols. Modern radical historicism provides its own horizon for reality, making the question of divine being merely a distraction from the function of the idea of God in societies legitimated by that idea. The modernist negation is more willing to bracket questions of divine being and is better represented in historicist feminist theologies than the classical negation that continues to assert divine greatness. But both forms of negation are present across the spectrum of feminist theological writings and offer, as they have offered theologians for centuries, a response to the paradox of skepticism and confession.

A note of caution is advisable here. Conceptual schemes are always vulnerable to premature closure and oversimplification. To classify the metaphoric exemption as a kind of skepticism that undermines theological ontology and also as a form of negative theology can gloss important ontological, and even mystical, possibilities in negative theology. Indeed, the negative theological tradition, particularly in Jewish and Christian history, offers a variety of examples suggesting a closer and more interdependent relationship between experiential confession and negation than a purely skeptical deconstruction allows. Whether it is Moses in the very presence of the divine, unable to "see" the face of God (Exod. 33:18–23), walkers to Emmaus unable to recognize Jesus until he is gone (Luke 24:13–35), or any of a multitude of mystical visions reported in early and medieval Christianity, Islam, Judaism, and so on, the metaphoric exemption as negative theology can support rather than oppose ontological claims in theology. So the metaphoric exemption is not simple criticism nor need it be thoroughgoing deconstruction. But the only way that it can support experiential affirmation of the divine is through *mystical* negation—experiences that cannot be described concretely or put into words.

Perhaps some examples can clarify this point. Mysticism from the Eastern branches of early Christianity often served as inspiration for negative theology in its most traditional form. Many mystical visions provided the lens, on the one hand, for direct awareness of the incomprehensibility of God and, on the other, for the necessity for establishing limits to this knowledge. Gregory of Nyssa wrote in the fourth century C.E. that true knowledge of God "is the seeing that consists in not seeing, because that which is sought transcends all knowledge, being separated on all sides by incomprehensibility."[11] Dionysius the Areopagite began a systematic tradition of categorizing the apophatic and cataphatic traditions in a triune scheme, calling them the *via negativa*, *via positiva*, and *via mystica*, whereas Maximus the Confessor argued in the sixth century C.E. for the inadequacy even of negative speech, claiming that the "two names of Being and Non-Being ought both to be applied to God, although neither of them really suits Him. . . . He possesses an existence that is completely inaccessible and beyond all affirmation and negation. . . . For the ignorance about God on the part of those who are wise in divine things is not a lack of learning, but a knowledge that knows by silence that God is unknown."[12] The mystical strains of piety do not necessarily generate negative theology, but it is helpful to remember that they do not always work against it.

Later on, medieval scholars in Christianity took up negative theology quite apart from mysticism in the hopes of establishing proofs for God's existence, either through Anselm's double logic or through Thomas's arguments from nature in which he attempted to prove the incomprehensibility of God by demonstrating the limitations of human intellection. "Since our mind is not proportionate to the divine substance," Aquinas claimed, "that which is the substance of God remains beyond our intellect and so is unknown to us. Hence the supreme knowledge which we have of God is to know that we do not know God."[13] It was when Cartesian philosophy began, in the late seventeenth century, to give shape to the worldview we now call modernity that negative theology turned from a positive exercise in mystical rationalization or metaphysical proofs *for* God to a first line of theological defense *against* the radical skepticism slowly emerging as scientific inquiry in Western thought.

Contemporary negative theology, from Karl Barth to the metaphoric exemption of constructive feminist theologies, reflects a necessary preoccupation with the skepticism of modernity. Experiences of divine presence are a problem insofar as they demand ontological affirmation about divine being. Gordon Kaufman therefore argues that religious experiences of divine presence mistake the "true" aseity of God with delusional longings for God's presence. We are confused when we long for God's presence to be discernible like that of other persons. He claims that often "believers, in their enthusiasm for their faith, have spoken as though God were in our midst in this way and have even supposed that they directly felt the divine presence.... We only confuse ourselves and others by thinking this, however important to us may be our faith, or the experiences in which we feel our faith has been confirmed."[14]

Kaufman's point is very much like Tillich's, namely, that God is always understood symbolically, even in experience, and therefore cannot be confused with the metaphors we use for or toward God. This is the iconoclastic assertion of all constructive theology, the positive claim of the "not that" of symbols and metaphors even as the symbols and metaphors enflesh and enrich language for and about God. This metaphoric exemption is the constructive theologian's foundation upon which the socially responsible work of theological symbol, image, metaphor, and model making can be built.

Without the metaphoric exemption, constructive theologians, and particularly feminist constructive theologians, fear the return or renewal of the idolatrous confusions and conflations of patriarchal theology. The metaphoric exemption is the linchpin of constructive theology and the tool of functional social constructionism, the reminder that everything we can say, do, or experience of God is mediated through the social constructions of culture. This reminder is kept rigidly to the fore precisely so that new metaphors will not be mistaken for divine identity and so that, in the tradition of negative theology, the great mystery and incomprehensibility of God cannot be reduced to the convenience of persons in positions of political or social power.

Unlike radical functional social constructionism, however, the metaphoric exemption of constructive theology cannot successfully *eliminate* the possibility of divine existence. It only exempts the possibility of unmediated knowledge of or about that existence. The assumption underlying the metaphoric exemption is that all knowledge is historical, mediated through the lenses of history and culture for purposes of social cohesion and meaning, and that all shared beliefs can be explained by their supportive role in the creation and maintenance of social meaning. Theologians who use the metaphoric exemption are therefore faced with the difficult and ancient task of speaking about something about which they cannot speak except through socially constructed (and culturally mediated) symbols and metaphors that *do* also happen to function in social ways. The "real" God beyond all human construction and imagining, in the constructive theological view, remains there and must be kept apart, distinguished from our conceptions, ideas, symbols, or images, written or enacted. This is what Barth means when he insists that theology must let God be God.[15] It is what Tillich means when he argues that "God does not exist. He is being-itself beyond essence and existence."[16] It is what Kaufman means when he claims that "the idea of God, the symbol which is built up through the variety of images . . . remains just that: an idea, a symbol."[17] McFague also makes clear that "theology as construction . . . supports the assertion that our concept of God is precisely that—*our concept* of God— and not God."[18] It is what Elizabeth Johnson means when she says that the "unfathomable mystery of God is always mediated through shifting historical discourse,"[19] what Peter Hodgson means when he likens constructive theology "to a work of fiction,"[20] and certainly what Anselm meant in the eleventh century when he claimed to prove that God's existence, being both real and great, could only be that than which nothing greater could be conceived.

From this vantage point, French philosopher Jacques Derrida's argument that negative theology is always really avowal makes real sense.[21] The proponents of negative theology are never arguing against the existence of God, even if the metaphoric exemption indicates that this is the end to which contemporary constructive theologies point. Constructive theologians making use of the metaphoric exemption resist this final skepticism, attempting instead to assert the existence of God through the negation of all that might fall prey to or betray itself ultimately as not-God. Thus, Mark C. Taylor can argue that the "not" also negates itself: "The return of, or to, negative theology is, in most cases, a gesture of recuperation. . . . All too often, the return of, or to, negative theology involves a dialectical move that is supposed to negate negation. If apparent opposites are really one, then the negative is at the same time positive and thus it becomes possible to discover resources for defense in criticism itself."[22]

Constructive feminist theologies have discovered in negation a useful tool for affirmation. The metaphoric exemption, far from destroying the possibility for construction, shores up the theological propositions that serve their primary commitments to social justice by ensuring orthodoxy and nonidolatry. In general, however, negation of correspondence to divinity in feminist metaphors tends to be less important than the legitimacy of the metaphors for specific groups and communities in justice struggles. More often than not, arguments for new and sometimes explicitly female language, images, rituals, and names for the divine are made in terms of their benefit for women, for human beings, for living things, or for the earth, and in terms of their consonance with basic religious values, not because of their support for the negative claims of divine incomprehensibility. The metaphoric exemption is an insurance policy in case of backlash.

The real concern, the "critical principle of feminist theology," Rosemary Ruether asserts, "is the promotion of the full humanity of women."[23] Elizabeth Johnson develops this point further. Christian feminist theology to her means "a reflection on God and all things in the light of God that stands consciously in the company of all the world's women, explicitly prizing their genuine humanity while uncovering and criticizing its persistent violation in sexism, itself an omnipresent paradigm of unjust relationships."[24] Delores Williams claims that womanist theologians need most of all not to lose their "intention for black women's experience to provide the lens through which we view sources, to provide the issues that form the content of our theology and to help us formulate the questions we ask about God's relation to black American life and to the world in general."[25] And Mary Daly argues for "the metaphoric language of 'Elemental spirits'" not so much because of the importance of the metaphoric and hence negative referent of that *kind* of language, but because the idea of "Elemental spirits is crucial for the empowering of women, for this conjures memories of Archaic integrity that have been broken by phallic religion and philosophy."[26]

In other words, the *function of the content* of theological and metaphoric language drives feminist theological construction, not the vastness of the divine that metaphors explicitly do not describe. Some go so far as to argue that divine existence matters little or is irrelevant to the task of feminist theologies. Sheila Ruth argues, for example, that it "makes little sense to ask whether God or a god exists, not because it does not exist, nor, in fact, because it does. *Exists* in the material sense is not the appropriate concept to apply here. *Serves* or *suffices* would be better terms. . . . This is slippery business, to be sure."[27] The slippery business is the likelihood that if divine existence is the inappropriate concept whereas service and sufficiency are appropriate, divinity is in danger of being reduced entirely to function, and feminist theologies become reduced to specialized social advocacy.

So functional social constructionism, the political root of feminist theological criticism, fuels the work of new construction. This in turn necessitates negation in the form of metaphoric exemption. This is the genius of feminist theologies, but also their greatest vulnerability. New proposals are judged on the basis of whether or not they help, as McFague says, to make things better—"things" being the relevant social, political, environmental, economic, and spiritual conditions of all victims of injustice, and the world in general.[28] Existing metaphors are interrogated not only for their suitability as models for human thriving, justice, or ecological survival, but also for their compatibility with accepted and acceptable traditional norms, which are themselves subjected to this critical analysis.[29]

Her concern with the social functioning of names and images sends Mary Daly out into constructive spirals of "Elemental" philosophy on behalf of bewitching furies, hags, and crones. This concern with function allows Cynthia Eller to suggest that "if in his maleness God sanctions a patriarchal social structure, it would seem that there is none better than a goddess to remedy the situation."[30] Likewise, Daphne Hampson can claim that "if a symbol does not symbolize what one thinks good or true, there can be no reason to retain it."[31] And this concern with function more than her characteristic concern with ontology brings Elizabeth Johnson to the conclusion that "at this point in the living tradition, I believe that we need a strong dose of explicitly female imagery to break the unconscious sway that male trinitarian imagery holds over the imaginations of even the most sophisticated thinkers."[32] Like Elisabeth Schüssler Fiorenza, Kelly Brown Douglas, Rosemary Ruether, and Sallie McFague, Johnson applies the standard of function to the traditional canon in search of retrievals that will help make things better. "Taking a cue from feminist methodologies in related fields," she says, "I ask whether, when read with a feminist hermeneutic, there is anything in the classical tradition in all its vastness that could serve a discourse about divine mystery that would further the emancipation of women."[33]

One of the powerful contributions of feminist theologies is their focus on function in the context of theological negation. In fact, the feminist theological insistence upon function *and* negativity, or the function *of* negativity, has preserved feminist theologies in many cases from a tendency to oversimplification, indicating through the metaphoric exemption the need for negativity precisely so that divinity is not ultimately reduced to utility. But at the same time, the metaphoric exemption does not in the end protect feminist theologies from the danger of reductive oversimplification. The vulnerability carried by the metaphoric exemption is that it creates the possibility of reducing feminist theologies to irrelevance by emphasizing function to begin with. This is the dilemma, the constitutive vulnerability, of constructive feminist theologies. Without a countering balance, the metaphoric exemption drives feminist theologies past the caution of theological negation to the endless loop of absolute negation.

The other dynamic that spurs negative claims in feminist theologies is the same one that spurred negative theology in the early centuries of Christian practice, namely, mystical enthusiasm. However, most claims from feminist religious experience do not tend toward incomprehensibility; they are generally quite the opposite. It is not typically the case that feminist mystical experience is inexpressible or indescribable, requiring a turn to negation to brush in the outlines of the divine encounter (although that may sometimes be true). More often the experience of divinity stemming from feminist accounts offers clear, colorful, specific, and embodied images of deity or divinity, what Northup calls the embrace of the ordinary, and it is this relatively simple clarity that sends theologians rushing to the "nots."

The strength of the metaphoric exemption is that it allows feminist theologies to continue both their focus on social construction and their emphasis on lived experience by dampening the effects of both. Feminist theological emphasis on functional social construction is useful, despite its reductive tendencies, because the metaphoric exemption negates the referential capacities of the patriarchal "bad" metaphors and the feminist "good" ones. The vulnerability, however, is a tendency to the cynical conclusion that ultimately there is no divinity to which the metaphors and images point. In other words, it does not matter what language is used for or about divinity except its efficacy in human terms, its ability to point toward postpatriarchal, postracist, and postimperialist possibilities. Thus, self-referencing human judgments and wagers about the flourishing of creation become the most important criteria for theological construction.

In addition, the hermeneutic of suspicion applied to all religious sources for language and images of God (i.e., Scripture, tradition, and doctrine) renders these sources valid only insofar as they serve the primary liberationist goal of justice.[34] Human thriving, the flourishing of women, and the good of creation are the leading stars in a small constellation of liberationist criteria for judging the worthiness of language and images for God. The arguments on behalf of this overall approach are both compelling and good, funded by the insights of functional social constructionism and fueled by a real concern for the injustices of human structures of authority and for the injuries sustained by the nonhuman world. They also tend toward cynicism.

The greatest strength of the metaphoric exemption in feminist theologies is the powerful corrective criticism it lodges against any privileging closures. It dismantles the revealed authority of the monarchical Father. It clears a space for new images and visions that, being exempted, resist filling the ontic (read oppressive) void left by the former. And so it is clear that at its most fundamental level, constructive theology is made possible by the metaphoric exemption.

The greatest vulnerability of the metaphoric exemption is the temptation toward certainty that persists in its unremitting critique. The metaphoric exemption by itself is necessarily cynical toward any reality claims outside social construction and is unable to affirm anything but negation. So negation becomes the certain, ahistorical assertion, clothed in colorful metaphor and image. Because the elemental human passion for reality yields too often to the temptation of certainty, the negation of divine accessibility or knowability threatens, logically, to become a certainly negated divinity. Because independent divine existence cannot be proven, the metaphoric exemption constituting feminist theologies also makes that theology vulnerable to certainty about divine nonexistence. In proving the unprovability of divine presence, it tends toward the error of disproving it.

In addition, systematically negating the referential quality of constructed images and metaphors gives to feminist theologies their critical standard of functional social construction, presumably without making social function the sum of their work. Divinity itself is, however, limited by the negation of incomprehensibility. For example, when theologians insist that God can only be greater than anything conceived, they are in essence limiting God to greatness. It is not acceptable for God to choose to be small. If the metaphoric exemption insists upon the complete noncorrespondence of metaphors to divinity, nowhere is there a ground from which to affirm specific or embodied presence, great or small.

Merely negating or denying something, in other words, does not necessarily make the negation always true. "The repressed," Mark C. Taylor argues, "always returns."[35] And as philosopher Richard Grigg points out, "We cannot blithely suppose that what ought to be the case about God is in fact the case."[36] This could mean that what the metaphoric exemption and the negative theological tradition are trying to protect (God's ultimate otherness and incomprehensibility) might not always be the case. The divine might, on occasion, choose otherwise, notwithstanding human iconoclastic concerns and theological constructions of divine incomprehensibility and greatness.

In theological terms, the metaphoric exemption offers modern theologians a reasonable means for restoring the negative theological tradition and adds to it a modernist epistemology. Constructive theologies can still let God be God by refusing any reductions to correspondence between their constructions and divine being. But at the same time, they are vulnerable to the opposite, a reduction of divinity to otherness and greatness, to a prison of incomprehensibility. I think that this reverse reduction masks a deeper cynicism about divine existence altogether. It becomes a methodological negation of determinacy, presence, and embodiment.[37]

The Strength and Vulnerability of Religious Experience

Given the constitutive strengths and vulnerabilities of the metaphoric exemption, we can now turn to the issue of experiential confession, the other taproot in feminist theologies. I suggest that feminist theologies must account for the possibility that the metaphors they construct can, at times, cross the threshold into real embodiments of real divinity. While the metaphoric exemption does not eliminate divine freedom, it does disallow human apprehension or comprehension of divine being and so casts a deeply suspicious eye on religious experience as evidence of divine presence. The problem for constructive feminist theologies is the persistence of experiences that confound the metaphoric exemption's restrictions.

Robert Cummings Neville argues that "powerful religious symbols in devotional use tend to be abrupt and absolutistic, making their demands difficult to harmonize with other demands."[38] Faced with absolutism, feminist theologies are ill served by modernist skepticism, which dismisses what cannot be theorized. Tempting as it may be to turn to the helpful certainties of psychology, sociology, and deconstructionist philosophies to explain experiences of divine presence, the certainty they offer merely closes off the unanswered question of divinity rather than addressing it. For example, psychology can analyze the role of symbols in the formation and functioning of human identity, but it must also bracket, or deny altogether, the possibility of a real divinity acting upon, through, or in response to the symbol because it can offer no insights into or clarification of that possibility outside a self-referencing psychological loop. The mind creates the image because it has a need for the image, the image fulfills the need, thus becoming real to the mind, and so on. Psychology tends to reduce things religious, as Neville suggests, to epistemological "terms of the finite/infinite contrast," a persuasive and illuminating form of functionalist meaning-making.[39]

Also, postmodern literary and performance theory can offer explanations for experience in terms of metaphors and symbols as they become speech acts that enact and construct meaning. As both performative and constitutive action, speech is explored extensively in contemporary deconstructionist and phenomenological analysis, but these theories, too, must bracket the possibility that there might be a divine response.[40] The insight of deconstructionist theory in terms of speech is that the performance and actualization of culture occur through language, in strong form undermining and denying, and in weak form causing to be bracketed, any certainty of reference outside the linguistic structure. Philosophers such as Michel Foucault and Ludwig Wittgenstein are principal among those who represent this approach to language and culture.[41]

The question of feminist invocational language, however, is one that posits the enduring possibility of speech, and hence ritual enactment to refer to or even to *invoke* a so-called true-real divine. What is more, real divinity may make itself accessible, even if "it" is always already mediated through the constructions of language. The complexities of experience, identity, reference, and the grammar of interpretation do not eliminate this possibility, provided that we are more than windowless monads and that our experience does not collapse into unremitting subjectivity.

Making room for the *possibility* of religious experience that apprehends something that is "real" is not the same thing as hardwiring a necessary correspondence between invocation and response. It is merely clearing a space that allows for divine activity on its own terms that might include irruption into human speech, consciousness, and other constructed acts and states of existence. Terrence Reynolds puts the issue this way in his discussion of Ludwig Wittgenstein's *On Certainty:* "Believing one's claims to be ontologically true in a strong or bad sense of correspondence is incoherent because as Wittgenstein reminds us: 'All testing, all confirmation and disconfirmation of a hypothesis takes place already within a system.' Yet, it seems possible to hold such a view and still allow for the hope of a post-historical convergence of one's claims with the 'real.'"[42]

Thus, the idea of an independent "real" divinity that acts on or through the constructions and imaginings of feminist (or any other) reflection and practice becomes possible in theology only if some kind of intelligible room is made for it.

While feminist claims of direct experiences of the divine prove nothing conclusive about the independent existence or actual nature of that divine (a point William James asserted in his *Varieties of Religious Experience* at the same time that Durkheim was writing *The Elementary Forms of the Religious Life*), feminism's general concern with women's experiences of oppression and liberation as basis for theological reflection places theologians in the position of having to account for the wider range of women's experiences in the communities for which the theology is written. Indeed, it would seem strange for any theologian to take seriously one set of experiences— in this case experiences of structural oppression—that help to ground an individual or community's encounter with the divine and to reject the encounter itself as an important source of information for the theological enterprise.

But on what basis should feminist theologies, to the extent that they are "logos about theos," acknowledge experiential confession as a constitutive foundation of their work? The fact that we cannot systematize religious experience and that it is always implicated in and shaped by forces of social construction should not *necessarily* mean that it cannot have a significant bearing on constructive theological work. The elemental passion for reality is poignantly expressed in the fragile experiences of individuals or communities for whom religious experience is real, as is their claim that such experience reveals something of what they profess to be divine.

The strength of experiential confession in feminist theologies is its ability to retrieve the insights and wisdom of persons traditionally silenced or diminished by patriarchal and racist culture. Given the overwhelming erasures of women and nondominant men in Western history, lived experience has often been the only source of information and knowledge available to them for resistance and protest against dominant truths. This is its essential strength in feminist theologies, which in turn exposes its vulnerability.

Tillich argues that experience is only the medium and not the source for theological reflection because of its vulnerability to misinterpretation. If it does more than merely transmit, if it produces, if it is a source, then, he claims, it falsifies.[43] Despite the essential strength that shared and named experiences impart to oppressed groups of people, falsification or, more gently, confusion is the great vulnerability of experience. That is because experience, even within the constraints of social construction, is profoundly open. Individual experiences are, as Burrell and Farley claim, notoriously protean and thus resist systematization unless they are abstracted into perduring themes and become history, or human experience in its more thematic sense. The very skepticism that spawned Enlightenment historicism was, in one sense, an insight into the tendency of discrete experiences to become oppressively normative, masquerading as universal truths. Autobiographical experiences, in their mundanity and in their occasional breathtaking uncanniness, can only serve descriptively to stand against and correct the overwhelming normativity of universalized claims.

But the always resident danger accompanying the entry of particular experiences into theological discourse is the temptation to colonize the particular content of a religious experience (especially if it is attractive, for some reason) and to turn an individual experience of God into a normative description of the divine. In terms of religious experience, for example, the temptation would be to argue that if the experience of a woman who claims to have "seen" the distinctively female face of God is to be granted credence, then the content—a female face—is taken as normative rather than the capacity of the divine to be "really" there and visible in a face, responsive to and embodying a temporal and perhaps temporary construct.

What is revealed here is our human vulnerability embodied in our elemental passion for reality. This passion fuels human curiosity and creativity, but it also drives interpretation toward closure, and uncanny experience toward domestication, including uncanny experiences of divine presence. This is the necessary impulse toward making meaning out of experience. This impulse produces boundaries of meaning that shut out untamable experiences and that tame others by naming them. Theory and interpretation are, after all, a kind of domestication in that they order and relate otherwise disordered parts.

Theology is much the same. Religious experience threatens the meaning erected by theology only when that experience is put in place of theology, becomes the sum of theology. Religious experience corrects theology when it stands opposite the normative theory or the systematic proposition in a tensive balance, reminding theology of its interpretive limitations and confounding its hubris. Divinity is, if nothing else, free. And this means that it is also free of theology and doctrine.

Thus, the vulnerability of feminist religious experience is a temptation toward closure that reduces divinity to the content of specific experiences, a temptation that comes naturally from the elemental passion for reality. It is, as Tillich declared, a temptation toward falsification, although it is not, as he believed, a falsification that comes from the constructive impulse but from the idolatrous impulse toward closure.

The categories of both thematic and specific experience are foundational to feminist theologies, grounding their claims against patriarchal erasures and providing a vital spring of information and sustenance from which women, nondominant men, and feminist men can draw. "I know what I have experienced" is an abrupt, absolutistic claim that cannot be denied without new erasure and colonization. Unmodified by skepticism, however, it becomes tyrannical. This is the core strength and the vulnerability of religious experience.

Revelatory experiences of divine presence, especially in the shapes and forms of feminist constructions, must be taken seriously by theologians despite the real consequences of backlash because of what the fact of the experiences, apart from their specific content, suggests about divine activity and multiplicity. This extremely important distinction clarifies how experiences of divine presence should inform theological reflection. The specific contents of feminist religious experiences are important in that they may be real expressions of real divinity. But because the metaphoric exemption also reminds us of the fallibility of our interpretations, feminist theologies cannot treat the specific contents of religious experiences as normative or even revelatory in terms of enduring descriptions of divinity or in terms of *enduring* correspondence. They can only acknowledge that the divine chooses to correspond to metaphor here, in this place, in that chalice, in those hands, or in that mute mountain. And they must then apply themselves to the task of understanding what this relationship of intimacy between the divine and the fragile world of experience means in this generation.

The fact that experience is a constitutive foundation in feminist theologies does not mean therefore that the task of those theologies is to adjudicate between competing claims of particular religious experiences. Feminist theologies are competent to explore more deeply the relevant structures of experience in general and to adjudicate competing claims at that abstracted level. What results from this argument for religious experience is a corrective for the primary negation of the metaphoric exemption. In essence, constructive feminist theologies do not want to be trapped by the metaphoric exemption into a final, Durkheimian reduction of divinity to human social processes or into a final, Barthian negation of the possibilities for divine coming forth in/to human consciousness. Constructive feminist theologies, therefore, must avoid functional social constructionism's ultimate *denial* of the possibility of authentic and revelatory religious experience even when that experience confounds normative traditions.

So long as constructive feminist theologies concern themselves with women's experience and experiences in some way, and concern themselves with the spiritually focused interests and needs of feminists living and enacting these theologies, they cannot shrink from the implications of their constructive proposals. Their proposals might engage women and men in powerful religious experiences that are related to the constructive content of those proposals. Assuming the divine to have some real existence apart from human imagining and to relate itself to the world in some way, feminist theologians do not create or re-create divine existence, intention, or activity in itself. In this, the metaphoric exemption is an essential and accurate correction. But the opposite correction means that feminist theologians do not through negation control divine existence, intention, or activity by deferring it.

To the extent that theology is not a matter of proof, neither is it a matter of disproof—a point that contemporary theologians occasionally forget. This is the primary negation of the metaphoric exemption (and negative theology) balanced by the correction of religious experience. If religious experiences of the divine are allowed the possibility of being real (even if we cannot adjudicate between the true and the delusional), then a theological method that concerns itself with experience at a foundational level must somehow take into account the possibility of correspondence.

CONCLUSION

I can now describe constructive feminist theologies as constituted by a fundamental tension between the negation carried by the metaphoric exemption and the assertion carried by experiential claims. The poles of this tension are mutually corrective rather than oppositional; they constitute the foundations of feminist theologies. But also, being dynamic, they make those theologies vulnerable. The vulnerability emerges when too much of one ends up negating rather than correcting the other. Thus, a true tensive balance carries with it for each of the two taproots in feminist theologies a corresponding corrective negation. The metaphoric exemption negates the knowability of divinity, both because of divine greatness (as in classical negative theology) and because of epistemological embeddedness in social construction (as in modern functional social constructionism). Experiential confession, on the other hand, negates the metaphoric exemption's reduction of divinity to incomprehensibility, asserting the power of the divine to be fully present, to embody metaphors, to take on human constructions of temporality and spatiality, and to do so sometimes in fully comprehensible and concrete, if transient and multiple, ways.

Both sources of constructive feminist theologies are mutually constituting, mutually correcting, and mutually vulnerable. The vulnerability attending the metaphoric exemption is the negation of divine existence and freedom, while the vulnerability attending religious experience is confusion of correspondence, or attempts to make divinity permanently and coherently tied to specific constructions. Vulnerability itself in feminist theologies is never, however, the problem because vulnerability makes its strengths possible. Any attempt to remove vulnerability removes the strength. This can occur when religious experience becomes universally normative or when constructive feminist theologies drift too far into the dismissals of metaphoric exemption to protect themselves from charges of heresy.

From the dynamic strength of their foundations in the skeptical deferrals of metaphor and the resilient affirmations of experiential confession, feminist theologies as critically constructive endeavors come more clearly into focus. If feminist theologies are constituted as I have suggested here, they do not start from doctrinal claims of any kind but make all such claims available to the hermeneutic of suspicion and available to the "stuff" of divine embodiment. They can be, therefore, more thoroughly consistent in their criticism because they need not gloss any doctrinal assumption. But they are also more freely open to the revelatory capacity even of traditional notions of divine presence, since none of these notions are universally normative. None restrict divine freedom in intimate commerce with the world.

A sharp eye will note the formation of some assumptions about divinity here, principally its ontological status as "there" and its freedom. Feminist theologies, founded on the dynamic and corrective interplay between metaphoric exemption and experiential confession, still must make some founding assumptions about divinity itself in order to proceed with their theology as theology. But how clearly articulated are these assumptions, and most important, how well do they navigate the confluence of metaphoric exemption and experiential confession? Assumptions that feminist theologians are willing to make about divinity itself, shaped like river clay by the carving insistence of both tributary sources, can better serve women and men who put feminist theologies into spiritual practice and can also more coherently defend them (though not protect them) from the sting of backlash.

Metaphoric exemption and experiential confession form the poles between which a bright, tensive web can be cast. It can hold spiritual imagination and embodiment, idea and untheorizable encounter. As the dynamic shape of feminist theological foundations comes into focus, the question that emerges is theological to its core. The mutual correction of metaphoric exemption and experiential confession supports some assumptions about divinity better than others. Given the living, vibrant push and pull of this interaction, how shall we then speak of the divine? How can feminist theologians re-imagine the divine itself in ways that meet the rigorous critiques of these twin roots? By way of conclusion, it is to this question, and suggestions for an answer, that I now turn.

CHAPTER SEVEN

Beyond Monotheism

I am surprised to be human,
to have senses and desires,
to have a mind and a body,
and an expiration date.

I am learning not to fill
my day with footsteps,
to sit and even hate stillness,
to learn why I fear
the lofty solitude of space.

I can't separate myself,
I feel the constant dripping of spirit,
I feel the fire of my maker
like a pilot light
and the purity of warmth
inside me trying to
create something that
isn't cold and undrinkable.
—Dianne Bilyak[1]

G IVEN THEIR MUTUALLY CORRECTING FOUNDATIONS, I suggest that feminist theologies at their best support assumptions of multiplicity in
their concepts of divinity. Together, their two root commitments give shape
to a theological task that, on the one hand, appreciates the imaginative and
poetic nature of human apprehension (metaphoric exemption) and, on the
other, appreciates the vitality and specificity with which the divine addresses particular communities and persons (experiential confession). In
the end, neither commitment can fully support exclusivist notions of di-

vinity because exclusivity implies a limitation of divine scope and a certainty of divine correspondence to exclusive notions. Both the metaphoric exemption and the robust experiential confession deny such limitation and such correspondence. And I suggest that this denial must include the most exclusively limiting theological construction of all—monotheism.

Monotheism is a theological construction that affirms divine greatness by seeing the existence of other divine realities as competition or denying the existence of other divine realities altogether. Although prior to the eighth century B.C.E., Yahweh was a tribal god among other tribal gods, he became increasingly triumphal through the generations, culminating in his declaration of superiority to all others on Mount Sinai. Regina Schwartz suggests in her provocative critique that monotheism arises in situations of scarcity in which the harsh realities of tooth and claw determine survival. It is common sense that perception of scarcity necessitates winners and losers. It breeds competition, which adjudicates between winners and losers. Yet scarcity is a perception that has nothing to do with actual means for human survival since cultures with vast material wealth still operate under principles of scarcity (such as the modern United States) and cultures with great poverty do not (such as the majority of rural India).

Scarcity is, in addition, a problematic means of understanding divine reality, yet it characterizes the monotheistic traditions that compete for divine favor. When divine favor is selectively given, as Schwartz points out that it is repeatedly in biblical narratives, competition for scarce rewards is tragic and ugly. Ancient and modern competitions for power, land, money, prestige, and ethnic or social identity are "encoded in the Bible as a principle of Oneness (one land, one people, one nation) and in monotheistic thinking (one Deity)." Schwartz argues that the ultimate claim of the One "becomes a demand of exclusive allegiance that threatens with the violence of exclusion."[2]

The triumphalist assumptions embedded in exclusivist notions of divinity raise disturbing specters of imperialistic violence. These specters are particularly poignant at the close of the twentieth century, one of the bloodiest on record. Feminist theologies have begun over the years to entertain the possibility that monotheism itself, the doctrinal heart of the religious traditions of the West, is part of the problem. The One emerges in feminist theories and theologies as a colonizing entity, leading some feminist theologians to suggest that monotheism itself is problematic. In some cases, such critiques guide them past theism altogether to poststructuralist and postmodern critiques of the very possibilities of presence.[3]

For the most part, however, the construction of monotheism in twentieth-century theology strives to undercut what Schwartz calls its violent legacy by turning monotheism (apart from the postmodern problem of presence) into a universal basis for judgment of worldly powers. A unified and unifying relationship to the one deity affirms a single human or worldly identity and orientation in the cosmos. Such theology is concerned pragmatically with human claims of allegiance in an era of fascists and ideologues, ethnic cleansings and genocides. A single supreme deity clarifies the proper orientation of otherwise widely disparate people and relativizes their potentially explosive differences under the aegis of its commanding and just supremacy.

The universalistic and inclusive idea of one God is that of a single Sovereign whose very existence humbles all human kings; a solitary Governor who unites nations; a Perfection under whom all ideologies are imperfect; and a supreme, if lonely, Parent who erases distinctions by loving without distinction.[4] But even this universalistic notion of the One excludes difference at ultimate levels of reality insofar as it ends up erasing particularities or substantive diversity in concepts of the divine. To claim universal monotheism by saying that all gods are really one God potentially resolves problems of incompatibility at the level of ultimate reality, but it also erases the incompatibilities altogether as if they do not exist. This is akin to earlier dismissals of theological content in anthropology's search for the "nature of all religions."[5] Ideas of universal monotheism that erase differences in concepts of divine existence also undermine or deny possibilities for human apprehension of that existence in terms of its freedom, embodiment, and participation in variable worlds. Such renderings of monotheism are intended to help us see that the differences over which we agonize and fight are petty, and to clarify human and nonhuman identities in an essentially unified and internally related cosmos. A single divine being who presides over all of the cosmos indicates the existence of a unified cosmos and puts all human agonies and egocentrisms in a humbling light. That is the theory at any rate.

It is a pity that monotheistic cultures have historically had such a difficult time understanding themselves in these humbled and unifying terms, however. They seem more often to associate their monotheistic beliefs with boundaries of exclusion and imperialism rather than with indications of cosmic unity. The one God is understood to be not only superior to all other concepts and experiences of divine existence, but "He" exclusively opposes all others by colonizing and absorbing them, or by outright denying them.

Because universal monotheism theoretically requires strong negative claims of infinity, inconceivability, and eternity to maintain its universality in a world of particularity, anything less than superlative and solitary greatness can undermine its universality and so must be rejected as material for imagining and describing experiences of divinity. If there is only one God, there is only one truth. Particularity, embodiment, and finitude all undermine this concept, as Plato insisted many centuries ago. So monotheism ends up protecting divine greatness through denials of particularity, finitude, conceivability, and temporality, which in turn end up as denials of multiplicity. The modern theological articulation of the metaphoric exemption supports this, of course, allowing particular, finite, conceivable, and temporal images into theology precisely because they do *not* express or imagine *real* divinity. God conceived as One thus ineradicably remains in heaven, safe from the messy particularity of the world. There appears to be room for only One at the top after all.

Although the theological aim of universal monotheism is to dissolve boundaries between peoples and to assert a kind of mystical unity to the disparate and dissenting parts of the cosmos, one reason that it does not tend to translate into popular understanding or into social or political practice may be the scriptural and doctrinal traditions that emphasize the exclusive over-againstness of the divine rather than its possibilities for a mystical unity that does not diminish multiplicity in sacred realities. Indeed, the Hebrew, Christian, and Qur'anic texts speak over and over of a deity who proclaims himself superior to and exclusive of others. The First Commandment that God gives to Moses, "You shall have no other gods before me," sets the monotheistic standard, picked up in the Christian claim that there is no way to heaven but through Jesus, and in the Muslim Shahada in which "there is no God but Allah."

It is not that monotheism itself is the problem, although the idea of a single divine being has troubled and fueled theological inquiry for centuries. Monotheism itself does not negate the possibility of divine presence by any means, as the Jewish tradition of spirit and the Christian trinitarian tradition attest. It would certainly overstate the case to claim that all scriptural and doctrinal sources for the monotheistic construction are purely exclusivist. The prophet Isaiah's messianic visions suggest a universal peace brought about by an equally universalistic deity: "They will not hurt or destroy on all my holy mountain; for the earth will be full of the knowledge of the Lord as the waters cover the sea."[6] But even here the knowledge of the Lord that fills the earth is knowledge of the monotheistic conception of deity that denies other sacred realities. This is a slightly more inclusive understanding of monotheism because it absorbs all that is into itself, but it is still a denial of divine multiplicity.

Christian theology is traditionally slightly more open to an inclusive idea of divinity than its Jewish and Muslim counterparts, having already modified strong monotheism in the divinity of Jesus. Paul, for example, told the Greeks that their preexisting altar to the unknown God was really an altar to "the God who made the world and everything in it, he who is Lord of heaven and earth, [who] does not live in shrines made by human hands."[7] There is certainly a bit more wiggle room here for understanding the single deity who made the world and everything in it as inclusive, rather than exclusive, of other ideas of divinity. The history of Christian evangelism and practice has tended to incorporate this approach to monotheism, over the centuries seeking to convert non-Christians with the argument that their indigenous ideas of sacred reality are fundamentally encompassed by the one sacred reality of Christian theology. Generous tolerance of non-Christian cultures that refused to revise their own ancient beliefs in the evangelists' terms has not, however, been a hallmark of Christian history.

Islam is more consistently exclusive in its affirmations of monotheism. Until the modern era and the rise of fundamentalism, however, Muslims interpreted Sura 109 in the Qur'an, which ends "to you your religion and to me my religion," as a basis for tolerance of difference in belief, if not difference in actual sacred constructions. Despite the acknowledged existence of other religious ideas of divinity, the unity of the divine in Islam is expressed in its complete comprehension and absorption of all that is, a characteristic common to each of the three main monotheistic faiths. But God's comprehension of all that is does not include other sacred realities and deities because they are denied existence altogether. Islamic scholar Kenneth Cragg explains the profound Islamic negation of divine multiplicity in terms of the prophet Muhammad's crusade against the polytheism of his neighbors in Mecca: "The Prophet's mission was not to proclaim God's existence but to deny the existence of all lesser deities. . . . It was not enough to confess that God was; He must be recognized as God alone. All the partners whom the pagan Arabs associated with God were truly nonentities. They did not exist and they had no right to recognition."[8] Monotheism so constructed is incompatible with multiplicity. It is contrasted to, rather than inclusive of, polytheism and possibilities for multiplicity in divine existence.

Because monotheistic doctrines are historically so exclusivist, ethnically bounded, and unitary instead of inclusive, Schwartz argues that the monotheistic idea is intolerant of multiple allegiances and so engenders intolerance of multiplicity and difference in social and political life. Philosophically speaking, what cannot be resolved to the One is rejected, and the One is itself defined by exclusion, a move that can take violent forms. The numerous and horrific ethnic, ideological, and religiously motivated wars of the twentieth century may be explicit examples of such exclusion at work—the creation and the valorization of a unitary identity through violent acts of expulsion. Correlation is not necessarily causation, but the correlation of monotheism with violence in pursuit of power, identity, supremacy, and coherent unity in a universe of divergent cultures and worlds of meaning is relevant to the questions that theology must ask in its constructive task.

THE CHALLENGE OF MONOTHEISM TO FEMINIST THEOLOGIES

The problem with monotheism for feminist theologies is more narrowly contemporary if we look at it in light of the corrective balance between metaphoric exemption and experiential confession. Monotheism is a metaphor. Monotheism also traditionally shores up negative theology in defense of divine greatness. In constructive feminist theologies, however, the metaphoric exemption provides more than enough corrective to the confusions of identity between real divinity and the constructs of human creativity. That is, the metaphor of monotheism is not necessary for iconoclastic caution. If it remains as a condition for feminist theological constructions, it functions as a pre-given doctrinal limit to which new metaphors must conform rather than providing any methodological coherence to theological construction. Feminist theologies that are self-conscious of their grounding in the metaphoric exemption and experiential confession are hard-pressed to support a normative claim to one metaphor above all others. They must recognize that the metaphoric construction of monotheism, while still powerfully resonant within the great traditions of Christianity, Judaism, and Islam (and indeed still functioning in these traditions as a confessional condition for membership), is not exempt from confusions of correspondence itself, contrary to the demands of the metaphoric exemption. What is more, the monotheistic construction of divinity supports what McFague suggests is a historic "passion to remove God from any real connection to the world," contrary to the freedom inherent in experiential confession.[9]

Robust feminist experiences of divinity, even if they are understood only as correctives to the metaphoric exemption's tendency to final negation, still suggest that divinity itself might be too big, too much with us, for the exclusivist metaphor of monotheism and its constraints. This does not mean, of course, that monotheism is therefore a wrong or incorrect metaphor for divinity. It may simply be incomplete and too easily corrupted by the totalizing tendencies of human hopes for certainty, the elemental passion for reality. Monotheism is complicit in the misogynistic religious history of the West, and as a metaphor for divinity, it is incomplete.

Still, the idea of monotheism solves numerous general epistemological problems by positing a unitary coherence to ultimate reality and by essentially denying the existence of other possibilities. Traditionally, the one God exists and has being in distinction to the messy particularity and temporality of the world. The conceptual distinction between a single deity and multiple worlds undergirds the monotheistic idea. But this distinction binds theology and ideas of the divine to abstract ideas and to dominant tendencies toward imperialism, which is an irritation that feminist theologians have rubbed raw. The problem is this: if divinity is truly embodied in any concrete way as feminist theologies often want to assert, the idea of monotheism as an overarching principle of theological and political unity threatens to crumble. The God who is One in a universal sense cannot remain both One and universal when embodied, since concrete embodiment by definition is particularistic and bounded by its existence in space and time. Any embodiment that is not particularistic embodiment—a here-and-now kind of thing that is both real and present—is abstract embodiment. The Torah is, theologically speaking, abstract embodiment of divine presence in the written and spoken word, though extreme caution must be taken with such a statement. The Qur'an is much the same thing. The limitation of divine embodiment in Christianity to a single historical figure and to the figurative embodiment in church membership draws boundaries around the scope of divine particularity that effectively limits divine universality.

If what is divine actually participates in time and space, occasionally becoming embodied in real, concrete stuff, then presumably divinity can become limited in some way, diminished and no longer capable of a global or cosmic idea.[10] To be sure, this is an assumption. There may well be globally unifying things that theologians can suggest about divinity in general without resorting to the restrictions that universal monotheism places on divine freedom and unlimitedness, including the freedom to be particular and limited in the world. If theologians are willing to make the ontological wager that divinity exists, and even more so to assume that it truly is beyond all imagining yet is "closer than breathing, and nearer than hands and feet,"[11] they must be open to the challenges that accompany a full re-imagining of transcendence in terms of unlimitedness and of embodiment in terms of multiplicity. The demands of the metaphoric exemption insist upon unlimitedness, and the demands of experiential confession insist upon embodiment.

Historically, exclusively universal monotheism falls short of the requirements of both metaphoric exemption and experiential confession because it pushes divine being into an abstract cell of One and reinforces the bars with "final" revelations that are universal, absolute, and complete.[12] Therefore, challenges accompany a truly balanced poise between metaphoric exemption and experiential confession because theology cannot begin with particular ecclesial commitments or doctrinal constructions such as monotheism. Doctrines of exclusive monotheism cannot form the starting place for theology grounded in the metaphoric exemption and experiential confession because such doctrinal commitments are themselves constructions. Like all the constructions of normative religious expression, they cannot escape the rigor of critical evaluation. All commitments and constructions come under the critical gaze of the metaphoric exemption and so cannot form the starting place for theologies that see deep problems of racism, misogyny, and ethnocentrism in those very traditions.

This move to a nondoctrinal starting place reflects a shift in the general work of theology from its traditional role as interpreter of denominational church doctrine to interpreter of divine activity in the broader context of human and nonhuman life. Indeed, church doctrine from Scripture to polity is as much the object of white, womanist, *mujerista,* and other feminist critiques as it is the base from which they may begin. Nevertheless, even though they make use of both the metaphoric exemption and warrants from women's experiences to clear space for their own constructive work, some feminist theologians may find it difficult to accept fully the foundation upon which their theology stands since it displaces all doctrine and tradition to the realm of historical construction.

A gardening metaphor may clarify this difficult situation. The distinction that gardeners make between weeds and flowers is ultimately based on what they want to harvest. Any plant that interferes with the harvest is therefore a weed. There is no essential weedness—one person's weed is often another's flower. So the distinction is pragmatic, determined by the gardener. Feminist theologians are in the difficult position of knowing that the distinctions they make between bad metaphors and good ones are also determined pragmatically, since both "good" and "bad" are socially constructed. Because of the metaphoric exemption, they have lost any basis on which to claim that better ideas and metaphors are closer to divine essence. This could be depressing if the goal of theological construction were to describe that essence in authoritative, universally normative, and final terms. Authoritative finality and universality, however, are the first things to go in the acids of metaphoric exemption. And this is not a problem if divinity is understood metaphorically in terms of multiplicity and responsive participation in the world. Multiplicity and responsive participation are authoritative and universal only insofar as they allow for divine response and for multiple embodiments. They do not determine response or embodiment.

In a move that may appear alarmingly Barthian, I suggest that the only normative statement that feminist theologies can make about divinity is that it is free. Much more free, in fact, than Barth himself would allow. The divine freedom that I propose understands transcendence as unlimitedness and embodiment in terms of multiplicity. For those whose sense of belonging depends upon the exclusion of others, the vitality of divinity conceived in terms of transcendent unlimitedness and embodied multiplicity is a stumbling block. Transcendent unlimitedness does not allow the restrictions that monotheism places upon divine expression, and multiple embodiments undermine the claims and control of final revelations. This is no small challenge to traditional thinking about divinity in the modern Western world. In psychological terms, exclusivity in concepts of the divine provides comfort and protection to the insecure by clearly marking identity and belonging. In social terms, it does much the same thing by clearly marking boundaries and rules of acceptance and rejection.

One way to look at this is to see exclusivist monotheistic religions and their doctrines as jealous lovers who would attempt possession by making their beloved (the divine) chaste. The commandment that "you shall have no other," seen in its social constructedness, goes both ways. Final revelations, exclusively disembodied transcendences, exclusively abstracted embodiments, biblical literalism, and doctrinal certainty all mask the fear and hubris of the insecure lover who wants to know that there is no other in the beloved's heart. It may be too difficult for some to realize that their own assertions about divine greatness and experiential confession suggest a divinity that not only exists, not only is related to the universe in meaningful ways, but is promiscuous in its intimate relations with the world.

Divine exclusivity, whether it is understood in terms of embodiment or of transcendence, cannot withstand the rigor of metaphoric exemption or the vitality of experiential confession. This is a problem only when theology gets into the business of making universally normative claims about an idea or metaphor. If, for example, the instruction that Yahweh gives to Moses on Mount Sinai, that Moses and his people shall have no other God but the one speaking to him, is interpreted to mean that *no one* in all space or time shall have another God (which, incidentally, has been the dominant interpretation), theology has the task of making the interpretation stick. An experiential confession such as this becomes, in the hands of Jewish, Christian, and Islamic theologies, a universally normative and exclusivist claim about the divine. The only way that theology can make such a triumphalist and universal interpretation stick is to give it the status of a final, infallible revelation.

That is why feminist theologies must account for the reasons they choose to accept a constructed idea of universal and exclusive monotheism as normatively true—as a taken-for-granted delimiter of their constructive tasks—while discarding so many other ideas from the tradition. The epistemological foundations of feminist theologies in the metaphoric exemption make uncritical acceptance of monotheistic metaphors a shaky proposition. If even part of the reasoning behind an interpretive theological choice is, as it is for so many feminist theologians, human or global flourishing and just relations in the world, it would seem that exclusively normative interpretations and doctrinal claims would be the first things to go.

In effect, the root commitments of feminist theologies in skepticism and lived experience put the exclusivist claims of tradition and creed in jeopardy. Persons unwilling to subject certain of their doctrinal traditions to the metaphoric exemption may hope thereby to retain claims to exclusive revelations. But if they make use of the metaphoric exemption at all, they become caught in the contradictions associated with picking and choosing what they will and will not deconstruct in the doctrinal tradition. This is quite close to the dilemma of biblical literalists who must pick and choose which passages of Scripture are clear instructions and which passages are understood only by God.[13]

The metaphoric exemption reminds us that divinity transcends even our dearest interpretations and images, some of which may be required for entrance into congregational membership. If to be a Christian, Muslim, or Jew means that I must reduce divinity to monotheism and its attendant final revelations, then I am faced with a choice between having membership in the religious community and regarding divinity as something that transcends and confounds human interpretation. Also, if to be a Christian, Muslim, or Jew means that divine embodiment occurs only in the abstraction of words and final events validated by ecclesial authorities, then I must choose between being identified with one of these religions and regarding divinity as truly free, responsive, and intimate in ongoing relationship to the world.

Ironically, feminist theologies that do not accept the full implications of their foundations in skepticism and in experiential confession are unable to assert either transcendence or embodiment in the fullest, most vital senses of the words. In theologies that are structured by metaphoric exemption and experiential confession, transcendence and embodiment are both more compelling and more complete. The idea of transcendence is expressed through the metaphoric exemption because *all* language, ideas, and images of the divine are human constructions. Truly divine realities, if they exist, transcend all such constructions. All religions, doctrines, creeds, traditions, and interpretations are partial, fallible, suggestive, and imaginative. They do not represent the divine itself in the sense that they comprehend or express divinity. But some, for a time, might.

The metaphoric exemption in feminist theologies suggests a more radical transcendence in which even ideas of revealed doctrine like monotheism and the Ten Commandments, like the Beatitudes and the resurrection of Jesus, like the Five Pillars of Islam, fall short of presence and correspondence in any definitional or enduring sense. All such foundational doctrines are generously and unalterably mixed with the leaven of social construction. They are accounts of powerful divine–human relationality and as such invite attention and perhaps even devotion unless one chooses to see them as delusions. But on what basis can one tell? There is no basis other than traditional authority for discerning the difference, and because of the constructedness of traditional authority, there is no basis for saying that only one type of experience or interpretation is correct.

In any case, the transcendence embedded in the metaphoric exemption insists that no idea or doctrine or revelation is exclusive or final because we cannot claim to know divine reality to that extent. Accepting a revelatory experience of divine presence as exclusive or final assumes a level of certainty across all time and space that cannot be supported by the skeptical insights of historicism. Such acceptance assumes that the divine limits itself by enacting final revelations (which it might) and that we know this to be true (which we do not); it assumes that divinity is One (which it might be) and that we know this to be true (which we do not); and it assumes that the recipients of the exclusive revelation heard correctly (which they might have) and interpreted correctly for the rest of creation (which we can never know). According to the metaphoric exemption, turning "might be's" into certainty is insupportable wishful thinking.

A double negative is the closest we can come to affirmation about divine oneness in the balanced poise between metaphoric exemption and robust experiential confession. Just as feminist theologies get themselves into internal contradictions when they assume monotheism to be a sound starting point, they also cannot claim that the divine might not, after all is said and done, indeed be One. Feminist theologians concerned with concepts of divinity must address the fact that *what we can know* of divinity, which comes to us from the multiplicities of experiential confession, is not singular. In addition, feminist theologies that insist upon exclusive doctrines such as absolute monotheism are unable to affirm divine embodiment except in the abstract senses, such as Word, Torah, or Qur'an, or a single historical figure like Jesus, or universalized concepts like "church" and even "world." Abstract embodiment is tentative embodiment. It is not messy, fleshy, transient, and resilient, like bodies or elements with scent and consistency. It is not particular, and it resists the temporality that conditions bodies. But anything more concrete than abstract embodiment threatens the exclusivity of the monotheistic idea. Embodied embodiment is everywhere embodiment, since the universe and its multitude of inhabitants mostly have mineral, animal, or vegetable bodies that interact vigorously. They circle, attract, crash, sniff, elbow, repulse, and exchange. Conceiving of divinity as embodied means conceiving of it as *really* participating (not just nominally participating in a panentheistic way) in this multitudinous array. Given all the possibilities for divine embodiment and multiplicity, abstraction seems the least defensible, not to mention the least engaging.

But a full notion of divine embodiment that is freely expressive in the world and absolute, universal monotheism are conceptually incompatible. Monotheism as a universal and exclusive norm is an abstraction that can abide only abstract embodiment. The Christian claim of Jesus' divinity may be the closest thing to concrete divine embodiment in a monotheistic tradition, and it is the theological basis of the schism between Christianity and its monotheistic siblings. Judaism maintains that the divine in a historical human form defies the iconoclastic requirements of the one God, while Christianity maintains that this one form transforms and determines divine relatedness to the world without undermining divine transcendence or unity.

The Christian idea would work if the particular embodiment of the divine in Jesus was not exclusive or final. Its very exclusivity and finality assert theological hubris and diminish divine freedom in the same way that limiting the divine to disembodied otherness does. Limiting divine embodiment to a single form in a single point in time puts Christian theology in the difficult position of accounting for the apparent contradiction between embodiment and divine greatness. The Trinity of Father, Son, and Holy Spirit is a tentative concession to polytheism as a means of accounting for the multiplicity embedded in any concept of divine embodiment. Christians fought among themselves for centuries over this dilemma and concluded their arguments with the nonsensical ruling that the three are really one, neither polytheistic nor subordinate to a higher singular deity. Monotheism remains a Christian doctrine by virtue of ecclesial fiat rather than internal coherence.

The confusing monotheistic doctrine of the Christian Trinity is an example of divine embodiment distorted by the required singularity and universality of God. Exclusivist monotheism cannot tolerate divine embodiment that occurs in multiple ways and in various forms. Primarily, it cannot tolerate the implication embedded in multiple embodiments that divinity may not be One, or that its unity may not be comprehensible in monotheistic terms. Contrary to historic monotheistic fears about paganism, conceptions of divine reality that can include stones, pieces of writing, loaves of bread, glances, or things discernible only to trees do not have to risk loss of transcendence and greatness through the particularity of the here and now. For the divine to be here and now, or variously embodied with variable intents, reveals nothing certain about the completeness of divine revelations or the scope of divine existence. Such an open conception of divine embodiment enhances the greatness, vitality, and wonder of divine relationships to the world, to the community, and to the individual because they are not limited or conditional.

Concepts of divinity that incorporate multiple rather than monotheistic claims re-imagine the divine-world relationship in mature terms that do not mandate exclusive or final revelations in order to ensure devotion or religious identity. Indeed, concepts of divine multiplicity offer little solace to theological jealousy that isolates and ultimately destroys the very divine greatness that it seeks to protect. Revelatory experience in which divinity is present and comprehensible, fully embodying a temporal and finite thing, is problematic for theology only when theology limits divine existence to eternal or final or exclusive abstractions. For a divine reality to be fully alive and present in a corporeal form (which means that it is then finite and temporary) does not exclude the possibility of other divine realities that may be eternal or incorporeal. The only thing it does exclude is the possibility of a divine reality that is entirely exclusive. Divinity as an adjectival concept, as a quality or attribute of truly sacred reality, is the unity that makes multiple divine realities or occurrences compatible with transcendent unlimitedness.

It behooves feminist theologies to address the fear behind assertions that the divine must be absolutely and exclusively One at the expense of voluptuous embodiment and divine responsiveness to metaphoric constructions. I have suggested that absolute monotheism is a kind of prison that identifies the boundaries of belonging; a chastity belt on divine possibility that has to do with the insecurity of persons who understand belonging only through possession and exclusion. Some like Kathleen Sands have argued that exclusivist claims to divine oneness represent a nostalgic longing for absolutes that must regress to a concept of One for coherence. And there is always the simple social coercion of religious affiliation and the central creeds that make one a Christian, Jew, or Muslim, against which divine multiplicity stands as heresy (or at least grounds for social exclusion).

Sharon Welch's helpful notion of the "ethic of control" offers another possible explanation for the fear that undergirds monotheistic assumptions. She suggests that Western Euro-American (monotheistic) cultures are generally motivated by values and intents that valorize the final and the complete, rather than the partial and the ongoing. An ethic of control evaluates potential actions on the certainty of their outcomes, rather than on the potential for further actions that they may create.[14] This notion is relevant to the problem of monotheism in that monotheistic concepts offer conceptual control through certainty and finality vis-à-vis divine revelation or embodiment. A variously embodied divinity that maintains free and intimate relations in the universe and that even dares to contradict itself (if it is One) or other divine realities (if it is not) is divinity that will not be controlled. And divinity out of (whose?) control is an embarrassment to theology that is intent upon absolute certainty.

What happens when a feminist theology threatens the most basic creeds of the tradition and community for which and to whom it attempts to speak? Backlash, certainly. This is the risk that theology, as honest inquiry into the roots and shapes of human response to divine relationship to the world, must take. It is by no means a new risk for feminist theologians or for people exploring feminist religious ideas. Feminist theologies have always claimed a pragmatic grounding of their work in the lived experiences of fully embodied communities, often in opposition to and sometimes at the expense of traditional claims. The task is not always comfortable.

Feminist theologies remain, after all, committed to redressing the wrongs that patriarchal religious ideas have done in the name of divine authority. In this, the metaphoric exemption and the negative theological tradition have served to great effect. But the challenges of the *via negativa,* whether as classical ontology or as metaphoric exemption, remain what they have been throughout the centuries. Worship and experience rarely, if ever, work negatively. By itself and uncorrected, the negation carried by the metaphoric exemption must always negate revelatory experience that gives specificity and substance to images of the divine, leading to a theological negation or trivialization of religious experience itself. And we see this throughout twentieth-century theology, from neoorthodox assertions of exclusive monotheism against the dangers of idolatrous experience to feminist theological assertions of the metaphoric exemption in contradiction to lived experiences of heretically concrete divine realities.

The correction that these so-called traditional theologies attempt to establish against idolatrous correspondence between ideology and God, between church and divinity, between personal experience and normative revelation, and between one group's historical experience and ecclesial authority, are lost on the women and men who experience divinity in transient particularity and uncanny presence. The unremitting negations of exclusivist monotheism or of uncorrected metaphoric exemption are themselves idolatrous insofar as they equate one type of monotheistic construction more closely with correspondence, negating experiences of communal and relational sacramentalism, negating ongoing embodiments and comprehensible presences, and ultimately negating the authority of women's experiences simply as real. It is unthinkable to most feminists that feminist theologies can do away with religious experience even in its problematic particularity since they understand so well the corrective that this experience provides against the important but dangerous abstractions of negation.

Were feminist theologians not conscious of this correction and were they entirely pragmatic and able to dispense with the assertions of real divinity altogether, feminist goals of human and ecological flourishing would suffice for theology, and a cynical reduction of divinity to utility would not be a problem as a means to those goals. But feminists who take constructive theology seriously, as we have seen, tend to be pragmatic *and* committed to assumptions of sacred realities. With perhaps a very few exceptions, feminist theologians do not want to give up as one of their aims the worship of or appropriate attention to a divinity that is real.

Constructive feminist theologians, even as they retreat to the metaphoric exemption to hedge against charges of heresy, do not want to fully negate the aim of appropriate attention to a divinity that is understood to be real, unlimited, multiple, and responsive. But what is a feminist theologian in the context of traditional doctrinal constraints to do? Orthodox monotheism demands an absolute rejection of referential insinuations of correspondence, although orthodox Christianity, even in its Protestant forms, has little trouble with the referential insinuations of masculine images. The metaphoric exemption appears to be the only bulwark for feminist theologians in traditional religions against rampant polytheism and paganism (the very accusation made against them by conservative Christian champions of backlash). What I suggest about experience and multiplicity, however, is beyond the pale of traditional monotheism. Experiences of divinity in the world reveal the limitedness of monotheistic constructions and embodied divine unlimitedness. This revelation may be too much for some feminist theologians, even though they then diminish the coherence of their foundational warrants for doing feminist theology.

Polytheism and paganism, while they may be compatible outgrowths of a methodological balance between metaphoric exemption and experiential confession (so long as they do not limit divinity in normative ways to particular ideas, things, or rituals), are themselves culturally constituted labels with little real contemporary content in mainstream Western theology or culture.[15] They have become effective boundary posts for traditional religions and are subsequently seldom examined or analyzed as such. The lack of specific content but powerful resonance and association that polytheism and paganism both have in mainstream consciousness with a number of vague sedimented images (mostly female) make them useful supports of a status quo orthodoxy. The cultural association of both with heresy lends support to exclusivist monotheism and disguises its constructedness by confusing metaphoric content (the construction of monotheism) with foundational warrants for traditional theology. But monotheism is a construction, and it puts even neoorthodox theologies intoxicated with divine greatness into contradiction when it comes to unlimitedness and freedom. It does not protect against idolatry, but is a form of idolatry when it is exclusive. It does not humble the human ego or will to dominate, but exalts the human mind and dominating will that can conceive of a One superior to all, yet is shocked into incomprehending awe by multiplicity without hegemony.

The problem for feminists in traditional religions, however, will not go away so long as exclusivist monotheism is a requirement for membership. Feminist theologians know that their speech about Gaia, goddesses, rituals, sacraments of milk and honey, erotic power, embodiment, and so forth rings many of the associational bells of polytheism and paganism. This is so much the case that many feminist theologians believe that their constructions, without the strongest metaphoric exemption, send them spiraling out into the "pagan" exterior. The problem is, the pagan exterior is the dirt that defines the purity of the monotheistic One; it is the disorder that reveals the patriarchal order. Paganism will always be attached to feminist theologies no matter how orthodox feminist theologians try to make their propositions sound. Having transgressed boundaries of white masculine divinized purity at the very first steps, feminist theologies are always already pagan because their commitments to inclusion and multiplicity place them always outside the exclusions of the One. Deep levels of ambivalence within feminist theologies about monotheism stem from the illusion that the One will admit feminist multiplicity and experiential confession without dissolving its divinized purity or traditional, comforting exclusions.

Nostalgia for the monotheistic One is the illusion that the divinized core of monotheism can bear the multiplicity of embodied metaphors and still remain essentially One. This is, in the end, illusion. The pagan exterior is the boundary on which feminist theologies walk; it is the vitality that

feminist theologies bear. Without it, the new constructions that feminist
theologies offer merely drape the Father God in drag; they do not break
through or transgress upon the limitedness of patriarchal conceptions. But
when they do, exclusivity is lost. This is the cost of feminist theologies, and
it is a significant one.

To those still wedded to a monotheistic construction, the fact that the
metaphoric exemption serves as orthodox reminder that *all* images, symbols, and manifestations of divinity are inadequate to describe divine being
is cold comfort. The fact that it reminds feminist theologies of their own
partiality and finitude is a minor salve, however crucial. It is nevertheless
important to remember that the whole project of feminist construction as
explicitly nonreferential is legitimated and required by the prior and indispensable critique of preexisting claims to authority that exclude and de-
mean women. To justify the fall of God the Father as an idolatrous social
construction but to then extol the rise of Goddess the Mother as referen-
tially true is hypocritical, and all serious feminist theologians know this and
avoid this simple, uncritical reversal. But at the same time, if feminist constructions and reconstructions are *never* referential, the revelatory quality of
human-divine encounters has no legitimate place within constructive
methodology except as a fiction that enhances the emotive or aesthetic
quality of theological propositions. And then feminist theologies do not
offer anything substantially different from the exclusions of patriarchal religion.

In any case, the metaphoric exemption is still foundational. It is both
important and persuasive enough to persons who put feminist theologies
into practice that they engage in the work of substituting female for male
images in worship and are shocked at the habituated resistance they encounter even in traditional communities that otherwise extol liberal justice
issues. They design and lead new liturgies based on the metaphoric constructions of feminist theologies, they approach spiritual practice with new
disciplines, and they become ever more open to new experiences and ap-
prehensions of divine presence, including what Tillich dismisses as new
revelations outside the principal circle of the scriptural experience. The
metaphoric exemption is persuasive as a justification for the work of altering liturgies, invocations, prayers, and other rituals because it serves as a
protection against charges of heresy (which abound anyway). But the metaphoric exemption is silenced in worship or spiritually focused experiences
when metaphors are, even briefly and intimately, enfleshed.

To be sure, some so-called religious experiences or awarenesses are nostalgic imaginings or mistakes in perception, or delusion. But I have argued
that this certainty does not then support certainty about all experiences or

a negation of divine freedom in the concretely particularistic and socially constructed world. The metaphoric exemption, in other words, does not protect feminist theologians from heresy because it does not protect them from the possibility that the monotheistic metaphor itself, the constructed— or revealed—heart of the Western religious tradition, is flawed.

There is no doubt that this proposition about divine unlimitedness and multiple embodiments raises particular challenges for feminist theologians who prefer a circumscription of theological discourse to the contents of a specific monotheistic experience and tradition. A few feminist theologians have begun to apply the metaphoric exemption to monotheism itself, leading to a deeper evaluation of its history as a metaphor, but for most, monotheism retains a revealed and therefore unquestioned status.[16] Most constructive feminist theologies therefore struggle to make room for the multiplicity of their metaphors without disrupting the coherence of the monotheistic norm. I suggest that this is a nostalgic and unrealistic hope because the monotheistic norm is already incoherent in feminist theologies. But not all feminist theologians may agree, particularly if they remain convinced that doctrinal claims are a legitimate starting point for their work, despite the acidic reductions of the metaphoric exemption. It seems clear, however, that the struggle to retain exclusively monotheistic claims alongside feminist theological commitments to social critiques of hegemonic norms can only become more difficult within the context of the metaphoric exemption and experiential confession.

Constructing Divine Multiplicity and Radical Embodiment

If feminist theologies cannot support exclusivist claims to monotheism or final revelations, how might we begin to conceive of the ways that divinity apart from monotheism or exclusivist claims might exist? Nurtured by the two roots of metaphoric exemption and experiential confession, divine transcendence can be conceived as complete noncorrespondence to human constructions and yet remain untroubled by particular embodiments. Divine embodiment can be voluptuously sensual and immediate, temporary or lasting, individual or communal, without diminishing itself in meaning or in possibility. It does not have to be controlled through finality. And lived religious experience, particularly in feminist communities, suggests that while human imaginings may not correspond to the divine, the divine may sometimes correspond to human imaginings.

There are some important assumptions here about divine existence and activity. The first is that what is truly divine both exists (has being) and is free. What is truly divine (whatever its name/s) created, creates, and may embody the universe. It relates to the universe and all of its animate and inanimate inhabitants intimately and awesomely. This is a premise of theology insofar as it is willing to accept the ontological assumption that the divine exists in some manner independent of human imagining and, what is more, that it relates to the world in ways that should matter to human beings. In other words, theology as I refer to it makes the ontological assumption that what is truly divine both exists and attends to human affairs in some relevant way. This is an ontological assertion, however, that resists closure and the finality of absolutes. Following Daly, it is an ontological assertion that is more along the lines of verb than noun, and following Sands, it is an ontological assertion that accepts problematics of the One and the crumbling ruin of the Absolute, without letting go of possibilities for multiple ontologies. Divinity, I suggest, is an adjective that connects the multiplicity of the divine and its unlimitedness into the language of theology. This is a unifying abstraction that does not diminish the concrete and incommensurate realities of divine coming forth into the world, as the world, of the world, and for the world. There is unity, but it is an abstract unity for the sake of our sanity perhaps. All we can know of the divine is its multiplicity, its intimacy, its awesomeness, whatever it shows us. Its transcendence is unlimited freedom. Its embodiment is as numerous and as fragile as the droplets of fog that hushed Loren Eisley into reverently still worship.[17]

Given this ontological assumption, feminist theologies that are answerable to the twin roots that nourish and legitimate them can better evaluate their constructions of divinity in terms of intellectual coherence and in terms of effectiveness in real life. These constructions remain "just imaginative products" as the metaphoric exemption insists, but they also evoke and embody divine response in the real communities to whom feminist theologians must answer. This bedrock theological claim—that the divine exists and involves itself in intimate and promiscuous relationship to the world—complicates the work of constructive theology in the problem of accounting for the myriad and multiple ways in which it does so. In essence, it does so, and that is enough warrant for feminist theologies to conceive of divinity in ways that allow for profound multiplicity and recurring embodiments that do not shy away from temporality, partiality, smell, taste, texture, heresy.

The epistemological problem of how we know divinity when we "see" it is incompletely resolved by modernist skepticism with its indisputable claim that, quite simply, we never can know divinity when we see it. The strength of this argument comes from modernist notions of proof, the burden of which rests on the divine to submit itself to tests, to reveal itself in such a manner and to such an audience as to dispel doubt once and for all. It does not help that the divine, to the extent that it is truly free, is also maddeningly uncooperative when it comes to objective tests. Because of this notorious reluctance of the divine to placate human obsessions with doubt, and because of the notoriously chaotic nature of individual experiences, it is easier to theorize divinity in its cosmic and unifying sense in terms of universal doctrines and absolute truths than in terms of specific and poetic things like blades of grass or the immediate experiences of particular communities. To theorize the divine as unlimited and yet temporally expressive in multiple forms, or to theorize multiple sacred realities without losing a quality of unity and organic order to reality, is the challenge before feminist theologians who would take seriously the foundations upon which their theologies rest.

Of course, the narrative traditions of the great monotheistic religions rely upon the immediate and specific experiences of particular individuals and communities, and sometimes upon blades of grass, bushes that burn, or rocks that house water. The specific experiences of a few particular individuals—a man named Moses with a speech disability 4,000 years ago; a small group of messianists from Nazareth 2,000 years ago; a single man named Muhammad in the desert outside Medina 1,500 years ago; an upstate New York farmer named Joseph Smith 150 years ago—form the founding myths of global traditions. Are these immediate experiences so different in character from other possible immediate experiences of divine relationship to specific people? Perhaps the only difference is that these individual communities transformed their experiences into normative claims with universal finality. They spawned massive followings and shaped cultural histories. Notwithstanding their incompatibility with each other, the exclusivity and finality of their revelatory claims do not hold up in feminist theologies that are grounded on the metaphoric exemption and experiential confession.

The validity of the tensive relationship between the metaphoric exemption and experiential confession is its ability to be a useful template for constructive feminist work. I have argued that this is a theological frame that is always in motion. It is more relational process than oppositional stasis, and so it offers a more appropriate means for analysis of theological constructs. The constructions of feminist theologies are, in this scheme, qualified by the metaphoric exemption, but they are also open to divine response. This means that no theological construction can take on descriptive certainty, can make claims to divine being. But it also means that theological construction is, in the metaphors and images it offers, open to the possibility that divinity may at times become concretely and actually present in them, making present divine being in real and perhaps comprehensible ways.

The monotheistic tradition in its strongest iconoclastic forms cannot support concrete, fully present multiple embodiments of divinity that are also recognizable. This is anathema to the negative theological tradition, and it does not correct the hubris of the tradition that limits divine being to incomprehensibility and inconcrete immanence.[18] The monotheistic metaphor tends to support the important negation of the metaphoric exemption, but it is weak in support of the possibility that divinity can appear freely in a multitude of real and present forms. Thus when we apply the feminist theological template as I have constructed it to the metaphoric idea of monotheism, we are likely to emerge not with an outright rejection of it, but with a correction to it. If monotheism will have any viability in feminist theologies without silencing the robust vitality of religious experience, it must incorporate some notion of multiplicity that is real, temporal, and concrete. For this to be the case, monotheism as a construction must recede to the abstraction of unlimitedness, a retreat that weakens it considerably, given the nature of unlimitedness to be also unlimited to One.

The place to which we have now come, therefore, is appropriately a beginning, balanced between the foundational poles of metaphoric exemption and experiential possibility. The dual foundation of constructive feminist theologies in the Enlightenment critical legacy, on the one hand, and robust religious expression and experience of the divine, on the other, suggests a new avenue of theological inquiry that opens up at the same time a space for experiences and embodiments of the divine as profoundly free and unerringly "there." A correction to the exclusions of traditional monotheism is, therefore, a construction of divinity whose unlimitedness rather than unitary disembodiment is its transcendence, and whose multiplicity in time, space, form, fragrance, allegiance, presence, and so on is its always free and real embodiment.

If divine unlimitedness is also its freedom to become embodied in real and temporal ways, to be multiple and chaotic and wholistic and ordered, monotheism can no longer be constructed as an exclusivist claim to oneness, but it can potentially serve the abstract and unifying adjective divinity. An image of how this abstract unity may work comes from Elizabeth Johnson. She offers a rich and suggestive description of the manyness embedded in multiplistic piety, a manyness that also demands the rejection of any One as ultimate. Her fluid image also suggests a buoyant, if fragile, connectivity that implies some organic unity to reality as we know it even though it is not a firm foundation. To this fluidity the idea of monotheism might eventually aspire:

> Taking all the names together will not deliver definitive understanding of God.... Persons who seek to know God by compiling the names of God do not resemble misers amassing a heap of gold, a summa of truths, which can go on increasing until a rare purchase can be made. Rather, such persons are better compared to swimmers who can only keep afloat by moving, by cleaving a new wave at each stroke. They are forever brushing aside the representations that are continually reforming, knowing full well that these support them, but that if they were to rest for a single moment they would sink.[19]

A principal advantage for feminist theologies of a more fully developed concept of divine unlimitedness and multiplicity is that, unlike negative theology, it lends authority and legitimacy to revelatory religious experience in all of its diversity without reducing the experiences to problems, conundrums, delusions, or pietistic enthusiasms. It is true that divine multiplicity and unlimitedness do not rest easily with iconoclastic orthodoxy, despite connections, at least in Christianity, to orthodox traditions of trinitarian sacramentalism. It is true that divine multiplicity and unlimitedness can all too easily be interpreted as hopelessly posttraditional and thus be dismissed or abused. This is their vulnerability. A stricter and more restrictive monotheism at least bears the weight of familiarity and the habituated sagacity of sound iconoclasm, even if it stumbles into incoherence.

It is possible that a construction of divinity as unlimited and multiple might also be conceived in Christian or (more tentatively) in Jewish terms. Divine multiplicity and unlimitedness do not, after all, represent the opposite of monotheism and negative theology since all theoretically reject idolatrous and therefore exclusivist claims. The possibilities attending a traditional or even posttraditional conception of divinity as unlimited and multiple are intriguing in that ideas of multiplicity translate well into ritual practice and restore the place of spiritually focused experience in theological reflection. There is a space in this idea hitherto difficult to find in feminist theologies for a depth of sacramental devotion and experience that can flourish, not only in spite of the metaphoric exemption as it now stands, but because of it.

Divine unlimitedness and multiplicity are ultimately suggestive of the balance that forms the relational foundations of feminist theologies. I have discussed that balance primarily in terms of a mutually correcting double negative between the metaphoric exemption's negation of divine comprehensibility and experiential confession's negation of absolute divine incomprehensibility. This corrective balance, however, can also be viewed as a double assertion of divine greatness and of divine particularity, of divine unity and of divine incommensurability. Neither side is complete without the other; both are vulnerable to colonization by the other. Divine unlimitedness and multiplicity suggest all of these relations and reassert feminism's first commitment to the validity and truth aspect of autobiography *as it relates* to the larger autobiographies of living communities with real burdens and real scars, real failings and real hopes.

Divinity conceived as unlimited and multiple resists colonization by any one community and by any one identity, but offers itself to them without hesitation. Divine transcendence as unlimitedness is incomprehensible in its scope, but infinitely comprehensible in its expression. Divine embodiment in multiplicity is breathtaking in its immensity and heartbreaking in its intimacy. Divinity so conceived is immediate fragility and unending recurrence. It overwhelms theory but meets life on its own terms. Feminist theologies, casting a webbed net between the analysis of metaphoric exemption and the robustness of experiential confession, found an imaginative project that finally allows for divinity that responds to the world in real and meaningful ways. We experience the green-gold earth, the hard and unyielding tragedy of it, the vital and overwhelming life of it; we embrace the ordinary; we breathe; we stretch thought; we ask our questions. And sometimes here, in the smoky fabric of the world that makes us, like the rare vulnerability of a truth, divinity folds into shape and answers.

Postlude

For years, when she told the dream, she ended with her decision to turn away, with the awful weight of it, the silent loss, the wondering remaining. For years, she continued to wonder why she had been taken to that spot, why she was given that choice, and why she had turned away. She wondered what it meant, and she wondered sometimes if God really was that cruel, that capricious a deity to entrust such an important decision to such a young girl. She even wondered if it had been "just a dream." She did not, however, wonder at the incapacity of therapists to explain it. She was not particularly disappointed when their pronouncements came up dry. Then, once, she told a friend the rest of the dream. Why she told the rest, she could not say. But in the telling, she saw her decision, and even the whole strange story, in a new light.

AFTER COMING BACK AROUND the outcropping of rock, after hearing the buzzing electricity of that strange shaft of light fade into silence, she sat down on the cold rocks and stared down the sloping mountainside into a now dark valley. She was too empty to cry. She was too awed by her rejection of the light and its awful demand. She wondered if she would die in this place so far from home.

So the child startled her. He seemed to appear out of the gloom in front of her with no warning. He was dirty, at home and akin to the rough ground. He said her name in his high, childish voice and told her that there were "two feminists in that farmhouse who want to see you." He pointed, and she saw, for the first time, a shape that was too square to be a boulder in the sloping field below. With a feeling of nothing to lose, she stumbled after him to the dark house, vaguely wondering how he knew her name, why he called the women feminists, and how they knew she was there. When she came close, a door was flung open, and a warm, decidedly unelectric light poured out into the night. She could not make out their faces, silhouetted as they were in the doorway, but their voices were kind. They asked her if she wanted to return home. She could only nod. One of them, in her textured, thoroughly solid voice, said that after they gave her some supper, they would take her there. They would take her back to the place where she lived.

Notes

1. How Disclosive of Reality Are Symbols of the Divine?

1. The term "feminist theology" has in recent years come to be identified by some solely with the scholarship of white, middle-class, North American academic women. Since the mid-1980s, important criticisms of feminist theology began to emerge from scholars outside this mainstream and sometimes from individuals outside the academic mainstream as well (cf. Rita Nakashima Brock, *Journeys by Heart*, 1988; Susan Thistlethwaite, *Sex, Race, and God*, 1991; and Marjorie Procter-Smith and Janet Walton, *Women at Worship*, 1993). Womanist scholars such as Katie Cannon, Audre Lorde, and Delores Williams, *mujerista* scholars such as Ada María Isasi-Díaz, Asian and Asian American scholars such as Hyun Kyung Chung, Virginia Fabella and Sun Ai Lee Park, and Kwok Pui-lan, and lesbian scholars such as Mary Hunt and Carter Heyward helped to expose the internal limitations of the feminist theologies generally defining the field, to broaden constructive opportunities, and to establish discourses important to the individual communities of women outside the white academic mainstream. Although this is a significant development (and it is certainly significant to the education of white North American scholars, though this is not the point of that work), I argue that the term "feminist theology" can still have use as a general indicator of a shared, though not exclusive, concern with sexism that is evident in this scholarship across cultural, ethnic, class, and other differences. If feminist theology refers only to white middle-class and upper-class academic scholarship, however, the point of this project is unnecessarily and, I believe, inappropriately foreshortened. If the term "feminist theology" is hopelessly essentialized as white, then a broader, more inclusive term should be applied in its stead. It is my contention that identifying white feminist theology as such remains of vital importance whether or not the term "feminist theology" is put to broader use.

2. Elizabeth Johnson, *She Who Is: The Mystery of God in Feminist Theological Discourse* (New York: Crossroad Press, 1992), 36.

3. Sharon Welch, *A Feminist Ethic of Risk* (Minneapolis: Augsburg Fortress Press, 1990), 156.

4. Mary Daly, *Beyond God the Father: Toward a Philosophy of Women's Liberation* (Boston: Beacon Press, 1973), 19.

5. Elizabeth Cady Stanton, *The Woman's Bible* (Seattle: Coalition on Women and Religion, 1974), 9–13.

6. The Re-Imagining Conference took place in November 1993 in Minneapolis, Minnesota. It was a gathering of several thousand women and men from a number of mainline Christian denominations to explore feminist theological issues and to "re-imagine" worship. The conference sparked widespread and vitriolic attacks on feminist theology, with numer-

ous challenges of heresy. The Drew Divinity School eucharist was a student-led worship service honoring women that used a Sophia-based liturgy. Thomas Oden, a senior faculty member at the Divinity School, launched a widely publicized attack on the faculty member (Heather Murray Elkins) responsible in an advisory role for the service.

7. Edward Farley, *Divine Empathy: A Theology of God* (Minneapolis: Fortress Press, 1996), 70.

8. Peter Berger, *The Sacred Canopy: Elements of a Sociological Theory of Religion* (New York: Anchor Books, 1967).

9. Marjorie Hewitt Suchocki, "God, Sexism, and Transformation," in *Reconstructing Christian Theology,* ed. Rebecca S. Chopp and Mark Lewis Taylor (Minneapolis: Fortress Press, 1994), 25.

10. Sallie McFague, "Human Beings, Embodiment, and Our Home the Earth," in *Reconstructing Christian Theology,* ed. Chopp and Taylor, 141.

11. Kelly Brown Douglas, *The Black Christ* (New York: Orbis, 1994), 4.

12. Delores Williams, *Sisters in the Wilderness: The Challenge of Womanist God-Talk* (Maryknoll, N.Y.: Orbis, 1993), 162.

13. Elisabeth Schüssler Fiorenza, *Discipleship of Equals: A Critical Feminist Ekklesia-logy of Liberation* (New York: Crossroad Press, 1993), 61–62.

14. Rosemary Radford Ruether, *Sexism and God-Talk: Toward a Feminist Theology* (Boston: Beacon Press, 1983), 53.

15. Nelle Morton, "The Goddess as Metaphoric Image," *in Weaving the Visions: New Patterns in Feminist Spirituality,* ed. Judith Plaskow and Carol Christ (San Francisco: Harper & Row, 1989), 111–18.

16. Geoffrey Wainwright, "United Methodist Women Defend Re-Imagining," *Good News: The Bi-Monthly Magazine for United Methodists,* May–June 1994, 19.

17. James V. Heidinger II, Faye Short, Dottie Chase, and Steve Beard, "The Good News Response to 'A Time of Hope—A Time of Threat,'" *Good News,* May–June 1994, 23.

18. Allison Stokes, *Women Pastors: The Berkshire Clergywomen* (New York: Crossroad Press 1996), 132.

19. Sallie McFague, *Models of God: Theology for an Ecological, Nuclear Age* (Philadelphia: Fortress Press, 1987), esp. chap. 2.

20. Bishop William R. Cannon, "The Cult of Sophia," *Good News,* March–April 1994, 17.

21. "Experience" is a hotly contested term, and no one is quite willing at present to make too rigid a definition. In this context, I mean by experience (and will discuss it at much greater length in part 2) assertions of a "coming forth" of divine presence that seems to the individual or group to be real. I am depending throughout on Gellman's excellent analysis and means of defining experiences of God (*Experience of God and the Rationality of Theistic Belief,* 1997) even though I do not find it necessary to agree with all of his conclusions about the existence of God as a result.

22. Pat Schneider, "Confession," in *Wake Up Laughing* (Montgomery: Negative Capability Press, 1997), 184–85.

2. Can Feminist Theologies Be Historicist and Disclosive?

1. Daly (esp. 1973) and Ruether (1975) are two of the earliest to make these claims, but the majority of feminist writers in the field of religion accept this premise.

2. See Jürgen Habermas, "Three Perspectives: Left Hegelians, Right Hegelians, and Nietzsche," in The *Philosophical Discourse of Modernity: Twelve Lectures,* trans. Frederick G. Lawrence (Cambridge, Mass.: MIT Press, 1993), 51, for a discussion of Hegel's introduction of historicism as the idea of modernity.

3. Claude Welch, *Protestant Thought in the Nineteenth Century*, vol. 1 (New Haven, Conn.: Yale University Press, 1977), 32.

4. See Kant's discussion of the function of the idea of God in religion in general (*Religion Within the Limits of Reason Alone,* trans. Theodore M. Greene and Hoyt H. Hudson [New York: Harper & Row Torchbooks, 1960], bk. 4, pt. 1), especially his definition of the rationalist as one who interprets natural religion as morally necessary and of the "true," i.e., universal church, "with the concept of God as moral Creator of the world" (sec. 1, p. 145).

5. See esp. ibid., bk. 4, pt. 1, sec. 1, p. 148.

6. Hegel, in particular, explored the possibilities of understanding the Absolute as a concept of motion and development; otherwise, he claims, it is reduced to a "monochromatic formalism," which "maintains that such monotony and abstract universality are the Absolute" (G. F. Hegel, *Phenomenology of Spirit*, trans. A. V. Miller [Oxford: Clarendon Press, 1977], preface, sec. 16). While Hegel by no means argued against an absolute truth at work objectively in the world, its currency in Spirit gave him the opportunity to argue for a process of truth coming to know itself in history, opening the door to historicism and relativity, despite his intentions. "The True," he argued, "is the whole. But the whole is nothing other than the essence consummating itself through its development. Of the Absolute it must be said that it is essentially a *result*" (ibid., preface, sec. 20).

7. Marx's theory of history as an affair of competing material interests clouded, obfuscated, and lubricated by religion appears throughout his writings. A particularly clear exposition of this theme occurs in his essay entitled "The German Ideology" in sec. 2, "Concerning the Production of Consciousness" (*The Marx-Engels Reader*, ed. Robert C. Tucker, 2d ed. [New York: W. W. Norton & Co., 1978], 163–200, but esp. 165–66).

8. Hegel foretells sociology in his discussion of *Zeitgeist*, the so-called "spirit of the times" and of "national genius" in terms of the political state's functional relationship to religion: "Religion is the sphere in which a nation gives itself the definition of that which it regards as the True. A definition contains everything that belongs to the essence of an object; reducing its nature to its simple characteristic predicate, as a mirror for every predicate—the generic soul pervading all its details. The conception of God, therefore, constitutes the general basis of a people's character. In this aspect, religion stands in the closest connection with the political principle. . . . The form of Religion, therefore, decides that of the State and its constitution. The latter actually originated in the particular religion adopted by the nation; so that, in fact, the Athenian or the Roman State was possible only in connection with the specific form of Heathenism existing among the respective peoples; just as a Catholic State has a spirit and constitution different from that of a Protestant one" (*The Philosophy of History*, trans. J. Sibree, rev. ed. [New York: Willey Book Co., 1944], 51; see also *Encyclopedia of Philosophy*, trans. Gustav Emil Mueller [New York: Philosophical Library, 1959], esp. sec. 449). Hegel's argument provided an entire systematic philosophy for historicization that, in its early-twentieth-century manifestation in sociological theory, further weakened the independence of Absolute Spirit.

9. Schleiermacher's intention, unlike Feuerbach's, is *not* a reduction of God to feeling or to subjectivity, but a response to the problem of *knowledge* implied by Enlightenment historicity by reducing the knowing subject thus. See *The Christian Faith,* ed. H. R. MacKintosh and J. S. Stewart (Edinburgh: T. & T. Clark, 1989), esp. chap. 1, sec. 4.

10. Marx, *Marx-Engels Reader*, 165.

11. See Ludwig Feuerbach, *The Essence of Christianity*, trans. George Eliot (New York: Prometheus Books, 1989).

12. Lowe's introduction to *Theology and Difference: The Wound of Reason* (Bloomington: Indiana University Press, 1993) is an excellent exposition of these same themes; see esp. pp. 23–27.

13. Emile Durkheim, *The Elementary Forms of the Religious Life*, trans. Joseph Ward Swain (New York: Free Press, 1965), 87.

14. Ibid., 269.

15. Ibid., 170.

16. Ibid., 116.

17. Victoria Lee Erickson, *Where Silence Speaks: Feminism, Social Theory, and Religion* (Minneapolis: Augsburg Fortress Press, 1993), 25.

18. Durkheim, *Elementary Forms*, 30.

19. Ibid., 333.

20. Ibid., 466.

21. Durkheim's rigid bifurcation of reality into realms of the sacred and the profane has deeply influenced twentieth-century anthropology, sociology, and theology. It has also come increasingly under fire as fieldwork and critical analysis have grown more sophisticated and sensitive. Not only have objections by people whose cultures and religious systems are the object of anthropological study called into question the veracity of the dichotomy, but the application of social theory and ideas of historicity to social theory itself has called into question the biases and interests that the dichotomy serves. Some of the strongest of such functional critiques come out of feminism. Victoria Lee Erickson, for example, argues that in Durkheim's dichotomous scheme, "religious force (the force of collective opinion) creates a collective force (from a membership that upholds the sacred by means of violence) used to legitimate domination, and it establishes gendered power and gendered social life. Without this concept of sacralizing force, Durkheim would have no theory of social life" (*Where Silence Speaks*, 23). Erickson's conclusion here can be true only if the sacred-profane dichotomy is necessary to Durkheim's more fundamental claims about the origin and function of religious ideas in social life. She suggests that the dichotomy falters as a descriptive and explanatory tool not because it fails in all cases to describe and even adequately explain some social systems but because its elevation to the status of universal phenomenon ultimately makes it neither descriptive nor explanatory of anything but Durkheim's ideological commitments. Perhaps because Durkheim placed so much emphasis on the dichotomy in his attempt to adequately account for social practices and their function in the maintenance of society, his critics and followers have made this dimension of his contribution to functional theory primary and, like Erickson, equate the success or failure of his theory of social life with the explanatory success or failure of the dichotomy.

22. Durkheim, *Elementary Forms*, 388–89.

23. I am indebted to Rebecca Schneider (*The Explicit Body* [New York: Routledge Press, 1997]) for this eloquent turn of phrase.

24. Max Weber, *The Sociology of Religion,* trans. Ephraim Fischoff (1922; reprint, Boston: Beacon Press, 1991), 1.

25. According to Talcott Parsons, Weber's "central problem was whether men's conceptions of the cosmic universe, including those of Divinity and men's religious interests within such a conceptual framework could influence or shape their concrete actions and social relationships, particularly in the very mundane field of economic action" (Weber, *Sociology*, xxxi). He identifies this as the "primary difference of emphasis" between Durkheim and Weber (ibid., xl n. 12). Parsons argues that Weber principally understood "the importance of the development of conceptions of the supernatural order, the claims of this supernatural order upon human attention and performance, and the implementation of these claims through agencies . . . to exert leverage upon that social order and change it" (ibid., xl–xli).

26. Ibid., 37–44. For his discussion of religion determined by the needs of social classes, see *The Protestant Ethic and the Spirit of Capitalism,* trans. Talcott Parsons (New York: Scribners, 1952), passim; and *Sociology*, chap. 6.

27. Weber, *Sociology*, 223.

28. Robert Merton, *On Theoretical Sociology* (New York: Free Press, 1967), 88.

29. Weber does not, according to Howard Harrod, necessarily believe that religious and ethical interests can be reduced to economics or politics, but he does not attempt to determine the status of divinity as Durkheim does. However, his claim, for example, that ineffectual gods are abandoned (cf. *Sociology,* 32) implies a vast sacred pantheon from which human beings pick and choose (making monotheistic claims delusional) or implies a reductive functionalism that assumes divinity to be a function of social processes. In any case, the point here is that he is not particularly concerned to determine this issue, and that in itself is significant evidence for the persuasiveness of functional social constructionism—his argument does not need "real" gods behind their social ideas.

30. Alfred Schutz and Thomas Luckmann, *The Structures of the Life-World*, vols. 1–2 (Evanston, Ill.: Northwestern University Press, 1973).

31. Peter Berger and Thomas Luckmann, *The Social Construction of Reality: A Treatise in the Sociology of Knowledge* (New York: Anchor Books, 1966), 97.

32. Robert Wuthnow, "The Phenomenology of Peter L. Berger," in *Cultural Analysis: The Work of Peter L. Berger, Mary Douglas, Michel Foucault, and Jürgen Habermas,* by Robert Wuthnow, James Davison Hunter, Albert Bergesen, and Edith Kurzweil (London: Routledge, 1991), 26–27.

33. Berger, *Sacred Canopy*, 1–15.

34. Ibid., 24–25.

35. Ibid.

36. Clifford Geertz, *The Interpretation of Cultures* (New York: Basic Books, 1973), 107.

37. Ibid., 108.

38. Berger, *Sacred Canopy*, 29.

39. Ibid., 33.

40. Although order is the concern of social construction and of the functional view of religious ideas, it should not be understood simplistically as static, airless, or the opposite of human creativity and freedom. Rather, order understood in this sociological sense is not just the delineation of the boundaries of meaning and sense, but the barometer of possibility. Revolution is as much a function of socially constructed order as is compliance; it is, after all, a reordering rather than a dissolution of order altogether. Chaos and nonsense—not freedom and possibility—are the opposite of this understanding of order.

41. This particular formulation of Geertz's argument comes from Howard Harrod, Vanderbilt University (unpublished lectures, 1993).

42. Berger and Luckmann also articulate this idea of negative affirmation in their somewhat clumsy example of homosexuality in *Social Construction of Reality* (113–16).

43. Mary Douglas, *Purity and Danger: An Analysis of the Concepts of Pollution and Taboo* (London: Routledge, 1966), 36.

44. Ibid., 42.

45. Ibid., 122.

46. Mary Daly, "After the Death of God the Father: Women's Liberation and the Transformation of Christian Consciousness," *Commonweal,* March 12, 1971. Reprinted in *Womanspirit Rising: A Feminist Reader in Religion,* ed. Carol P. Christ and Judith Plaskow (San Francisco: Harper & Row, 1979), 54.

47. Elisabeth Schüssler Fiorenza coined the term "kyriarchy" to denote a wider concept than the term "patriarchy," which tends to limit itself to ideas of gender. "Feminist liberation movements and theorists around the globe have unmasked the universalizing and essentializing gender discourse on woman as mystifying and reproducing patriarchal or, better, *kyriarchal* (master) relations of domination. Their historical analyses have pointed out that not only the

nature of elite women but also that of subordinated and colonialized peoples has been construed as the devalued and deficient 'other' of elite Western Man." See "Spiritual Movements of Transformation? A Critical Feminist Reflection," in *Defecting in Place: Women Claiming Responsibility for Their Own Spiritual Lives*, ed. Miriam Therese Winter, Adair Lummis, and Allison Stokes (New York: Crossroad Press, 1994), 224.

48. Rebecca Chopp, "From Patriarchy into Freedom: A Conversation between American Feminist Theology and French Feminism," in *Transfigurations: Theology and the French Feminists*, ed. C. W. Maggie Kim, Susan M. St. Ville, and Susan M. Simonaitis (Minneapolis: Fortress Press, 1993), 48.

49. Mary Daly, *Webster's First New Intergalactic Wickedary of the English Language Conjured by Mary Daly in Cahoots with Jane Caputi* (Boston: Beacon Press, 1987), 75.

50. Mary Daly, *Gyn/Ecology: The Metaethics of Radical Feminism* (Boston: Beacon Press, 1978), 39.

51. Williams, *Sisters,* 185.

52. Christ and Plaskow, *Womanspirit Rising,* 1.

53. "Motherearth and the Megamachine," *Christianity and Crisis* (April 12, 1972). Reprinted in *Womanspirit Rising,* ed. Christ and Plaskow, 49.

54. Daly, *Beyond God the Father,* 19.

55. Elisabeth Schüssler Fiorenza, "Toward a Liberating and Liberated Theology: Women Theologians and Feminist Theology in the United States," *Concilium* 15, no. 1, 22–32. Reprinted in *Discipleship of Equals,* 32.

56. Johnson, *She Who Is,* 5.

57. Rita Nakashima Brock, *Journeys by Heart: A Christology of Erotic Power* (New York: Crossroad Press, 1988), 8.

58. The "solipsistic ellipse" of functional social constructionism is a helpful insight into the problem of this latter dichotomy, whereby "all ideas, and especially the idea of God, have direct and indirect effects in all aspects of human life … [but] the ability to trace and describe the functional effects of ideas on human life, on the one hand, and the functional effects that all aspects of human life have on ideas on the other hand is a process most critical of itself. Thus the process of self-criticism becomes the new basis of objectivity, as opposed to revelation. What is more, revelation, or the ability of a deity to function outside of the solipsistic ellipse of functional social constructionism, i.e., to transcend the restraints of remaining only an idea, and become an actor who is not restrained by the self-critical catch-22 of the ellipse is itself an idea outside of the ellipse, and therefore unable to be addressed by it" (Peter Schneider, correspondence, January 15, 1996).

59. Joachim Wach, *Sociology of Religion* (1944; reprint, Chicago: University of Chicago Press, 1949), 1, emphasis mine.

60. Anthony Giddens (*Studies in Social and Political Theory* [London: Hutchinson, 1977]) has suggested two major variants of phenomenological methodology that have informed the evolution of social and cultural theory. The first is hermeneutic, represented by theorists such as Hans Gadamer and Paul Ricoeur, and refers to the collective aspect of culture carried in and concerned primarily with language. The second variant he describes is existential, represented by Alfred Schutz and Peter Berger, referring to a more individual understanding of culture as it is internalized in subjective consciousness and transformed into everyday meaning. I have added to these variants, the material, represented by Marx and Malinowski, referring to economic and biological/physical forces as determinants of meaning and cultural formation.

3. CAN FEMINIST THEOLOGIES HAVE BOTH METAPHOR AND SUBSTANCE?

1. Daly, "After the Death of God the Father," 54.

2. Sheila Greeve Davaney, "The Limits of the Appeal to Women's Experience," in *Shaping New Vision: Gender and Values in American Culture*, ed. Clarissa W. Atkinson, Constance H. Buchanan, and Margaret R. Miles (Ann Arbor, Mich.: UMI Research Press, 1987), 31.

3. Chopp, "From Patriarchy into Freedom," 32.

4. Pascal, *Pensées* 552, trans. W. F. Trotter (New York: E. P. Dutton & Co., 1958), 66–68. For a helpful and brief synopsis of Pascal's wager, see Placher's introduction to the Catholic reformations (*A History of Christian Theology: An Introduction* [Philadelphia: Westminster Press, 1983], 212–14).

5. See Paul Tillich, *Systematic Theology*, vol. 1 (Chicago: University of Chicago Press, 1951), 8–28.

6. Farley, *Divine Empathy*, 62.

7. Peter Berger, *A Rumor of Angels* (New York: Doubleday & Co. Anchor Books, 1970), 18. Quoted in Placher, *A History of Christian Theology*, 291.

8. Karl Barth, "Feuerbach," in *Theologian of Freedom*, ed. Clifford Green, The Making of Modern Theology Series (Minneapolis: Fortress Press, 1991), 93.

9. Barth, "The Humanity of God," in *Theologian of Freedom*, 49.

10. Barth, "Feuerbach," 97.

11. Barth, "The Humanity of God," 47.

12. Paul Tillich, "What Is Wrong with the 'Dialectic' Theology?" in *Paul Tillich: Theologian of the Boundaries*, ed. Mark Kline Taylor, The Making of Modern Theology Series (Minneapolis: Fortress Press, 1991), 107.

13. Barth, "Feuerbach," 90–97.

14. Barth, *The Church Dogmatics*, vol. 1, pt. 1 (Edinburgh: T. & T. Clark, 1956), 299.

15. Barth, "The Humanity of God," 60.

16. Barth, "The Barmen Declaration," in *Theologian of Freedom*, 149.

17. Green, ed., *Theologian of Freedom*, 148.

18. According to Barth, "What the 'German Christians' wanted and did was obviously along a line which had for long enough been acknowledged and trodden by the church of the whole world: the line of the Enlightenment and Pietism, of Schleiermacher, Richard Rothe and Ritschl. And there were so many parallels to it in England and America, in Holland and Switzerland . . . that no one outside really had the right to cast a stone at Germany because the new combination of Christian and natural theology effected there involved the combination with a race nationalism which happened to be rather uncongenial to the rest of the world, and because this combination was now carried through with a thoroughness which was so astonishing to other nations. Now that so many other combinations had been allowed to pass uncontradicted, and had even been affectionately nurtured, it was about two hundred years too late to make any well-founded objection" (*The Church Dogmatics*, vol. 2, parts 1 and 2, "The Doctrine of God," trans. T. H. L. Parker et al. (Edinburgh: T. & T. Clark, 1956], 174).

19. Barth, *The Epistle to the Romans*, 5th ed. (London: Oxford University Press, 1960), 50–51.

20. McFague, *Models of God*, 21.

21. Brock, *Journeys by Heart*, 2, 51.

22. Judith Plaskow, *Standing Again at Sinai: Judaism from a Feminist Perspective* (San Francisco: Harper & Row, 1990), 6–7. And see Feuerbach, *The Essence of Christianity*; and H. Richard Niebuhr, *Radical Monotheism and Western Culture with Supplementary Essays* (1947; reprint, New York: Harper and Brothers, 1960).

23. Jacquelyn Grant, quoted by Karen Baker-Fletcher in "Womanist Theology," in *Dictionary of Feminist Theologies,* ed. Letty M. Russell and J. Shannon Clarkson (Louisville: Westminster John Knox Press, 1996), 317.

24. James Cone, *Speaking the Truth: Ecumenism, Liberation, and Black Theology* (Grand Rapids, Mich.: Eerdmans Press, 1986), 7.

25. See for example Renita Weems, *Just a Sister Away: A Womanist Vision of Women's Relationships in the Bible* (San Diego: LuraMedia, 1988); Elisabeth Schüssler Fiorenza, *In Memory of Her: A Feminist Theological Reconstruction of Christian Origins* (New York: Crossroad Press, 1984) and *But She Said: Feminist Practices of Biblical Interpretation* (Boston: Beacon Press, 1992); Phyllis Trible, *Texts of Terror: Literary-Feminist Readings of Biblical Narratives* (Philadelphia: Fortress Press, 1984); and Regina Schwartz, *The Curse of Cain: The Violent Legacy of Monotheism* (Chicago: University of Chicago Press, 1997).

26. Johnson, *She Who Is,* 40.

27. Tillich, "What Is Wrong with the 'Dialectic' Theology?" 111.

28. Ibid., 110.

29. Ibid., 111.

30. Ibid.

31. Tillich, "On the Idea of a Theology of Culture," in *Tillich: Theologian of the Boundaries,* 36.

32. Ibid.

33. Ibid.

34. Ibid.

35. See Sandra Harding, *The Science Question in Feminism* (Ithaca, N.Y.: Cornell University Press, 1986), chap. 6.

36. Tillich, *Systematic Theology,* 1:93, emphasis mine.

37. Ibid., 4.

38. *Systematic Theology,* vol. 1. See esp. 147–50.

39. "Religion and Secular Culture," in *Tillich: Theologian of the Boundaries,* 121.

40. Ibid.; see also *Systematic Theology,* 1:148.

41. Ibid.; see also *Systematic Theology,* 1:149.

42. Ibid., 235.

43. Ibid., 236.

44. *Systematic Theology,* passim; but esp. vol. 3, pt. 5.

45. *Systematic Theology,* 1:238.

46. "The Church and the Third Reich: Ten Theses," in *Tillich: Theologian of the Boundaries,* 118.

47. Tillich has a highly refined concept of the demonic, and it is central to his theology and to his understanding of social construction, symbols, and the tendency of human beings to forget God in their intellectual creativity and psychological intensity. What Barth calls idolatry, Tillich calls the demonic. He develops this concept at length in all three volumes of *Systematic Theology,* but at heart it refers to the disastrous and infinitely various error of mistaking God for the symbol of God or, worse, for something else altogether. In one place he succinctly describes it as the "confusion between the medium and the content of revelation. It tends to make the medium and its excellencies into the content. It tends to become demonic, for *the demonic is the elevation of something conditional to unconditional significance*" (*Systematic Theology,* 1:140, emphasis mine). H. Richard Niebuhr developed this idea also in *Radical Monotheism and Western Culture.*

48. McFague, *Models of God,* 78.

49. See Tillich, *Systematic Theology,* vols. 1–3, esp. vol. 2.

50. Tillich, *Systematic Theology*, 1:241.

51. Davaney, "The Limits of the Appeal to Women's Experience," 44–48.

52. Ibid., 44.

53. Sheila Davaney, "Problems with Feminist Theory: Historicity and the Search for Sure Foundations," in *Embodied Love: Sensuality and Relationship as Feminist Values*, ed. Paula M. Cooey, Sharon A. Farmer, and Mary Ellen Ross (San Francisco: Harper & Row, 1987), 93.

54. Kathleen Sands, *Escape from Paradise: Evil and Tragedy in Feminist Theology* (Minneapolis: Fortress Press, 1994), 63.

55. Patricia Hill Collins, in a speech delivered at Vanderbilt University in January 1995, echoed the sentiments of many white feminist and womanist scholars when she argued that although important for analytical purposes, particularly against dominant (what she calls central) forms of inquiry, postmodern critiques are also a nihilistic attack upon the tentative gains of feminist scholarship. This is a common complaint, but it suggests a caricature of the difficult and often highly nuanced analysis feminist scholars such as Sands bring to their work. A close reading of some so-called postmodernists and radical historicists like Sands and Fulkerson displays a much more sophisticated understanding of the perils of nihilism than their critics tend to allow. But just as they are aware of the dangers of the infinite deconstruction suggested by radical historicism, they are equally concerned, as Sands suggests, with the perils of escapism accompanying absolutes or any return to the monolithic (monotheistic?) One.

56. Sands, *Escape from Paradise*, 66. In *Pure Lust: Elemental Feminist Philosophy* (Boston: Beacon Press, 1984), Daly cites Tillich's question, "Why is there something, why not nothing?" as a particularly insidious example of what she calls patriarchal fascination with death, or necrophilia. Equating phallicism with necrophilia, she suggests that Tillich's conflation of the two quite different questions is an example of the way that biophilic thinking can be undermined. She says, in contrast, that a "Wonderlusty woman might imagine that the question thus posed corresponds to her own ontological experience, to her Lust for Be-ing. She might imagine that the ontological question thus posed expresses an attitude identical to her own Wonder and gratitude that things *are*. Caught up on this Wonder, she might fail to notice anything suspect about the second half of Tillich's question: 'why not nothing?' Musing women would do well to ask ourSelves whether this question would arise spontaneously in biophilic consciousness" (29).

57. Sands, *Escape from Paradise*, 66.

58. Quoted in Williams, *Sisters*, 178.

59. Sands, *Escape from Paradise*, 46.

60. Davaney, "Problems with Feminist Theory," 92.

4. MULTIPLE CLAIMS OF DIVINE PRESENCE

1. Donna S. Gates, "Untitled," 1996.

2. A fabulous example of this is *Found Goddesses: Asphalta to Viscera*, as revealed to Morgan Grey and Julia Penelope (Norwich, Vt.: New Victoria Publishers, 1988). See especially the authors' introduction for a discussion of the self-consciously imaginative practice of invocation that, at times, yields response. In a lighthearted manner, these women are identifying and embodying the very theological point that I want to make in this book.

3. Marjorie Power, "Why I Gave Tishku Shampoo," in *Tishku: After She Created Men*, A Lone Willow Press Chapbook (Omaha: Lone Willow Press, 1996), 21.

4. I use the term "spiritually focused" to broaden my reference to experience. Religious experience suggests church- or temple-related experience rather than the range of experi-

ences that individuals and communities may have whether they are involved in traditional or posttraditional spiritual settings.

5. Janie Marshall, "Untitled," 1997.

6. Jerome Gellman, *Experience of God and the Rationality of Theistic Belief,* Cornell Studies in the Philosophy of Religion (Ithaca, N.Y.: Cornell University Press, 1997).

7. Cindy Davenport, "Untitled," 1997.

8. See Mary McClintock Fulkerson, *Changing the Subject: Women's Discourses and Feminist Theology* (Minneapolis: Fortress Press, 1994).

9. Paul Tillich is the principal architect of the "method of correlation" by which he argued that theology poses answers to existentially generated questions. "Systematic theology," he argued, "uses the method of correlation. It has always done so, sometimes more, sometimes less, consciously, and must do so consciously and outspokenly, especially if the apologetic point of view is to prevail. The method of correlation explains the contents of the Christian faith through existential questions and theological answers in mutual interdependence" (*Systematic Theology,* 1:60). This method links theology, in Tillich's system, indissolubly to culture. It is ironic that his purpose in developing the method of correlation was to privilege the "apologetic point of view" whereas its development in feminist scholarship was for the purposes of undoing so-called traditional apologetics. Many feminist theologians, Mary Daly principally among them (cf. *Beyond God the Father,* and Laurel Schneider, "From New Being to Meta-Being: A Critical Analysis of Paul Tillich's Influence on Mary Daly," *Soundings* 75, nos. 2–3 [1992]: 421–39), are deeply indebted to this method since it requires close attention to the burning questions of contemporary life as instructive of theological response. David Tracy (*The Analogical Imagination: Christian Theology and the Culture of Pluralism* [New York: Crossroad Press, 1981]) has linked Tillich's method of correlation and its various applications in contemporary culture to older analogical methods.

10. See Ruether, *New Woman/New Earth: Sexist Ideologies and Human Liberation* (New York: Seabury Press, 1975) and *Sexism and God-Talk*. Also Dorothee Sölle, *Thinking About God: An Introduction to Theology,* trans. John Bowdon (Philadelphia: Trinity Press International, 1990), 71.

11. See *Bread Not Stone: The Challenge of Feminist Biblical Interpretation* (Boston: Beacon Press, 1984) for Elisabeth Schüssler Fiorenza's full description of her four hermeneutical principles of feminist liberation theology. Briefly, they are (1) hermeneutics of suspicion, which recognizes the patriarchal and androcentric bias of religious texts and involves the critical question of whose interests are served by the texts; (2) hermeneutics of proclamation, which assesses religious texts suitable for liturgical use; (3) hermeneutics of remembrance, which searches texts for traces of women's history and reconstructs a heritage for women in religious history; and (4) hermeneutics of creative actualization, which is the expression of feminist ritual and art based upon the products of the prior three endeavors.

12. Lisa Sowle Cahill, "Feminism and Christian Ethics," in *Freeing Theology: The Essentials of Theology in Feminist Perspective,* ed. Catherine Mowry LaCugna (San Francisco: HarperSanFrancisco, 1993), 213.

13. Suchocki, "God, Sexism, and Transformation," 36.

14. Johnson, *She Who Is*, 18.

15. Williams, *Sisters*, 185.

16. Davaney, "Limits of the Appeal to Women's Experience."

17. Welch, *A Feminist Ethic of Risk*.

18. Fulkerson, *Changing the Subject*, 56.

19. Wilhelm Dilthey, *Philosophy of Existence: Introduction to Weltanschauung* (Westport, Conn.: Greenwood Press, 1976), 195.

20.Victor Turner and Edward Bruner, *The Anthropology of Experience* (Urbana: University of Illinois Press, 1982), 17.

21. Fulkerson gives a helpful encapsulation of the function of "women's experience" in most feminist theology, despite its leanings toward a prelinguistic realm, which she disputes:"Making women a central topic in theological reflection has an important epistemic function, best seen in relation to entrenched views of theological reflection that refuse to recognize the imprint of the knower on the known. Feminists appeal to women's experience in two different conversations. First, experience is invoked against orthodox notions of Christian revelation in order to affirm the historical and constructed character of the tradition. . . . The appeal to women's experience also contests a second theological position, that of liberal theology. Liberal theology prides itself on its adoption of historical consciousness and its willingness to champion modern challenges to the heteronomy of church and tradition. In this latter relation, feminist appeal exposes the androcentric character of the humanism in liberal theology" (*Changing the Subject,* 51–52). Like Davaney, Thistlethwaite focuses on the problem of women's experience as a universalized white, privileged norm (*Sex, Race, and God: Christian Feminism in Black and White* [New York: Crossroad Press, 1991], see esp. 24–26).

22. Johnson, *She Who Is,* 61.

23.Anne Carr,"The New Vision of Feminist Theology," in *Freeing Theology,* ed. LaCugna, 25.

24.Thistlethwaite, *Sex, Race, and God,* 8.

25. Edward Farley, *Good and Evil: Interpreting a Human Condition* (Minneapolis: Fortress Press, 1990), 116.

26. Gordon Kaufman, *In Face of Mystery: A Constructive Theology* (Cambridge: Harvard University Press, 1993), 8.

27.Tillich, *Systematic Theology,* 1:40.

28. Ibid., 46.

29. David Burrell, *Freedom and Creation in Three Traditions* (Bloomington: Indiana University Press, 1994), 64–65.

30. Even white feminist scholars such as Sheila Greeve Davaney and Susan Thistlethwaite, who raise important questions about the universal applicability of specific experiences to all women, and womanist scholars such as Delores Williams, Emilie Townes, and Cheryl Townsend Gilkes, who consistently argue that experience delineates the priorities of historical cultures, thereby demonstrating the limitations of white feminism for black women's liberation, and *mujerista* scholars such as Elsa Tamez and Ada María Isasi-Díaz, who make similar claims for Hispanic women, do not seek to do away with the importance of women's various experiences both of particular cultural and historical settings and of divine presence as sources of some kind for theological reflection. What all are concerned with, in various forms, is the ossification of a particular experience or set of experiences into the normative source. Even within specific communities of ethnic, economic, racial, or other classifications, assumed characteristic experiences are increasingly challenged by divergent and multiple alternatives.

31. Sölle, *Thinking About God,* 178.

32. Elsa Tamez, "Introduction: The Power of the Naked," in *Through Her Eyes: Women's Theology from Latin America,* ed. Elsa Tamez (Maryknoll, N.Y.: Orbis, 1989), 4, emphasis mine.

33. Ursula King, ed., *Feminist Theology from the Third World: A Reader* (Maryknoll, N.Y.: Orbis, 1994), 3, emphasis mine.

34.Ada María Isasi-Díaz, *En La Lucha: Elaborating a Mujerista Theology* (Minneapolis: Fortress Press, 1993), 95.

35. Both Elsa Tamez (*Through Her Eyes*) and María Pilar Aquino (*Our Cry for Life: Feminist*

Theology from Latin America [Maryknoll, N.Y.: Orbis, 1993]) represent *mujerista* theologians who treat Hispanic women as both capable and interested in the work of theological reflection as a part of liberation. Tamez's edited volume quotes extensively from Hispanic women who express interest in language about God, who express opinions or beliefs about their images of God, and who engage in discussion about it (see particularly Verhoeven, Bidegain, and Gebara, in Tamez, ed., *Through Her Eyes*). Aquino attempts a sophisticated and systematic liberation theology in *Our Cry for Life*, where she writes that "systematic reflection on God has advanced more consistently in the identification of God's feminine and maternal aspects [in Latin American feminist theology]. This is not apart from the growing perception of the God of life but the identification of other characteristics that belong to the divine being. The suspicion that the patriarchal image of God that exists in Judaism and Christianity is rooted in the unequal relationship between men and women at the expense of true love and solidarity has shown the need to seek new ways of thinking and speaking about God" (*Our Cry for Life*, 134).

36. There is a growing range of theological reflection on the concept of God from North American women of color and from women outside Europe and the United States, making this a topic less and less the sole concern or purview of white middle-class theologians. One of the best examples of this expansion is Delores Williams's work. Indeed, the subtitle of Williams's most recent theological work is *The Challenge of Womanist God-Talk*. Kelly Brown Douglas has made important contributions to womanist conversations dealing with concepts of God, especially in terms of the merging of God and Christ concepts in the black community. Katie Cannon has moved more directly into this discussion since her Antoinette Brown lecture at Vanderbilt University entitled "Sacred Rhetoric in African American Texts." See also Katoppo, Chung, Hinga, Gebara and Bingemer, and Govinden in pt. 4 of *Feminist Theology from the Third World*, edited by King, for theological concerns with constructions of God outside the white middle-class North American context.

37. Cynthia Trenshaw, "Sickness and Death: The Anointing of Acceptance," 1997.

38. Lesley Northup, *Ritualizing Women: Patterns of Spirituality* (Cleveland: The Pilgrim Press, 1997), 19.

39. "Bar Mitzvah" by an anonymous author.

40. Joann Heinritz, CSJ, "The Winter of My Life."

41. Cf. David Hume, "Argument against Miracles," in *Dialogues Concerning Natural Religion*, ed. Norman Kemp Smith (Indianapolis: Bobbs-Merrill Educational Publishing, 1977).

42. Cf. Rudolf Otto, *The Idea of the Holy* (Oxford: Oxford University Press, 1958).

43. Inna Jane Ray, "To the Road Crew," in *Ruah: Power of Poetry—A Celebration*, vol. 2 (Berkeley, Calif.: Graduate Theological Union, 1992–93), 44.

44. Dianne Bilyak, "Canyon."

45. James Fernandez, *Persuasions and Performances: The Play of Tropes in Culture* (Bloomington: Indiana University Press, 1986), 164.

46. Farley, *Divine Empathy*, 73–74.

47. Deconstruction in its most rigorous forms denies ontological claims on the basis of the unsystematic concrete multiplicities of experience that such claims theoretically suppress. See esp. Martin Heidegger (*Being and Time* [San Francisco: HarperCollins, 1962]), Jacques Derrida ("How to Avoid Speaking: Denials," in *Language of the Unsayable: The Play of Negativity in Literature and Literary Theory*, ed. Sanford Budick and Wolfgang Iser [New York: Columbia University Press, 1989]), and Foucault (*The Archaeology of Knowledge* [New York: Pantheon Books, 1972]) for explications of this anticoncept that popularly characterizes postmodernism. See Mark C. Taylor (*Erring: A Postmodern A/theology* [Chicago: University of Chicago Press, 1984]) and Farley (*Good and Evil*, introduction) and Lowe (*Theology and*

Difference, introduction) for clarifications of these philosophical moves. The idea of a/theology, coined by Mark C. Taylor, expresses not antitheism, but "the negation of negation" without allowing for an oppressively unambiguous affirmation, truly deconstructionist in its attempt to depict theism in a carnivalistic motion.

48. Pat Schneider, "Temple," *One More River* (Amherst, Mass.: Amherst Writers and Artists Press, forthcoming).

5. LIVED FEMINIST SPIRITUALITY

1. The most helpful new research in this area has been done by Cynthia Eller (*Living in the Lap of the Goddess: The Feminist Spirituality Movement in America* [New York: Crossroad Press, 1993]); Charlotte Caron (*To Make and Make Again: Feminist Ritual Thealogy* [New York: Crossroad Press, 1993]); Lesley Northup (*Ritualizing Women: Patterns of Spirituality* [Cleveland: The Pilgrim Press, 1997]); Allison Stokes (*Women Pastors*); Patricia Lynn Reilly (*A God Who Looks Like Me: Discovering a Woman-Affirming Spirituality* [New York: Ballantine Books, 1995]), among others.

2. The conservative religious press offers a wide selection of texts and journals concerned with what are perceived as substantive claims about goddesses and female divinities in feminist theologies and feminist worship. Magazines such as *Good News* and the *Presbyterian Layman,* published respectively by the conservative United Methodist Good News and Presbyterian Layman organizations, took up this theme after the Re-Imagining Conference in 1993.

3. Nancy Berneking and Pamela Joern, eds., *Re-Membering and Re-Imagining* (Cleveland: The Pilgrim Press, 1995), 202.

4. McFague, for example, denies the deconstructionist claim of "words all the way down" by arguing that "all renderings of reality are metaphorical (that is, none is literal), but in our novel constructions we offer new possibilities in place of others. In this sense we create the reality in which we live; we do not copy it, or to put it more pointedly, there are no copies, only creations. The assumption here, however, is that there is a reality to which our constructions refer, even though the only way we have of reaching it is by creating versions of it" (*Models of God,* 26).

5. Theresa Berger, in Northup, *Ritualizing Women,* 31.

6. Eller's excellent study of spiritual feminism in the United States is a primary source for this chapter, and her definitions are both inclusive and precise enough to capture the meaning of this diffuse term. Other sources with useful descriptions of feminist spirituality include early writings in *The Politics of Women's Spirituality: Essays on the Rise of Spiritual Power Within the Feminist Movement,* ed. Charlene Spretnak (Garden City, N.Y.: Anchor Press, 1982), esp. Stone (64–70), Davis and Weaver (368–72), Rush (382–85), and Spretnak (393–98). See also Susan Cady, Marian Ronan, and Hal Taussig, *Sophia: The Future of Feminist Spirituality* (San Francisco: Harper & Row, 1986), esp. chap. 1; Carol Ochs, *Women and Spirituality* (Totowa, N.J.: Rowman and Allanheld, 1983); Sheila Ruth, *Take Back the Light: A Feminist Reclamation of Spirituality and Religion* (Lanham, Md.: Rowman and Littlefield, 1994), esp. 48; Elizabeth Dodson Gray, *Sacred Dimensions of Women's Experience* (Wellesley, Mass.: Roundtable Press, 1988); Maria Harris, *Dance of the Spirit: The Seven Steps of Women's Spirituality* (New York: Bantam Books, 1989); Marjorie Procter-Smith and Janet R. Walton, eds., *Women at Worship: Interpretations of North American Diversity* (Louisville: Westminster/John Knox Press, 1993); and Cheryl Demerath Learn, *Older Women's Experience of Spirituality: Crafting the Quilt,* Garland Studies on the Elderly in America (New York: Garland Press, 1996), esp. chaps. 4 and 6.

7. Eller, *Living in the Lap of the Goddess,* 3.

8. Ibid., 6.

9. The labels "Christian" and "post-Christian" can be limiting when used in reference to feminist spiritual practices and beliefs, and so I prefer "traditional" and "posttraditional." Even still, the boundaries blur. It is possible that women and men who take feminist reconstructions seriously in their religious lives may very well represent more of a blend of the two in a kind of inclusive spiritual syncretism indicated by the willingness to deviate from orthodox doctrines and practices. This study is more concerned with the minority of self-described Christians who take feminist ideas *of divinity* seriously rather than the majority who may perceive feminist theology more in limited terms of inclusive pastoral (female clergy) and lectionary (inclusive language) issues.

10. Many of the mainline Protestant denominations maintain offices that support feminist resources and spirituality, but extradenominational centers tend to have greater freedom and hence more actively support both Christian and non-Christian feminist spirituality events, communities, and publications with international scope. The ecumenical Women's Theological Center in Boston and the predominantly Catholic feminist organization Women's Alliance for Theology, Ethics and Ritual (WATER) in Silver Spring, Maryland, are two outstanding examples of the latter.

11. Eller, *Living in the Lap of the Goddess*, 141.

12. Myhre, in Berneking and Joern, *Re-Membering and Re-Imagining,* 166.

13. Eller, *Living in the Lap of the Goddess*, 141.

14. Carol Christ, *Rebirth of the Goddess: Finding Meaning in Feminist Spirituality* (Reading, Mass.: Addison-Wesley, 1997), 1.

15. Heather Murray Elkins, *Worshipping Women: Re-Forming God's People for Praise* (Nashville: Abingdon, 1994), 15.

16. Caron, *To Make and Make Again,* 227.

17. Eller, *Living in the Lap of the Goddess*, 83.

18. Terrence Reynolds, "Two McFagues: Meaning, Truth, and Justification in Models of God," *Modern Theology* 11, no. 3 (July 1995): 293. Christ presumably limits her understanding of feminist theologians to those who are engaged in the articulation of ontological claims (or who make assumptions of such claims) concerning independent divine being. But the historicism of contemporary cultural theory is not likely to go away in feminist theology or elsewhere, regardless of what Christ might hope. Feminist theologians, such as Davaney and Sands, who take the historicist critique to its logical extremes concerning God are not necessarily at the same time out to destroy feminist hopes of community or of religious experience (see chap. 4). However, both (and Welch might be included here) argue that the "ruin of the Absolute" is the dawn of a new pragmatism, and the possibility (in the case of Sands and Welch at least) of a radically more immanent and pragmatic understanding of divine existence.

19. Chris Smith, "A Movement from Christology to Christo-Praxis," *Re-Imagining: Quarterly Newsletter,* November 1994, 4.

20. Mary Hunt, "On Feminist Methodology," *Journal of Feminist Studies in Religion* 1, no. 1 (1985): 86.

21. Caron, *To Make and Make Again,* 192.

22. Joan Timmerman, "Can We Talk?" *Re-Imagining,* February 1995, 5–6.

23. Caron, *To Make and Make Again,* 150.

24. Gloria Feman Orenstein, *The Reflowering of the Goddess* (New York: Pergamon Press, 1990), 79.

25. Sue Seid Martin, "Can We Talk?" *Re-Imagining,* May 1995, 7.

26. Elkins, *Worshipping Women,* 16.

27. Joy Bussart, "Can We Talk?" *Re-Imagining,* February 1995, 5.

28. Richard Rorty, *Consequences of Pragmatism* (Minneapolis: University of Minnesota Press, 1982), xxxv.

29. Pat Schneider, *Wake Up Laughing,* 180–82.

30. Timmerman, "Can We Talk?" 5.

31. James Evans, *We Have Been Believers: An African-American Systematic Theology* (Minneapolis: Fortress Press, 1992), 53.

32. Berneking and Joern, *Re-Membering and Re-Imagining,* 3.

33. Caron, *To Make and Make Again,* 46.

34. Eller remarks on the uncanny ability of constructed divinities to satisfy the needs for which they were constructed, and she points to a tongue-in-cheek but utterly serious subset of feminist spirituality reflected particularly in lesbian communities that engage spirituality in creative ways. *Found Goddesses: From Asphalta to Viscera* reflects this self-consciously constructive dynamic. The authors, one a "Witch" and the other a "Linguist," indicate that they wrote the book after discovering a remarkable and often funny relationship between invocation and what they perceived as a new reality that emerged: "This seeking after Found Goddesses began with the Witch's disillusionment about the focus among women's spirituality groups on 'lost goddesses.' After several years of studying lost goddesses, talking about lost goddesses, teaching classes about lost goddesses, the Witch began to feel that these lost goddesses, while interesting, had no immediate bearing on her life as a Lesbian in the latter part of the Twentieth Century. Those goddesses were defined mostly through their relationships with men and gods, even in feminist writing that tried to recreate older, less male-centered myths, and few of them were Lesbian-identified. Furthermore, not a one of them had ever tried to find a parking place in Manhattan, or wondered, as far as we can determine, what to bring to a potluck. The Linguist, on the other hand, had not shown one Iota of interest in 'lost goddesses,' with the possible exception of Eris, the Discordian goddess of chaos. She was into fun and nonsense, being a Dyke in the latter part of the twentieth century, and figuring out how we can use language to create a reality that is comfortable for us. The Witch and the Linguist started playing with the idea of creating our own goddesses, FOUND goddesses who not only respond to the specific needs of 20th century Dykes but whose naming calls into being a reality grounded in the will and gynergy of Dyke envisioning. We chortled and guffawed as friends sparked and spun the weird realm of Found Goddesses with us. When we started finding parking spaces with noticeable regularity, and money appeared when we needed it, we knew that our naming and invoking were making a new reality immediate and visible in our lives. Linguists and Witches both, after all, practice the ways language creates and alters the world as we perceive it. What we conceive we name, and the naming makes it so. Our experience with these goddesses has been an empowering one, perhaps because we've had so much fun" (4).

35. Berneking and Joern, *Re-Membering and Re-Imagining,* 3.

36. Heather Murray Elkins, "The Bitterness of the Human Heart and the Sweetness of the Word," *Re-Imagining,* May 1995, 5.

37. According to the organizers of the conference, the "1993 Re-Imagining Conference was organized by an ecumenical group of volunteers called together by Rev. Sally Hill. Our dream was to respond to the goals of The Ecumenical Decade/Churches in Solidarity with Women. Nearly 150 people, clergy and lay, helped to move the Conference from a dream into reality. Due to the controversy following the Conference, we began to dream about another Re-Imagining venture. Over and over people spoke to us of isolation. We wanted to do something that would help us stay connected. It is our intention to work locally to mentor Re-Imagining groups for study, support, and theological exploration. . . . We believe

in the powerful potential of a grassroots movement, for history and our tradition have taught us that wherever two or more are gathered with holy intentions, the Spirit of Christ is present" ("The Re-Imagining Community" brochure; more information is available from Re-Imagining, 122 W. Franklin Avenue, Minneapolis, MN 55404).

38. Berneking and Joern, *Re-Membering and Re-Imagining*, 237.

39. Sally Nelson, "Theology Should Start with God, Not Women's Lives," *Good News,* March–April 1994, 15.

40. "Bishop Hunt Addresses Sophia," *Good News,* March–April 1994, 17. Nelson gives specificity to her call for discipline by arguing that, because of Re-Imagining, it "is time for pastors, presbyters, church councils, and religious orders to call to repentance those who worship false gods, and to remove from clergy rosters and membership rolls those who refuse to repent" ("Theology Should Start with God," 15).

41. See esp. McFague (passim, but esp. *Models of God*, 21–57) and Ruether (*New Woman / New Earth* and *Sexism and God-Talk*), among others.

42. A significant amount of feminist constructive theology addresses and develops the claim that feminism enriches and strengthens the central themes of divine love, compassion, power, and justice. The metaphorical approach also contends that the ancient *via negativa* is preserved rather than undermined by feminist images and models. Good examples of these claims can be found in Elizabeth Johnson's *She Who Is,* Sallie McFague's *Models of God,* Rita Nakashima Brock's *Journeys by Heart,* and Dorothee Sölle's *Thinking About God.*

43. Berneking and Joern, *Re-Membering and Re-Imagining*, 213.

44. Ibid.

45. Elkins, *Worshipping Women,* 169.

46. Riley Case, "Whither the Seminaries?" *Good News,* January–February 1994, 14.

47. Elkins, *Worshipping Women,* 169.

48. Ibid., 105.

49. Eller, *Living in the Lap of the Goddess*, 140.

50. See Grey and Penelope, *Found Goddesses.*

51. The great Kachinas of the Hopi tradition are ancestor spirits and deities who return to the people in ritual dances. Dancers are initiated into Kachina societies and wear the masks that represent individual Kachinas. A part of a Hopi boy's initiation into adulthood is the revelation of the mask as mask—the privilege of seeing for the first time not only that the face is a mask when before he saw it only as Kachina, but also that it is a vehicle for Kachina emergence. He is allowed to see, for the first time, the world through the eyes of the mask. Sam Gill writes that "we usually interpret this as a means of educating the initiates to the unreality of the masks; that is, we consider it as showing the uninitiated that, instead of a real being, the masked performer is actually only an impersonation. I think we are wrong in this understanding. Again it is a matter of perspective; the perspective from which one gains the fullest meaning and reality of the masks is not by looking *at* it at all, though this is certainly an essential stage in the process. The full meaning is gained by looking *through* the eyeholes of the mask and seeing the effect it has on the world. That is why it is a privileged view of the initiated" (Sam D. Gill, *Native American Religions: An Introduction* [Belmont, Calif.: Wadsworth, 1982], 71). A Hopi dancer articulates it more in terms of the transformation that comes when the mask is worn: "I am certain that the use of the mask in the Kachina ceremony has more than just an aesthetic purpose. I feel that what happens to a man when he is a performer is that, if he understands the essence of the Kachina, when he dons the mask he loses his identity and actually becomes what he is representing" (Emory Sekaquaptewa, quoted by Sam Gill, *Native American Religions,* 72). Benjamin Lee Whorf also writes of Hopi and other Native American understandings of the dynamic interrelationship between spo-

ken words and spiritual or sacred emergence. It is far too simplistic to suggest that Hopi peoples assumed their constructions to be anything other than that, but also misses the point to suggest that they did not see spiritual beings fully capable of making use of those constructions in mutually beneficial ways (Benjamin Lee Whorf, *Language, Thought, and Reality: Selected Writings,* ed. John B. Carroll [Cambridge: MIT Press, 1956]).

6. Re-Imagining the Divine

1. Lived experience, I noted in chapter 5, may be particular and individual (and so not descriptive of any group of women and men), or it may be communal and cultural (and so descriptive of whole communities). Either way, feminism in general has responded to the paucity of women's voices in history and theology and to the tendency of dominant culture to disavow women's contributions by historic tendencies to "forget" women by giving credence to them in its work.

2. Tillich is an example of the former, Farley of the latter. Indeed, Tillich explicitly asserts the normative "experience" of the Christ event to close off the "openness for the new which characterizes the pragmatic method, [with] the consequence that experience has become not only the main source of systematic theology but an inexhaustible source out of which new truths can be taken continually" (*Systematic Theology,* 1:45). Farley, on the other hand, abstracts from the Christian tradition not the contents of an explicit experience, but what he calls "a retrieved paradigm of a major world faith to interpret a human condition" (*Good and Evil,* xvii).

3. Farley offers a useful corrective to the problem of static "structures and features of regions of being," providing instead a concept that takes into account the dynamic quality of "the philosopher's own locus, situation, and condition [as] one aspect of whatever is under consideration. Thus, for instance, an ontology of the features of the human body should be differentiated from the reflective ontology of the lived body or embodiment" (*Good and Evil,* 2 n. 3).

4. Ibid., 106–8.

5. Daly, *Gyn/Ecology,* 39; and Ruether, "Mother Earth and the MegaMachine," 49.

6. See Elisabeth Schüssler Fiorenza (*Bread Not Stone,* 15–17) for a discussion of the hermeneutic of suspicion.

7. Eller has recorded some of the arguments of spiritual feminists who have rejected Christian theology on the basis of its demonic capacities. These feminists tend to be unconvinced by negative theology and thus by the purely metaphoric claims of Christian feminist constructive proposals. She points out that the "majority of spiritual feminists seek out a precarious balance between slamming traditional religions . . . and allowing that traditional religions have redeeming characteristics. Christianity, in particular, is the object of truly virulent rhetoric: it is 'a curse,' it is 'sado-sexual' (with praying on bent knee likened to fellatio); it is 'necrophilic,' 'fascistic,' 'nihilistic,' and of course misogynistic. Zusanna Budapest describes Christianity like this: 'It is an incestuous male homosexual concept that excludes the Mother, the female principle of the universe, and the creator. And of course the entire semen theology of the Pope, barring ordination of women, is completely supporting this' " (*Living in the Lap of the Goddess,* 224). More specifically concerned with ideas of God but still reflecting the general feminist spiritual view of positive theology, she notes that "Suzanne Courveline provides an unusual dissenting voice to the spiritual feminist consensus about the absence or ultimate harmlessness of evil spirits. She is convinced that Jehovah exists and that he wishes her—and indeed the entire world—no good. She describes him as 'a manifestation of the hatred and fear and killing wish of the patriarchal principle' and says, 'I think

that he has been thought about and invoked so often that he's completely insane, and I think he's out to destroy everything'" (ibid., 224).

8. Some of the clearest representatives of this sentiment are Rosemary Radford Ruether, Elisabeth Schüssler Fiorenza, Delores Williams, Sallie McFague, Kelly Brown Douglas, Dorothee Sölle, Marjorie Hewitt Suchocki, and Elizabeth Johnson. Johnson sums up the general sentiment of exemption by arguing that "human words, images, and concepts with their inevitable relationship to the finite are not capable of comprehending God, who by very nature is illimitable and non-objectifiable. Absolutizing any particular expression as if it were adequate to divine reality is tantamount to a diminishment of truth about God" (*She Who Is*, 112).

9. Rita Gross, "Female God Language in a Jewish Context," in *Womanspirit Rising*, ed. Christ and Plaskow, 169.

10. Sölle, *Thinking About God*, 171.

11. Gregory of Nyssa, *The Life of Moses 2.163*, trans. Abraham J. Malherbe and Everett Ferguson (Mahwah, N.J.: Paulist Press, 1978), 94.

12. Maximus the Confessor, *Mystagogia*, in *Patrologia Graeca*, vol. 91 (Paris: Garnier Fratres, 1865), col. 664; quoted in Philip Sherrard's *The Greek East and the Latin West* (London: Oxford University Press, 1959), 40.

13. Aquinas, *De Potentia* (Westminster, Md.: Newman Press, 1952), q. 7, a. 5. Quoted by Elizabeth Johnson, *She Who Is*, 45.

14. Gordon Kaufman, *The Theological Imagination: Constructing the Concept of God* (Philadelphia: Westminster Press, 1981), 71.

15. Barth, "The Humanity of God," 49.

16. Tillich, *Systematic Theology*, 1:205.

17. Kaufman, *Theological Imagination*, 70.

18. McFague, *Models of God*, 37.

19. Johnson, *She Who Is*, 6.

20. Peter Hodgson, *Winds of the Spirit: A Constructive Christian Theology* (Louisville: Westminster John Knox Press, 1994), 40.

21. Derrida, "How to Avoid Speaking: Denials," 3–70.

22. Mark C. Taylor, *nOts* (Chicago: University of Chicago Press, 1993), 38.

23. Ruether, *Sexism and God-Talk*, 18.

24. Johnson, *She Who Is*, 8.

25. Williams, *Sisters*, 12.

26. Daly, *Pure Lust*, 11.

27. Ruth, *Take Back the Light*, 75.

28. Sallie McFague, *The Body of God: An Ecological Theology* (Minneapolis: Fortress Press, 1993), 88.

29. McFague cites a number of criteria for judging the worth of a construct or model that includes embodied experience ("slippery philosophical status" noted), "the testimony [tradition] of the religious community in which one stands," the "view of reality current in one's time." It is only "finally and of primary importance [that] one adopts a model because it helps to make things better" (ibid., 85–88).

30. Eller, *Living in the Lap of the Goddess*, 49.

31. Daphne Hampson, *Theology and Feminism* (Oxford: Basil Blackwell, 1990), 44.

32. Johnson, *She Who Is*, 212.

33. Ibid., 9.

34. Rosemary Radford Ruether was one of the first to develop a feminist methodology that decisively delegitimizes and excises language and images inherited through the Chris-

tian tradition that support the subjugation of women and the earth (*New Woman/New Earth,* passim). Others, most notably Elisabeth Schüssler Fiorenza (esp. *In Memory of Her* and *Discipleship of Equals*), Judith Plaskow (*Standing Again at Sinai*), Gordon Kaufman (esp. *Theological Imagination*), Delores Williams (esp. *Sisters in the Wilderness*), Hyun Kyung Chung (*Struggle to Be the Sun Again: Introducing Asian Women's Theology* [Maryknoll, N.Y.: Orbis, 1990]), and María Pilar Aquino (*Our Cry for Life*), have developed this method further within the specific contexts of their work. Certainly, the oral tradition of African Americans as represented by Howard Thurman suggests a long history of excising traditional sources on the basis of oppressive function (*Jesus and the Disinherited* [1949; reprint, Boston: Beacon Press, 1976], esp. 30).

35. Taylor, *nOts*, 38.

36. Richard Grigg, *When God Becomes Goddess: The Transformation of American Religion* (New York: The Continuum, 1995), 55.

37. The critique of negation as limiting to God is by no means new to theology. One good example from contemporary scholarship is Kathryn Tanner's historical analysis of the importance of emphasizing a free relation of divinity to the world (see esp. *God and Creation in Christian Theology* [Oxford: Basil Blackwell, 1988], chap. 2).

38. Robert Cummings Neville, *The Truth of Broken Symbols* (Albany: State University of New York Press, 1996), 220.

39. Ibid., 217.

40. A wide range of literature in phenomenology stemming principally from Edmund Husserl (*Ideas Pertaining to a Pure Phenomenology and to a Phenomenological Philosophy* [The Hague: M. Nijhoff, 1982]) and from Schutz and Luckmann (*Structures of the Life-World*) and in pragmatism stemming principally from William James (*The Varieties of Religious Experience* [New York: Modern Library, 1936]), John Dewey (*Experience and Nature,* rev. ed. [(New York: Norton, 1929]), and illustrated by Cornel West (*The American Evasion of Philosophy: A Genealogy of Pragmatism* [Madison: University of Wisconsin Press, 1989]) has led to important analyses and philosophies of experience that link historicist claims about cultural formation with sociology of knowledge theories in language. See for example, Victor Turner's *Dramas, Fields, and Metaphors: Symbolic Action in Human Society* (Ithaca, N.Y.: Cornell University Press, 1974) and a collection he edited with Edward M. Bruner entitled *The Anthropology of Experience*. See also Catherine Bell's *Ritual Theory, Ritual Practice* (New York: Oxford University Press, 1992) for a more generalized but useful philosophical analysis and William Paden's *Interpreting the Sacred: Ways of Viewing Religion* (Boston: Beacon Press, 1992) for an introduction to the phenomenological approach to comparative religious theory. Julia Kristeva represents another branch of phenomenological theory that supports deconstructionist philosophy in semiotics. See especially *Desire in Language: A Semiotic Approach to Literature and Art,* ed. Leon S. Roudiez, trans. Thomas Gora, Alice Jardine, and Leon S. Roudiez (New York: Columbia University Press, 1980).

41. See esp. Wittgenstein's *On Certainty* (New York: Harper, 1969) and Foucault's "Discourse on Language" (*Social Science Information,* April 1971).

42. Reynolds, "Two McFagues," 308.

43. Tillich, *Systematic Theology,* 1:46.

7. BEYOND MONOTHEISM

1. Dianne Bilyak, "Mindfulness."

2. Regina Schwartz, *The Curse of Cain*, xi.

3. Cf. Sands, *Escape from Paradise,* and Luce Irigaray, *This Sex Which Is Not One* (Ithaca,

N.Y.: Cornell University Press, 1985), for example. For an interesting challenge to address the problems of monotheism, see Rebecca Chopp's article, "From Patriarchy into Freedom: A Conversation between American Feminist Theology and French Feminism," in *Transfigurations,* esp. 42–44; and Serene Jones's article, "This God Which Is Not One: Irigaray and Barth on the Divine," in the same book (109–42).

4. As process theologians have pointed out, there are essentially Hellenistic assumptions about greatness and perfection embedded in these traditional monotheistic ideas (that greatness is never small or particular, that perfection exists most fully in ideas, etc.).

5. See my discussion of the dichotomy that social theory places on theology in the conclusion to chapter 3.

6. Isaiah 11:9.

7. Acts of the Apostles 17:24.

8. Kenneth Cragg, *The Call of the Minaret* (New York: Orbis, 1985), 31.

9. McFague, *Body of God,* 136.

10. More modern notions of panentheism (divinity *in* the world) try to resolve this basic problem through abstract constructions of divinity as a shared principle of reality, an element in the makeup of the universe. Process theology in particular develops this idea, but is unable to conceive of divine existence in anything but abstract universalistic terms, even though it reconstructs concepts of God as being in the world and taking part in its physical existence.

11. Alfred Lord Tennyson, "The Higher Pantheism," from *Works* (London: Macmillan, 1891).

12. The absolutism of monotheism is supported by doctrinal claims of final revelation. Judaism is the most open to ongoing divine revelation through the process of rabbinic inquiry known as the oral Torah. But the written Torah is still the one place, once and for all, that God revealed himself to the Jewish people on Mount Sinai. In Christianity, Jesus is understood to be the fullest and the final revelation of divine being and intent. And in Islam, Muhammad's receipt of the Qur'an is believed to be the fullest and last direct experience of divine will. For all of these religions, revelation is ongoing in the sense that it is universally available through the revealed texts, but the delivery—on Mount Sinai, in the life of Jesus, and near Mecca—is complete. Further revelations that might cause confusion are therefore controlled.

13. I am grateful to Pat Schneider for this comparison.

14. See *A Feminist Ethic of Risk.*

15. Both polytheism and paganism have significant content in traditions that engage them, such as Hinduism, which is a profoundly polytheistic set of traditions, and Wicca, which associates itself with contemporary retrievals of medieval European pagan traditions.

16. A wonderful example of another corrective idea for monotheism is what Eller calls "an ultimate monism coupled with an intermediate or functional polytheism" (*Living in the Lap of the Goddess,* 134). There is as yet little contemporary work available in the area of monistic polytheism as a feminist proposition. This is, therefore, only an opening, a gesture toward a perspective that cannot be condensed or sketched in caricature for the purposes of pointing out its most obvious strengths and weaknesses. It is a gesture that suggests, however briefly, a potentially fertile area of exploration for future work in feminist theology, for those who are persuaded by and concerned with the critique raised in this study. Eller's reference to the provocative idea of monistic polytheism is fleeting, indicating only that the spiritual feminists of her study seem to demonstrate a widespread disagreement with the idea that the particular goddesses of their experience might negate a wholistic One or that, by the same token, they are anything less than really real. She points out that there are numerous cultures

(among which Hindu culture stands out) in which this perspective is taken for granted. Polytheistic piety is certainly categorized by traditional Christian doctrine and intellectual habit as idolatry, but there appears to be little evidence among the believers of various polytheistic sensibilities that idolatry, defined as the worship of *false* gods, is really the issue. H. Richard Niebuhr, in his compelling essay on radical monotheism, can be a helpful resource in a further development of the notion of monistic polytheism. He makes a strong case for understanding the worship of any particularity as idolatrous. He also defines monotheism as supreme loyalty to the "One beyond the many" (*Radical Monotheism and Western Culture*, 32) but makes an argument for the reverence of every "relative existent" that, he argues, is possible only in radical monotheism. It is an argument for monotheism that comes closer to pantheism, or to the possibilities of monistic polytheism, than any other orthodox writing of the twentieth century. Indeed, at the center of Niebuhr's understanding is a Tillichian ontology, in which "radical monotheism dethrones all absolutes short of the principle of being itself" but proclaims that "all that is, is good" (ibid., 37). How this is different from the sensibilities of spiritual feminists who worship both goddesses and Jesus Christ, who understand invocational speech to be referential and effective, but relativize all within a monistic notion of wholeness, is not yet established. The possibilities of monistic polytheism as a construct for future feminist theological work lie in the mutually correcting relation between unity and multiplicity, the one and many, that does not necessarily result in a one that has colonized the many, although this is always a possibility. In addition, Kathleen Sands represents one of the best examples of theology that explores "the ruins of the Absolute" as a direct critique on feminism's romantic adherence to monotheism. See especially her discussion of "tragic sensibilities in feminist theology" (*Escape from Paradise*, 60–65).

17. Loren Eisley tells a wonderful story in which he imagines God as a fog on the beach, taking that form in order to touch, with profound intimacy, the flesh of the world. See "The Innocent Fox," in *The Star Thrower* (New York: Harcourt Brace Jovanovich, 1978), 53–65.

18. This structure can offer another rationale for McFague's suggestion of a more radical transcendence that is radically immanent (*Body of God*, passim), and allow the proposition to evolve in religious practice without losing its corrective negations.

19. Johnson, *She Who Is*, 120.

Index